MOVING ON WI...

PLANNING, TRANSITIONS A...
FOR MIDDLE-AGED A...
WITH INTELLECTU...

MOVING ON WITHOUT PARENTS

PLANNING, TRANSITIONS AND SOURCES OF SUPPORT
FOR MIDDLE-AGED AND OLDER ADULTS
WITH INTELLECTUAL DISABILITY

Christine Bigby

B.A.(Hons), M.SocWk, PhD.

*Lecturer, Department of Social Work and Social Policy,
LaTrobe University, Melbourne, Australia*

MACLENNAN + PETTY
SYDNEY • PHILADELPHIA • LONDON

First published 2000

MacLennan & Petty Pty Limited
Suite 405, 152 Bunnerong Road, Eastgardens, NSW 2036

©2000 MacLennan & Petty Pty Limited

All rights reserved including that of translation into other languages. Except as permitted under the Act (for example a fair dealing for the purpose of study, research, criticism or review), no part of this book may be reproduced, stored in a retrieval system, or transmitted in any form or by any means without prior written permission. All inquiries should be made to the publisher at the address above.

Copying for Educational Purposes

The Australian *Copyright Act* 1968 (the Act) allows a maximum of one chapter or 10% of this book, whichever is the greater, to be copied by any educational institution for its educational purposes provided that the educational institution (or the body that administers it) has given a remuneration notice to Copyright Agency Limited (CAL) under the Act.

For details of the CAL licence for educational institutions contact:

Copyright Agency Limited
Level 19, 157 Liverpool Street
Sydney NSW 2000
Facsimile: (02) 9394 7601
E-mail: *info@copyright.com.au*

National Library of Australia
Cataloguing-in-Publication data:

Bigby, Christine
Moving on without parents: planning, transitions and sources of support for middle-aged and older adults with intellectual disability.

Bibliography
Includes index

ISBN 0 86433 152 5

1. Life-changing events – Australia. 2. Ageing parents – Australia. 3. Life change events in old age – Australia. 4. Developmentally disabled aged – Long-term care – Australia. 5. Mentally handicapped aged – Long-term care – Australia. 6. Handicapped – Long-term care – Australia. I. Title.

362.160994

Cover art based on image by Monica Burns 1998
Courtesy of Arts Project Australia

Printed and bound in Australia

Contents

Foreword (Matt Janicki)		vii
Preface		xi
Acknowledgments		xi

PART ONE
The context

Chapter 1	Introduction	3
Chapter 2	Planning for the future	14
Chapter 3	Sources of support in later life	30
Chapter 4	Older people with intellectual disabilities: A diverse and hidden population?	46

PART TWO
The nature and success of parental planning

Chapter 5	Key person succession plans	69
Chapter 6	The transition from parental care	82
Chapter 7	The post-parental care phase	99

PART THREE
Sources of support in later life for people with intellectual disabilities

Chapter 8	Informal support networks of older people with intellectual disability	125
Chapter 9	Formal support networks of older people with intellectual disability	152
Chapter 10	Understanding the post-parental care phase and ensuring adequate sources of support for ageing adults with intellectual disability	176

Appendix 1	Study design	205
Appendix 2	Glossary	220
Appendix 3	Additional tables	222
Bibliography		230
Index		249

Foreword

One of the universals in the developed world is the growing respect and recognition of the impact of general population wellbeing and improved health status on persons with lifelong disabilities. No less an international body than the World Health Organization has recognised that persons with lifelong disabilities, in particular intellectual disabilities, are surviving to new lengths and under conditions that heretofore have not been the norm. Yet, many Western societies have not yet truly adapted their societal resources to fully accommodate individuals with lifelong disabilities who are growing older in increasing number. In part, this deficiency is due to our general lack of appreciation for the life circumstances associated with growing older with a lifelong disability.

To enable us to better understand the life situations of persons with lifelong disabilities, we need to fully appreciate their life circumstances, family histories, patterns of support and care, and goals and aspirations for older age. Many older adults have had disadvantaged lives, some having spent a good portion of their lives in institutional or other segregated settings. Others have lived with parents who had to cope on a daily basis with the uncertainties and burdens posed by unavailable or underdeveloped community services. In many instances, parents were overwhelmed by their own problems and advancing age, and had not the time to ponder what would happen should they cease to be the primary carer. With core families becoming progressively smaller or less multigenerational in European heritage households, the transitions and assumptions of care, in such situations, have become more problematic. Further, with low expectations for longevity and the vagaries of public supports, carers often failed to take into account their relatives' personal plans and wishes for their own old age.

This text, *Moving On Without Parents*, so rich in detail and drawn from actual experiences, goes far to help us better understand the life histories, circumstances, and challenges of men and women with a lifelong disability as they age. This text is unique, for it is rich in resources and insight for those readers keen to better understand the nuances of lifespan development and family dynamics and their influences on decision-making in older age.

It is also unique in that it provides a richness of insight into the thinking and aspirations of older adults themselves, as they face their life situation and contend with older age. No doubt, this text will quickly become a primary reference and a classic in its field for its unique distillation of the research and available knowledge of a key element—family caregiving and transition planning—so crucial to our understanding of how to construct support systems for the older age of adults with intellectual disabilities.

It will also serve as primer on the thinking of older adults with lifelong disabilities as they adapt to older age and cope with being on their own.

Dr. Bigby has done her part. No doubt it will be heavily read by those who serve as advocates and who influence and shape pubic policy. It is hoped that what she has delivered in this text will result in a more responsive community, with fruitful services and supports, and a demonstrated first-rate investment into building a more secure and dignified old age for people with lifelong disabilities.

MATTHEW P. JANICKI
Chair, Special Interest Research Group on Aging
International Association for the Scientific Study
  of Intellectual Disabilities
University at Albany
Albany, New York (USA)

Preface

This book deals with crucial new phases in the lives of people with intellectual disabilities, the post-parental care period and later life. People with intellectual disability now live a relatively normal life span and are more likely than ever before to outlive their parents and survive into old age. Adults who have remained at home with their parents will lose their primary carers at some stage during mid-life. The major issues facing parents and service providers are how to plan for the transition from parental care and who or what services will substitute for the roles previously fulfilled by parents. 'What will happen when I die?' has become a major question and source of anxiety for parents of people with intellectual disability. The major issues confronting adults with intellectual disability are how to rebuild their lives away from parents and tackle ageing successfully. This book documents the results of a qualitative study that examined the nature and success of parental planning and the intersection of informal and formal sources of support for people with intellectual disabilities in later life. The book considers the implications that an increasing number of people ageing with a disability pose for the aged care and disability service systems.

The first part of the book reviews existing research on parental planning for the future and sources of support for people with intellectual disabilities in later life, the bulk of which is drawn from the UK and US. The second and third parts detail the results of a qualitative study of the transition from parental care and document the post-parental care experiences of 62 older people (aged 55 years and over) with intellectual disabilities who had remained at home with their parents until at least mid-life (40 years). The study used an extensive case-finding strategy to ensure inclusion of people who were unknown to the disability service system. Several chapters detail the nature of parental plans, the process of transition from parental care and the success in the long term of parental plans. These chapters draw on the rich qualitative data collected and use case vignettes to illustrate the prevalence and importance of informally based plans, their longer-term advantages and the manner in which informal arrangements avert crisis transitions.

Later chapters examine the myriad changes that occur in people's lives following their transition from parental care. The unexpected opportunities and broadened horizons experienced are counterpoised with vulnerabilities such as control by others, residential mobility, inappropriate environments and withdrawal of specialist services. The nature of the older people's current situation, their access to formal services and the nature of informal supports are documented. The complementarity of informal and formal supports is examined, together with the often conflictual relationships that occur between these two sources of support.

The final chapter considers the policy and service implications that arise from the study, focusing on how to optimise later-life opportunities and minimise vulnerabilities that arise during this period. The book draws on theoretical understandings of family and informal support networks, in particular the work of Litwak regarding the distinctive roles fulfilled by different sources of support.

Future planning and later life for adults with intellectual disabilities are major issues confronting individuals, parents and service providers. This book will be an invaluable resource for students studying disability in vocational courses, undergraduate and post-graduate levels, as well as to policy makers, planners and service providers in the field and to parents and adult siblings of people with intellectual disability.

In order to ensure their privacy, the names of all the individuals involved in the study have been changed, as has other information that may identify people. All the names used in the text are pseudonyms.

Acknowledgments

I am indebted to the older people, their families, friends and service providers who agreed to participate in this study. Without their cooperation it would not have been possible. Many friends and colleagues have provided me with encouragement and support during this undertaking. In particular Elizabeth Ozanne has been a source of unflagging support, confidence and inspiration for which I am extremely grateful. This study has been an integral part of the lives of my partner John and daughters Jessie and Jacquie, and their support and forbearance must be acknowledged.

PART ONE

THE CONTEXT

CHAPTER 1

Introduction

The dramatically increased life expectancy of people with intellectual disability over the past 50 years will result in many surviving into old age and outliving their parents. Thus, during middle age, adults with intellectual disability who have remained at home with their parents, are likely to lose their lifelong caregivers. Their transition from parental care is now inevitable rather than, as previously, a matter of choice. The management of this care transition and who or what services replace parental care and provide support to middle-aged and older adults with intellectual disability are critical issues confronting individuals, their families and service systems. This book explores parental planning for the future, the transitions and sources of support for middle-aged and older adults with intellectual disability in the post parental care phase of their lives.

Informal sources are central to the provision of support for adults with intellectual disability who live with ageing parents. Their support networks are small, dense and dominated by family members. Day-to-day caregiving is usually the exclusive domain of a parent. Siblings, friends and more distant relatives also provide support but usually of an affective, less intense nature (Grant, 1988; Krauss et al., 1992). As a group, ageing parents are not well connected to formal service systems and receive little formal assistance with the tasks of caring (McCallion & Tobin, 1995; Smith, 1997).

Informal support is also central to the provision of care for older people in the general community and provides the bulk of services they require (Australian Bureau of Statistics (ABS), 1995; Chappell, 1990; McDonald, 1997). An effective, informal support system, in later life, is associated with maintenance of lifestyle and functional abilities, continued participation in social activities, reduced use of formal services and avoidance of institutionalisation (Cantor & Little, 1985; Rosenman, 1991). In the 1990s, informal support occupied a pivotal position in disability and aged care policies, which focused on shifting the balance of care from institutions to the community. Central planks of these policies were support to informal carers, maintenance and development of informal support networks and a shift from public to private provision of care (Johnson, 1998; Bornat et al., 1997; Health & Community Services (H&CS), 1993a, 1993b).

Given the centrality of informal support in care for the aged, the availability of alternative sources will be a primary concern for middle-aged and older adults with intellectual disability, who face the loss of their main source of informal care—their parents. The nature of informal support in the post parental care phase is crucial to their wellbeing and a major determinant of the type of formal services they need.

Informal support is multidimensional and conceptualised in various ways. For example, Horowitz divides it into four components: emotional support, direct service provision, financial assistance, and management of relationships with formal organisations (1985). Seltzer and her colleagues dichotomise informal support into either instrumental (the provision of direct aid) or affective (the provision of emotional support) (Seltzer et al., 1991). Empirical research and theoretical models demonstrate the social processes and breadth of factors that influence who provides what type of informal support. These include the interaction of situational factors, individual characteristics and life course changes (Antonucci & Akiyama, 1987). Two primary mediating factors are family ties and gender (Finch & Mason, 1993; Land, 1995; Wenger, 1992). Litwak's theory of task specificity suggests that the tasks fulfilled by primary groups are dependent on their structure. Different primary groups fulfil different tasks that may not be easily substitutable (Litwak, 1985). His model suggests that single, childless adults with intellectual disability living with their parents constitute an atypical primary group. Parents fulfil tasks such as personal care, day-to-day supervision and household management which, when parents die, other kin cannot easily replicate. However, informal network members will continue with tasks they are already providing and may be able to substitute for some parental tasks, such as financial management, that require commitment but not proximity or frequent contact.

The multidimensional nature of informal support and the complexity of factors that determine its provision suggest that a full understanding of the type of support informal network members provide to an individual is important in considering and providing formal substitutes or developing strategies to foster additional or alternative sources of informal support.

Older people with intellectual disability have been characterised as 'the familyless elderly' (Hogg et al., 1988, p. 261) and predicted to have 'no significant others' (Gibson et al., 1992, p. 37). Broad indicators of informal support and measures, such as frequency and number of contacts are relied on to draw these conclusions and to suggest that they have poor informal support networks. For example, a higher proportion live in supported accommodation than their younger peers (Bigby, 1994; Meyers et al., 1985), while only between 33% and 50% have regular contact with relatives (Ashman et al., 1993; Seltzer, 1985). Since most people with intellectual disability are single and childless, they will lack the two key providers of informal care to older people. Their sources of informal support are likely to comprise siblings, more distant relatives and friends. The nature of their support while parents are alive suggests that in the post parental phase it may be limited, particularly in the realm of more direct caregiving. This proposition is supported by research concerning older people generally, demonstrating that distant relatives and friends are much more likely to provide affective than instrumental support (Cicirelli, 1992; Johnson & Catalano, 1981; Wenger, 1987).

In contrast, research on parental planning suggests that many parents of people with intellectual disability expect their other children to undertake roles, such as supervision of care and management of affairs, in relation to their brother or sister with intellectual disability (Heller & Factor, 1991; Krauss, 1990; Seltzer et al., 1993). These are roles that siblings do not normally fulfil for each other, although they are ones that Litwak's model suggests may be feasible. The extent to which parental expectations are fulfilled has not been investigated. It is commonly anticipated that older adults with intellectual disability have a high need not only for supported accommodation but will also be dependent on formal services to identify, articulate and advocate their service needs (Community Services Victoria (CSV), 1988; Gibson et al., 1992; Lakin et al., 1991).

The nature of informal support available to middle-aged and older adults with intellectual disability has not been fully explored and is largely unmapped (Seltzer & Krauss, 1994). Qualitative studies have not amplified the quantitative data and examined the types and quality of informal support. Most surveys have only focused on service users (Seltzer et al., 1991), neglecting the significant proportion who are unknown to specialist services. Study designs have not differentiated between the care background of individuals. Yet, adults who have lived in institutions or left home during young adulthood have very different ties to family and friends compared with those who have remained at home till middle-age, and this affects the informal support available to them in later life.

Ageing parents are often ambivalent about future care and only about 33% to 50% make plans, many of which remain at the informal level (Grant, 1986; Richardson & Ritchie, 1989). The anticipated high need for formal services combined with the pivotal role of parents in support networks, the reluctance of parents to formulate concrete plans and their wish to continue caring as long as possible suggest that the transition from parental care may be a time of crisis that occurs in an unplanned manner when a parent dies or is incapacitated. Such transitions are typically seen as involving emergency first time contact with services, inappropriate placement and multiple loss and trauma for the person with intellectual disability (Heller & Factor, 1988a; Janicki et al., 1985; Kaufman et al., 1991). A major response, aimed at facilitating the transition from parental care and to ensure the provision of appropriate later life support, has been to emphasise the importance of parental planning for the future and to provide assistance to elderly parents to formulate plans (Eloura Homes, 1995; H&CS, 1995a; Heller & Factor, 1988b; Smith & Tobin, 1989). Adequate planning, it is supposed, can avert the crisis of an ill-prepared transition from parental care, ensure longer term security and stability of the person with intellectual disability, and forecast future service demands (Heller & Factor, 1988a, 1988b; Kaufman et al., 1991). Planning can also promote the development and incorporation of methods to facilitate sharing costs of future care between parents and the state, whether desirable or otherwise (CSV, 1992a; H&CS, 1995b).

The notion of planning is straightforward for some researchers and writers on the topic, involving financial and guardianship arrangements, and finding appropriate placements (Heller & Factor, 1988b). Others conceptualise planning as a more complex process, considering that plans must be adaptable to changing needs and may be one means of ensuring the continued involvement of other family members in the life of the person with intellectual disability (Seltzer & Seltzer, 1985). The process of planning raises difficult psychological, ethical and practical issues for parents and those assisting them (Grant, 1988; Smith & Tobin, 1993a, 1993b; Wood, 1993). These difficulties are compounded by the lack of experience by practitioners in this area, together with a service system that emphasises throughput and not long-term work with families (H&CS, 1995b; McCallion & Tobin, 1995).

Despite planning and its suggested benefits being the focus of recent service responses to ageing parents, little attention is given to its efficacy, its role in the transition process and whether plans are implemented and parental expectations fulfilled. Research has not explored the type of plans that are most effective in facilitating transition and securing longer term stability and security for an adult with intellectual disability in the post-parental care phase. This book is primarily concerned with that phase and aims to explore the nature and efficacy of planning, the process of transition from parental care and the intersection of informal and formal support for people with intellectual disability in this latter life course stage. It is focused on a group of adults with intellectual disability who share a common care background of having been cared for at home by their parents until mid-life.

MAJOR QUESTIONS

The questions addressed in this book are:

- Planning: Do parents plan for the future of their middle-aged child with intellectual disability who has remained living at home with them? What is the nature of their plans? Are plans implemented? What is the effect of plans in the short and longer term?
- Transition: How do adults with intellectual disability who have remained at home with parents until mid-life make the transition from parental care? What further changes occur in their lives following this transition?
- Sources of support: Following their transition from parental care, what are the sources of support received by middle-aged and older adults with intellectual disability? What is the nature of this support and the relationship between formal and informal sources? How can aged care and disability service systems support successful ageing for people with lifelong intellectual disability?

The overarching framework used in this book for considering these questions is that of ecological systems theory that locates the individual in their familial, organisational and social structural contexts. This perspective recognises the interconnections and interdependence between these elements and changes that occur across the life course and historic time (Bowes & Hayes, 1999; Germain & Gitterman, 1980; Hareven, 1978; Hogg et al., 1988; Kahn & Antonucci, 1980). The study utilises social network theory (d'Abbs, 1982) and draws on empirical research and theoretical work from the traditions of social work (Challis & Davies, 1986; Whittaker, 1986) and social gerontology (Cantor & Little, 1985; Wenger, 1992). Litwak's task specific theories of substitution and complementarity are specifically explored (Dobrof & Litwak, 1977; Litwak, 1985; Litwak et al., 1995).

STUDY DESIGN

This book details the results of a qualitative study conducted in Melbourne, Australia between 1993 and 1996. Appendix 1 contains a detailed description of the study design and methodology and figure 1.1 provides a visual overview of the design.

A sample of 62 older people with intellectual disability, who had lived with their parents until mid-life but had since made the transition from parental care, was generated using an area-based case finding strategy. This ensured a more representative sample that included people unknown

8   Moving on without parents

FIGURE 1.1 **Overview of the study design.**

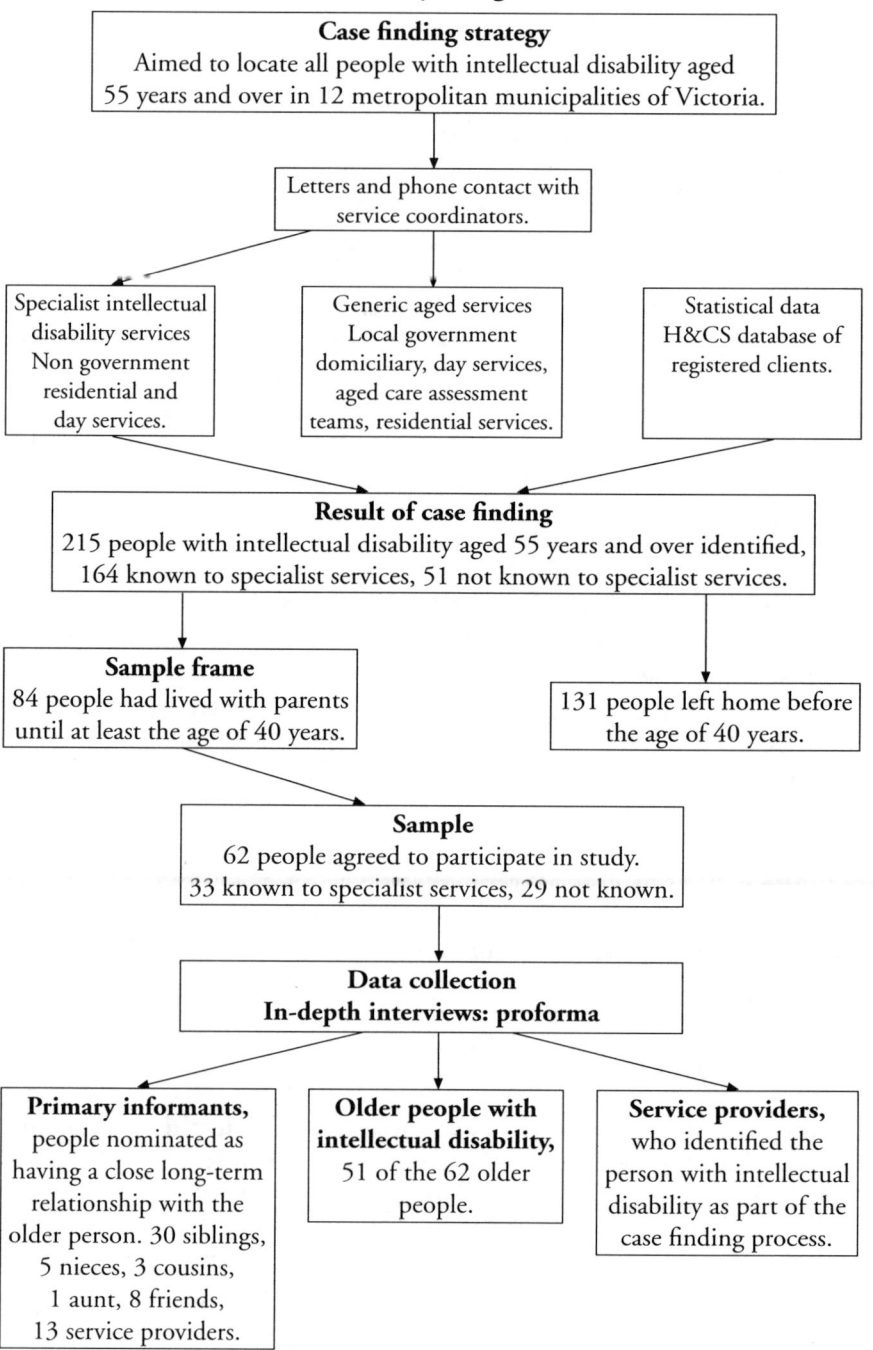

Case finding strategy
Aimed to locate all people with intellectual disability aged 55 years and over in 12 metropolitan municipalities of Victoria.

↓

Letters and phone contact with service coordinators.

| Specialist intellectual disability services Non government residential and day services. | Generic aged services Local government domiciliary, day services, aged care assessment teams, residential services. | Statistical data H&CS database of registered clients. |

Result of case finding
215 people with intellectual disability aged 55 years and over identified, 164 known to specialist services, 51 not known to specialist services.

Sample frame
84 people had lived with parents until at least the age of 40 years.

131 people left home before the age of 40 years.

Sample
62 people agreed to participate in study.
33 known to specialist services, 29 not known.

Data collection
In-depth interviews: proforma

| **Primary informants,** people nominated as having a close long-term relationship with the older person. 30 siblings, 5 nieces, 3 cousins, 1 aunt, 8 friends, 13 service providers. | **Older people with intellectual disability,** 51 of the 62 older people. | **Service providers,** who identified the person with intellectual disability as part of the case finding process. |

to disability service systems. Biographical data and detailed descriptions of relationships and social processes were collected by the author from multiple informants through in-depth semi-structured interviews.

The main source of data was one primary informant for each older person, who was someone with whom they had a close long-term relationship. These were mainly siblings (30) but also included friends (8), nieces (5), cousins (3), an aunt, service providers (13) and parents (2). Additionally, a person involved in formal service provision for each older person was interviewed. The study was not an ethnographic one as it sought to map a broader terrain than such methods would have allowed. However, with an awareness of the limitations of single interviews, where feasible, each person with an intellectual disability was interviewed to ensure they had some voice in the research. Fifty-one of the 63 older people were interviewed, one person declined, and the others were considered by the primary informant to be unable to participate. An interview guide, covering similar material was constructed for each set of informants, and sought detailed descriptive data about parental planning and expectations, changes of residence and primary carer and the nature of formal and informal sources of support used since the transition from parental care.

A mixture of quantitative and qualitative methods of data analysis was undertaken which relied on careful description and inductive analysis (Silverman, 1993; Taylor & Bogdan, 1984). Extensive notes were written after each interview and while listening to the audiotapes of interviews. A set of biographical details and social facts were pieced together for each older person from an examination of notes and comparison of data supplied by different informants. The method of data collection facilitated the development of ideas and analytical categories from the data rather than from preconceived and pre-structured operational definitions. The qualitative data were analysed for common themes using the constant comparative method (Huberman & Miles, 1994) and with the aid of a 'search and retrieve' computer program, the Ethnograph. It aimed to identify patterns, generate categories of things, people or events, and look for explanations and linkages between them.

Quantifiable details such as family characteristics and type of residence were categorised and entered on a relational database and analysed using descriptive statistics. Formal services were classified by their target group and funding source into two groups: 'disability specific' and 'generic aged care'. Disability specific services were those targeted only at people with disabilities but were not necessarily exclusively for people with intellectual disability. Generic aged-care services were those targeted at older people, irrespective of their health or disability status. Data was not sought in regard to health services. The strength of the study's design was that, instead of collecting superficial information about a large number of people, a detailed data set was compiled about a relatively small number of individuals who were fairly representative of a group of people whose biographies and relationships with formal and informal sources of support had not been investigated previously.

It must be noted, however, that this study included only one cohort of older people with intellectual disabilities, those born before 1938 and who were therefore aged over 55 years in 1993. Each future cohort of older people will have lived through a unique historic time and experienced different attitudes, expectations and opportunities which will inevitably affect their experiences of transition from parental care and later life.

PLAN OF THE BOOK

The first part describes the focus of the book and the issues addressed providing a succinct overview of the major themes. The relevant literature and policy are reviewed and the design of the study on which the book is based is summarised. The major questions the book seeks to address are posed: What sorts of plans do parents make? How effective are they in facilitating the transition from parental care and providing longer-term security? How does the process of transition from parental care occur? What sources of informal and formal support are available to older adults with intellectual disabilities? How can aged care and disability service systems support successful ageing for people with lifelong intellectual disability?

Chapter 2 reviews the research and literature on parental planning for the future. This includes both academic work and some of the more concrete 'how to' guides to planning in regard to legal, estate and financial planning. The bulk of material is drawn from studies conducted in the US and UK. Because of the dearth of published Australian material, use is made of unpublished local studies and service initiatives. The chapter examines the extent to which parents do plan, the type of plans they make and the challenges they and service providers confront in the planning process. The chapter concludes that, although planning has been widely explored and an emphasis has been placed on assisting parents in this task, little knowledge exists as to whether plans are actually implemented or the effectiveness of different kinds of plans.

Chapter 3 reviews the research concerning who provides what sort of support in later life for people with intellectual disability, drawing on the international literature in this field. The fundamental importance and roles of informal support are considered and parallels are drawn between the likely support networks of older people with intellectual disability and those without lifelong disabilities. The chapter concludes that although very little is known about the informal support networks of older people with intellectual disability, they appear to lack some of the crucial sources of informal support and, consequently, substantial need for formal support services is forecast.

Chapter 4 discusses the heterogeneous nature of the population of ageing people with intellectual disability, and the existence of a 'hidden group' who remain out of touch with disability services. Many of the hidden group are those who have remained at home with parents and data regarding the extent of this population in the US, the UK and Australia are presented. The implications of this hidden group for service development and practitioners and the importance of outreach strategies are discussed. The latter part of this chapter describes the group of older people involved in the study on which the remainder of the book is based. An overview of their characteristics is presented together with several vignettes of their lives, illustrating their diverse life histories and experiences of ageing.

The second part of the book examines the type of plans parents make and the success of their implementation. The contribution of different types of plan to the ease and experience of transition from parental care and the longer term stability and security of ageing people with intellectual disability in the post parental care phase of their lives is analysed. Case vignettes are interspersed throughout the chapters to illustrate the major points raised in the text.

Chapter 5 examines the importance parents attach to planning and the various types of plans that they make. It highlights the prevalence of open-ended informal plans that nominate a key person to succeed the parent and fulfil their 'caring about' rather than 'caring for' roles.

Chapter 6 documents the manner in which middle-aged people with intellectual disability experience the transition from parental care. A major theme is that, contrary to popular notions, transition is a process invariably managed informally, occurring gradually rather than being a sudden crisis event. The extent to which parental plans are implemented and contribute to the transition process is discussed, and the manner in which responsibility for transition is often handed over or assumed by others, thus relieving parents of this painful process, is highlighted.

Chapter 7 builds on the previous two chapters and tracks the ongoing changes and transitions that occur in the lives of people with intellectual disability after their transition from parental care. The continually changing nature of people's own characteristics, skills, interests, and that of their social and service contexts is highlighted. This chapter serves to illustrate the futility of attempting to make concrete plans for the rest of a middle-aged person's life and reflects on the vital role that a strong informal support network plays in ensuring longer term security, if not stability.

The second part of the book is concerned with the transition from parental care and the immediate post-parental care phase, that occurs at some stage during middle age for people with intellectual disability. In contrast, part three focuses more clearly on later life and examines the situation of members of the study population at the time of the study, when they were all over 55 years of age. Case vignettes are used in these chapters to illustrate the nature of informal support networks of older people with intellectual disability and their experiences of using formal support services.

Chapter 8 examines the composition of the informal support networks of older people with intellectual disability and the various roles that are played by different network members. It traces the ties that people maintain and the reasons for the durability of informal support into later life. The significance of the long-term relationships between family members and the person with intellectual disability, rather than a sense of obligation, is discussed. Informal network members replace some aspects of parental care but for most people they do not fully replace the roles played by parents. The chapter also highlights the vulnerability of informal networks as people age.

Chapter 9 examines the patterns and experiences of service use by older people with intellectual disability. In addition to describing the nature and quality of services used, the focus is on relationships and collaboration between disability and aged-care services, and between formal and informal sources of support. The importance of formal services in people's lives is highlighted, alongside the criticisms made by informal network members and the apparent lack of cooperation and collaboration between service systems.

Chapter 10 draws together the major threads from the previous chapters stressing the complementarity of informal and formal sources of support and the need for flexible planning. It considers the policy and service implications that arise from the study, focusing on how to optimise later life opportunities and minimise the vulnerabilities that accompany ageing for people with intellectual disabilities. Implications for direct practice, issues that should be addressed and strategies for working with aged parents, ageing people with disabilities and those who replace parents as key providers of informal support are presented. Many of these centre on the importance of informal sources of support and ensuring they are recognised and nurtured by professionals. A table format is used to highlight key issues for practitioners and summarise key themes of the book.

This book makes a significant contribution to the limited knowledge of the sources and nature of informal support available to older people with intellectual disability. It provides an indication of the outcome of various types of parental plans. This knowledge will provide an important foundation for professional workers who become involved with middle-aged people with intellectual disabilities and their families, around issues of future planning. The book also provides an important basis for understanding the formal service needs of the group and constructing policy and service responses. By documenting the intersection of formal and informal sources of support and this group's experiences of formal support, insights into unmet support needs and appropriate ways of meeting them are gained. The book suggests the need for a clearer articulation of policy to take into account the needs of middle-aged and older people with intellectual disabilities and members of their informal networks, and suggests directions such policy must take to achieve optimal outcomes for this group.

CHAPTER 2

Planning for the future

The duration of the caregiving relationship between older parents and their co-resident adult son or daughter with intellectual disability is much longer than for spouse or filial carers, and unlike other groups, it is the death or incapacity of the carer that often marks the cessation of caring. The caregiving relationship between parents and their adult child with intellectual disability is therefore particularly vulnerable to breakdown and the transfer of care is inevitable, although uncertainty surrounds the timing. These unique dimensions present parents with the challenging non-normative tasks of confronting their own mortality and planning for the future care of their adult child with intellectual disability. This chapter reviews research studies that have explored the extent and nature of parental planning. The characteristics of older parental carers, obstacles to planning and suggested strategies to encourage parents to plan are also considered. The chapter concludes by raising questions about the effectiveness, efficacy and legitimacy of parental planning.

CHALLENGES OF PLANNING FOR THE FUTURE

Parental planning for the future care of their adult child with intellectual disability is increasingly seen as a fundamentally important task with diverse goals and multiple beneficiaries (Smith et al., 1995). Adequate planning, it is supposed, can avert the crisis of an ill-prepared transition from parental care, ensure longer term security and stability of the person with intellectual disability and assist in forecasting future service demands (Heller & Factor, 1988a; Kaufman et al., 1991). The process of planning has also been suggested as psychologically important for elderly parents to resolve unfinished business (Grant, 1989; Kaufman et al., 1991; Heller & Factor, 1991; Smith & Tobin, 1993a, 1993b).

Planning is usually conceptualised into three areas: *guardianship*, *financial* and *residential* provisions (Heller & Factor, 1991; Seltzer & Seltzer, 1992; Smith & Tobin, 1993b; Smith et al., 1995; Wood, 1993). However, formal notions of guardianship planning are problematic in jurisdictions such as Victoria, Australia, where legislation precludes the anticipatory appointment of a guardian and is based on the notion of the least restrictive alternative (Carney & Tait, 1997). Planning is generally seen as straightforward: 'Proper planning includes making financial and guardianship arrangements and finding appropriate placements' (Heller & Factor, 1988b, p. 2). However, it is also regarded as a complex dynamic process whereby plans must be sufficiently flexible and adaptable to meet the changing residential, financial and legal requirements of adults who may survive their parents by 30 or 40 years (Kaufman et al., 1991; Seltzer & Seltzer, 1985). With this in mind, Seltzer and Seltzer (1985) suggest that planning may not achieve a secure permanent residential situation but may be important in ensuring that family members remain involved with the person with intellectual disability and monitor the quality and appropriateness of services. Plans have two major functions, facilitating the transition from parental care and ensuring, in the longer term, an optimum quality of life and security for adults with intellectual disability as they age.

It has also been suggested that planning should involve a guarantee of care (Freeling & Bruggeman, 1994). In their view, a plan encompassing all life areas should be made jointly by the person with intellectual disability, his or her parents, and professionals, and include a guarantee of services by the local political authority. Parental planning may also be used as a mechanism to promote cost sharing of future care between parents and the state (Community Services Victoria (CSV), 1988, 1992b; Health and Community Services (H&CS), 1995b; Sach & Associates, 1991).

Extent and nature of planning by parents

Parents of adults with intellectual disability hold three main attitudes towards planning: avoidance, ambivalence and active planning, of which avoidance is the most common (Richardson & Ritchie, 1986, 1989).

> With advancing years, carers became preoccupied, and somewhat fearful, about the future. Many carers and their families tended to live life on a day to day basis, preferring to blot out the agonies of contemplating the future when they are no longer able to cope or else themselves deceased. (Grant, 1986, p. 336)

Most studies show that only between one third to one half of parents make concrete plans for future care of an adult with intellectual disability who is living at home (Campbell & Essex, 1994; Freedman et al., 1997; Grant, 1989; Heller & Factor, 1991; Kaufman et al., 1991; Krauss, 1990; Prosser, 1997). Financial planning is the most common type undertaken. Smith et al. (1994) suggest that planning is not a simple act occurring at one point but has five stages, ranging from no discussion to definite plans. Some families may not move along the full continuum, and plans may remain implicit, comprising informal agreements or understandings between family members (Heller & Factor, 1991; Kaufman et al., 1991). Some are never formalised and may not even be discussed with the family members expected to be involved in future care for the person for whom the plan is being constructed. For example, one study found that parents paid little attention to the wishes of the adult with an intellectual disability, and when preferences were known, if they were incompatible with parental attitudes they were sometimes disregarded (Smith & Tobin, 1989). In contrast, however, another study suggests that most families who make concrete plans for a future residential placement have discussed these decisions with their adult child with intellectual disability and other children (Heller & Factor, 1991).

A quantitative analysis of parental planning can be misleading because of the different ways plans are conceptualised. For example, an early study found that 66% of elderly parents had applied for future placement of their adult child in residential accommodation and that this could indicate a high level of residential planning. But only 10% of the sample had any intention of ever taking up residential care and these 'plans' often represented multiple applications made long ago (Gold, 1987). Some families formulate several plans representing a series of back ups or different views among family members about the future. For example, Krauss and her colleagues found that in 22% of families where a sibling expected to co-reside with a brother or sister with an intellectual disability, the parent also placed the person's name on a waiting list for residential accommodation (Krauss et al., 1996). Similar inconsistencies between family plans and perceptions of the future were found in a study by Griffith and Unger (1994). In their study, a higher proportion of siblings expressed a willingness to act as carer in the future than was reflected in parental expectations and encapsulated in plans. Plans and expectations may also change over time; for example, Grant (1989) found that over a two-year period just over half the parents in his study changed their preference for future care.

Parental expectations of future care

The choices and options that plans contain often emerge from the social context of care, with preferences generally evenly split between continued family care, primarily by siblings, and residential placement (Grant, 1989; Heller & Factor, 1991; Wood, 1993). For example, when continued family care is chosen, caring is generally judged to be trouble-free, with little involvement by professionals, and a supportive network, made up predominantly of kin, is usually in place (Grant, 1989). In contrast, families who expected to rely on formal services for future care had fewer kin supports and were more involved with professionals (Grant, 1989).

Parents are more likely to expect a family member to provide indirect care for the adult with intellectual disability, by, for example, overseeing their wellbeing, than to expect a relative to provide hands-on support (Goodman, 1978; Krauss, 1990). Many of these parental expectations resemble the theoretical propositions derived from Litwak's model of informal care (1985), which is discussed further in chapter 3, and the conceptualisation of indirect informal care suggested by Sussman (1985). These types of expectations are usually informally based, although in some instances may involve formal guardianship arrangements.

Parental plans value protection and permanency rather than developmental opportunities. Instead of looking towards increased independence for their adult child in the future, parents seek residential accommodation to duplicate the care and protection that they have provided at home. Parents also want to select a residential situation where their adult child can remain for the rest of his or her life (Card, 1983; Gold, 1987). Griffin and Bennett (1994) found when parents discussed planning in a group, they generally emphasised security, attaining peace of mind and a safe, secure situation as most important to them. However, Brubaker and Brubaker (1993) suggest that the greatest concern that parents have regarding the future is the adult child's social and emotional wellbeing rather than concern about residential or financial needs.

Factors affecting planning

Most studies have found an association between the use of formal services and both the parental propensity to make plans and an expected reliance on formal services rather than other family members for future care. This suggests that use of services may lead to a greater knowledge of options and more trust in the quality of formal services (Essex et al., 1997; Grant, 1989; Heller & Factor, 1991; Seltzer et al., 1991, Smith & Tobin, 1993a; Smith et al., 1994; Wood & Skiles, 1992). The decision to plan is multifactorial, and has been associated with carer characteristics, stressors and resources (Essex et al., 1997; Heller & Factor, 1991; Seltzer & Krauss, 1994). For example, behaviour problems of the adult with intellectual disability, high unmet needs and small support networks are positively associated with planning, whereas age of the carer is negatively associated (Essex et al., 1997). Smith and his colleagues have constructed a model incorporating many of these factors, demonstrating the complexity of factors involved in parental planning decisions (Smith et al., 1995).

Obstacles to planning

Despite the suggested benefits of comprehensive planning, many parents do not undertake this task. The most common reasons proposed are parents' lack of information about service options and their distrust of or dissatisfaction with formal services (Card, 1983; Gold, 1987; Grant, 1989; Heller & Factor, 1988a; Kaufmann et al., 1991; Kropf, 1994; Smith & Tobin, 1989; Smith et al., 1995). Other suggestions are based on the perception that planning is emotionally challenging for parents, logistically complex and confronts professionals with difficult ethical issues. Formulating a plan forces parents to come to terms with their own ageing and mortality. They may also have to deal with the tension between a desire to continue caregiving and their anxiety about future care (Kropf, 1994; Seltzer & Ryff, 1994; Smith & Tobin, 1993a; Smith et al., 1994). The process may also require parents to balance their own needs and desires with the rights and needs of their adult child (Grant, 1986). The types of future care parents want for their offspring may conflict with the values and options preferred by professional workers. The resultant clash of values may be an obstacle to effectively working with older parents to develop plans. Research has noted that workers feel anger and frustration with elderly parents about their failure to make plans, and parental protective attitudes towards their adult child are perceived as having jeopardised the growth and development of the person with intellectual disability (McCallion & Tobin, 1995; Smith & Tobin, 1993a).

The nature of formal service systems may create systemic obstacles to parental planning. These include an emphasis on short-term interventions that make it difficult to undertake the long-term work with parents that is required to gain parental trust and confront complex issues. Inadequate linkages between specialist and generic service systems and poor knowledge of other systems by staff may also be an obstacle to planning (Smith & Tobin, 1993b; H&CS, 1993c). A lack of concrete alternatives available to parents, as well as long waiting lists, particularly for supported accommodation, may mean that parents see planning as pointless (AAMR, 1998; Walker & Walker, 1998a).

CAREGIVING RELATIONSHIPS OF OLDER PARENTAL CARERS

The role of formal services in encouraging and assisting parents to engage in planning has become a focus of discussion and service development (Eloura Homes, 1995; H&CS, 1995b; Lehman & Roberto, 1993, Smith & Tobin, 1993a, 1993b). An understanding of the characteristics of older parental carers and the nature of their caregiving relationship with adult offspring should inform such strategies.

On various dimensions, older parents of adult children with intellectual disability differ from their younger peers. For example, older carers tend to live in smaller households and are more likely to be single carers, have other caring responsibilities, have poorer informal support networks and use fewer formal support services (Hayden & Heller, 1997; Heller, 1993; Janicki, 1996; McGrath & Grant, 1993; Smith et al., 1994; Todd et al., 1993). Older parents are usually less optimistic about the progress of their offspring than younger parents although the dependency levels of their offspring have an inverse relationship to carer age (Todd et al., 1993). However, despite the offspring of older carers being less dependent, they are less likely to have a full time occupation and more likely to have unoccupied days than younger offspring (Todd et al., 1993).

Older parents confront planning issues when they are experiencing their own age related decrements such as reduced physical capacity and mobility, perhaps in addition to those of their offspring, especially if their offspring suffer from early onset Alzheimer's which is common among middle-aged adults with Down syndrome (Hawkins et al., 1993; Heller, 1993). For older parents, adaptation to age related changes, which may affect their caring ability, and planning tasks, occur in the context of ongoing parental responsibilities (Seltzer & Krauss, 1994).

Potential stresses involved in later life caring are seen to be unending dependency, chronic sorrow, age-associated decrements, lack of formal services, social isolation and financial pressures (Smith, 1996). Anxiety about the future care of their offspring is the most common stress mentioned. However, despite the factors indicative of greater stress, older parents are consistently found to experience greater satisfaction with caring and less stress than their younger counterparts (Hayden & Heller, 1997, Heller & Factor, 1991; Seltzer & Krauss, 1989; Smith & Tobin, 1993a). For example:

> Overall parents of children were more likely to be confronted with more demanding caregiving than parents of adults, because children were likely to be more highly dependant and to have more behaviour problems. (Todd et al., 1993, p. 141)

> Despite the long duration of their caretaking roles, many of the mothers seemed resilient, optimistic, and able to function well in multiple roles. Specifically the women were healthier than other non caregiving women their age, they had better morale than caregivers of elderly persons and reported no more burden than family caregivers of elderly residents and less stress than parents of young children with retardation. (Seltzer & Krauss, 1994, p. 7)

However, Smith and Tobin found that although older parents had greater subjective wellbeing than normative ageing mothers, they were less accepting of the ageing process and death, and their fears of death increased with age (1993a).

Factors that may account for the satisfactions of older parents and their relatively less stressful caring situations are the greater reciprocity and mutuality in caregiving relationships that develops as carers and their adult offspring grow older (Grant, 1993; Heller et al., 1997; Prosser, 1989), ageing parents' resolution of the disappointments associated with having a child with intellectual disability, accommodation to the child's strengths and a recognition of unexpected personal and familial benefits associated with having a child with intellectual disability (Seltzer & Krauss, 1994). Experiences of older parents have been found to conform to a model of adaptation over time rather than one of 'wear and tear' (Seltzer & Krauss, 1994). Relinquishment at earlier stages an the life course by parents for whom caring may have been more difficult could mean that older parents are a self-selected unrepresentative 'healthy survivors' group.

Wellbeing of older parents is strongly related to age, level of education, marital status, and income (Grant, 1993). The involvement of siblings with the adult with intellectual disability rather than their engagement with parents is also demonstrated as an important factor in maternal wellbeing (Seltzer et al., 1991). These findings suggest the importance of supportive family environment to caregiver wellbeing (Seltzer & Krauss, 1989, 1994). Findings from a study of older carers in Northern and Southern Ireland suggest that wellbeing of older parents was also linked to the range of services and supports offered to them (Walsh et al., 1993).

CONNECTIONS TO FORMAL SERVICE SYSTEMS

Most research suggests that many older parents are isolated from formal service systems and underutilise services from both the ageing and disability networks (Fullmer et al., 1997; Lehman & Roberto, 1993; McCallion & Tobin, 1995; McGrath & Grant, 1993; Smith, 1997; Todd et al., 1993). For example, an extensive study in New York State found that at least half of the older carers identified by an outreach project were unknown to formal services systems (Janicki et al., 1999). A survey of staff in regional disability services in Victoria, Australia showed older carers limited their service use to day centres and associated residential programs and were distrustful of new service types (Pierce, 1991).

This low use of formal support by older parents is often explained by reluctance and mistrust stemming from their negative experiences of government policies and service use in the past (Horne, 1989a; McCallion & Tobin, 1995; Stehlik, 1997). Accounts of the predominantly institutional and paternalistic services available between 1930 and the 1970s, the negativism of professionals towards children with intellectual disability and heartbreaking parental experiences clearly illuminate why some older carers are reluctant to approach formal services for assistance. For example, Pierce points out that the child rearing practices of older carers occurred in another era when values and ideologies were quite different from those currently prevailing. She suggests it should not be surprising 'if ageing carers are protective and cautious, and reluctant to choose new service options. Their life experience involved successive exclusions from generic community services and facilities' (1993, p. 22).

Despite their low level of service use, one study found that older carers have a high level of formal knowledge about the service system (Smith, 1997). This and another study suggest that low usage may stem from difficulty of access or lack of a full understanding about the operations and applicability of services, particularly more recent and innovative models (Smith et al., 1995; Smith, 1997). It is also suggested that the nature of their connections to formal services may be indicative of carer's characteristics and attitudes and provides clues to service needs and the manner in which the service system should attempt to engage them. For example, a comparison between offspring who did and did not use day services found the latter group were older, more disabled, more likely to be female, from lower socio-economic backgrounds and that their parents had fewer supports, lacked confidence and trust in services and were more likely to have had an unfavourable service experience in the past (Smith et al., 1995). In contrast to Smith's finding, several studies suggest that parents do not know about services and that the lack of knowledge about possible accommodation options is a major obstacle preventing parents planning adequately for the future (Collinson, 1997; Grant, 1989; Heller & Factor, 1988a; Kropf, 1994; Magrill et al., 1997; Walker & Walker, 1998a).

Smith (1997) suggests a qualitative difference between parents who have withdrawn from the service system and those who have never used the system at all. The first group is more likely to report a high need for services but be fearful of them and therefore need to re-establish their trust. In contrast, more important issues for parents who have never used services are their limited knowledge, isolation and concern about unwarranted intrusion into their lives (Smith, 1997). These findings reinforce the point made by several writers that older parents are not one homogeneous group and their experiences are likely to be mediated by cohort effect, culture and diverse individual biographies (McCallion et al., 1997; Todd et al., 1993).

UNMET NEEDS AND THE RATIONALE FOR INTERVENTION ABOUT PLANNING

Older carers do not express a high demand for services and are less stressed than other carer groups. From this perspective, their needs may not appear as complex or urgent, indicating no particular attention from service systems is warranted. However, studies consistently demonstrate that many unmet needs of older carers cluster around issues related to future planning and the transfer of care (Brubaker & Brubaker, 1993; Caserta et al., 1987; Heller & Factor, 1991, 1993; Smith et al., 1995). This suggests that attention to these issues must be added to the more normative service system tasks of sustaining the caring relationship and providing complementary services and support. Both researchers and advocacy groups make a strong case for the utility of proactive, preventative intervention around planning which will avoid future crisis and reduce both financial and emotional costs (Grant, 1986; Harris, 1998; Magrill et al., 1997; Smith and Tobin, 1993a; Walker & Walker, 1998a; Wood, 1993). For example:

> ... we strongly believe that when you assist an ageing carer, everyone benefits. The help provided can avert crises and keep the family intact. It can also help adults with a lifelong disability plan their own future and make a planful transition from their family home, if they choose to do so. We found that staff resources can be conserved and monetary resources can be preserved for when they are most needed. Contact now with families will permit timely consideration of more independent and therefore less costly options for services in the future. (Janicki, 1996, p. 110)

> Just because carers are coping now doesn't mean they don't need help.... an investment in preventative partnership work with families is at the core of meeting the needs of this user group and determining accurate, cost effective planning for future years. (Magrill et al., 1997, pp. 15, 16)

The literature indicates considerable agreement on the broad aims of service interventions with older carers (Caserta et al., 1987; Grant, 1986; Heller & Factor, 1991, 1993; Janicki, 1996; Kelly & Kropf, 1995; Smith et al., 1995; Smith & Tobin, 1993b; Wood, 1993). These include:

- identification of 'hidden' carers and their transformation into clients
- avoidance of crises of unplanned transition by facilitating parental planning
- creation of linkages to formal service systems
- prediction of future needs

- preparation of adults with intellectual disability for transition and greater independence
- support to maintain existing caregiving situations for as long as possible
- counselling parents to assist the resolution of conflicting demands and psychological issues and renegotiation of their caring role
- developing the capacity of the service system to meet the needs of this group.

Two common strands run through the various principles and service models that are suggested. These are the need for a dual focus of intervention on both carer and care recipient, and the value of a total family approach that takes into account broader networks of support than the caregiving dyad, with a particular emphasis on inclusion of siblings (Grant, 1986; Heller et al., 1997; Janicki, 1996; McCallion & Tobin, 1995; Seltzer & Krauss, 1994; Smith & Tobin, 1993a). In recognition that the bulk of research and advocacy report either the voices of parents or professionals, Walmsley stresses the inclusion of the voice of the adult with intellectual disability (1996).

Despite the consensus of aims, some writers suggest that, from the perspective of case managers, little practice wisdom and limited knowledge exist to guide development of services or direct practice with this group (Smith & Tobin, 1993a). They propose three levels for intervention essential for practices with older parents. First, the context of practice, which must include development of policies that support practice with ageing families, training for staff and possible development of geriatric specialists in the field of disability. Second, outreach to make parents into clients, including educational programs, peer support groups, and active outreach by services from both ageing and disability networks. Third, parental counselling, characterised by a slow pace, appreciation of parental experiences and fears, and incorporation of siblings on issues relating to the future (1993b). Figure 2.1 below summarises the various roles suggested for case managers or other professionals to fulfil in meeting the aims of service intervention. Key roles suggested are those of therapist and teacher, whereby parents can be assisted to confront death and anxieties about the future, and learn about potential care options (Smith & Tobin, 1993b).

Direct work with older carers

In regard to planning for the future, older parents confront many tensions and conflicting demands, which require particular skills from professionals working with them. Personal conflicts include: carer's rights versus the

FIGURE 2.1 **Roles for professionals in providing services for older carers**

Writer	Roles, tasks for professionals
Kaufman, Glicken & deWeaver, 1989	Outreach, advocate, teacher, therapist, enabler or facilitator, broker or coordinator.
Lehman, 1993	**For person with disability** Assessment, plan development, residential support, social support, day programs, education. **For ageing carers** Plan development, social support, education, transportation, congregate meals.
Smith & Tobin, 1993a	Outreach worker, advocate, teacher, therapist, and enabler or facilitator, broker or coordinator.
Kropf & Greene, 1993	Life review. Based on identification of points of stress, assessment of coping styles and age-related changes, understanding family history and environment supports, enhancement of social supports, resolution of issues of integrity.
Smith & Tobin, 1993b	Development of a context of practice that supports work with older carers, outreach, counselling.
Kelly & Kropf, 1995	Life review, pyschoeducation groups, long-term support services—comprehensive case management, information and referral.
Janicki, 1996	Outreach, information and referral, training and education of professionals, casework, advocacy, brokerage.
Kropf, 1994	Clinical interventions, resource management—access to multiple and diverse support to maintain care, service system modifications.

rights of the care recipient, maintenance of interdependence and reciprocity versus the rights of the 'care recipient' to independence, continued nurturance versus letting go, and known costs and benefits of informal care versus the unknown world of future services (Grant, 1993).

> Some carers recognised that they were treading a kind of emotional tight rope between fulfilling their own personal and social needs, often through the handicapped person, and trying to avoid exploiting their dependant by demanding too much of them, physically and emotionally. (Grant, 1986, p. 336)

Older carers have not experienced many of the rituals associated with 'letting go' and renegotiating their parental relationship from that of adult–child to adult–adult (Kropf & Greene, 1993; Richardson & Ritchie, 1986).

Parents face considerable guilt and anxiety in confronting decisions about the future (Smith & Tobin, 1993b).

Differences in the nature and demands of interpersonal work with older carers compared to younger carers is highlighted and linked to the need for development of expertise in working with this group (McCallion & Tobin, 1995). Continuity, longevity, and the development of acceptance and trust in the casework relationship are seen as vital components (Kropf & Green, 1993). The time required to develop trust, the slow progress of work and absence of quick tangible outcomes are noted (McCallion & Tobin, 1995). Kropf and Greene consider that in contrast to younger parents, older carers have greater needs for nurturance and support, and more diverse needs (1993).

> Case managers are aware of the emphasis on empowerment and also how the system's focus on quick outcomes hinders the necessary pacing in approaching and then addressing planning for the future. It is, however essential to go slowly and gingerly. Whereas pacing is always important in counselling, it is especially important to this group who resist planning. It takes time and clinical acumen to develop the trust necessary to overcome resistance. (Smith & Tobin, 1993b, p. 72)

Magrill et al. consider that the trust, developed from a long-term partnership between carer and professional, is central to work with older carers as is the assurance they have a reliable contact when necessary (1997). They suggest that fleeting social work relationships are not only dangerous but also common. Guides to practice stress the importance of respecting the contributions made by older carers, avoidance of blame and the delicate task of balancing the different needs of the caring dyad (Harris, 1998; Magrill et al., 1997; Walker & Walker, 1998a). The relative importance of traditional social casework elements of case management compared with service coordination and brokerage tasks appear to be characteristic of case management with older carers. Facilitating linkage and use of formal services, which in turn is associated with increased willingness to plan may also be an important strategy.

Outreach

Various outreach strategies have been used to locate 'hidden families', and establish linkages with formal service systems (McCallion & Tobin, 1995; Smith & Tobin, 1993b). Janicki suggests that by doing so a mechanism is established to assist with planning and maintaining the caregiving situation intact and viable for as long as possible (1996). Owing to the possibility of negative past experiences, outreach may be more successful if it is conducted by non disability agencies, such as those from the aged care system (Janicki, 1996; Seltzer & Krauss, 1994; Smith & Tobin, 1993b). The New York Caregiver Assistance Project funded a number of successful outreach demonstration projects that were auspiced by Area Agencies on Aging (Janicki et al., 1998). The tasks of outreach and follow-up assistance were assigned to a host agency, which undertook programs promoting community awareness and assessments. The project found that Agencies on Aging could provide a safety net for crisis and that by working through local community based ethnic organisations, some families were more willing to accept services (Janicki et al., 1998; McCallion et al., 1997).

Publicly advertised information and education sessions targeted at older carers is one strategy that has been used successfully by a number of programs (Janicki et al., 1998; McCallion & Tobin, 1995; Smith & Tobin, 1993b). Utilising agencies such as day programs or income support services that many older carers already know, in order to disseminate information and reach parents is a strategy suggested by Smith (1997).

Mutual support groups

The success of mutual support groups for older carers with the dual aim of education and emotional support are reported in the literature (Mengel et al., 1996; O'Malley, 1996; Smith et al., 1996). Parental outcomes have been increased use of services, taking steps towards future planning, being heard and understood by others and receipt of mutual support (O'Malley, 1996). Groups are often jointly auspiced by aged care and disability networks and provide a link between these often quite separate service systems. In the UK the development of support groups for older carers auspiced by local divisions of the national advocacy group Mencap and local government authorities, are reported by Walker and Walker (1998a).

Heller (1997), however, notes that drawbacks of groups may be issues around transport and their time limited nature. She considers they may also undermine parents' own sense of control and problem solving capacity (Heller, 1997). A concurrent group for co-resident adults with intellectual disability is reported by O'Malley (1996). The description of this group provides an example of supportive intervention for care recipients to assist them to deal with their own issues around the future transfer of care, the death of their parents and their own ageing. Other examples of this kind of work are found in work undertaken primarily by day programs which may run pre-retirement or seniors groups (Laughlin & Cotton, 1994).

Service system challenges

Developing a capacity for proactive work around future planning is the dominant theme highlighted in relation to older parents of adult offspring with intellectual disability. Recognition and resolution of value conflicts between older carers and professional worker or service ideologies are also important challenges. As indicated previously, blaming or judgmental attitudes often held by workers in regard to parental overprotectiveness can be an obstacle to work with older carers (Smith & Tobin, 1993a). It is suggested that service systems geared to quick tangible outcomes impede work with older carers and programs must be adapted to reflect the specific requirements of work with that group (Smith & Tobin, 1993a). Specialist workers and dedicated caseloads are often suggested as the ideal means of case management for this group (Lehman & Roberto, 1993; McCallion & Tobin, 1995). For example, Rinck and Calkins argue that case managers dedicated to working with older carers are more successful in addressing their issues than case managers with a mixed caseload (cited in Lehman & Roberto, 1993).

Documenting the extent of need among older parents and gaining a clearer picture of the size and location of this group is implicit in outreach strategies. The establishment of a comprehensive database in regard to this population is suggested by Walker and Walker (1998a) who, with many other writers, consider that service systems must respond strategically to older parents rather than just rely on picking up their needs in the normal course of assessment when carers or care recipients seek services.

The report prepared by Magrill and her colleagues (1997) detailing the perspective of older carers suggest six action priorities required to enable older carers to continue caring and face the future. These are:

- to be known by the service system and have regular contact to assist with planning and enable assistance to be sought when necessary
- provision of information regarding local services for both the short and long term
- to ensure system linkages and the availability of a central contact place for information and help
- a non-judgmental approach by workers and an awareness by them of the pressures experienced by parents, and their expertise
- reassurance that help will be available in crisis, that their dependent will be well cared for and have support to deal with loss, and
- involvement in planning, assessment and decision making processes regarding their dependent.

ISSUES IN EFFECTIVENESS AND IMPLEMENTATION OF PARENTAL PLANS

Despite the focus on the critical importance of planning, its outcomes, effectiveness, and whether or not parental expectations are met have not been well researched or documented. Findings consistently show that, although elderly parents make plans, they want to continue in their role of primary carer for as long as possible (Card, 1983; Goodman, 1978; Grant, 1989; Heller & Factor, 1991; Kaufman et al., 1991; Krauss, 1990; Richardson & Ritchie, 1986, 1989). The centrality of caring to the lives of older parents and the significance of this role to their identity may account for parents' continued commitment (Seltzer & Krauss, 1989; Todd et al., 1993). Increased interdependence between the carer and care recipient in later life may also provide a strong disincentive to relinquishment (Seltzer & Krauss, 1994). Predictors of a transfer from care by older carers are primarily related to parental health problems, parental subjective burden and their offspring's high physical dependency (Heller & Factor, 1993). Some research suggests that relinquishment by older parents is preceded by a crisis and circumstances beyond the control of the parent (Essex et al., 1997; Walker & Walker, 1998a). At a more pragmatic level, continuation of caring may stem from dissatisfaction with the quality of alternative forms of care or a realistic appraisal of the lack of alternatives (Grant, 1993).

These factors inevitably impinge on the implementation and effectiveness of plans, as services such as supported accommodation may not be immediately available on demand and plans may be made a number of years prior to implementation. Some indications of the outcomes of planning and the effect of resources on this are highlighted by the longitudinal study of aged carers undertaken by Seltzer and her colleagues (Seltzer et al., 1991; Essex et al., 1997). Findings suggest a poor fit between parental planning and service system resource decisions. For example, low level parental planning (e.g. adding the person's name to a local service residential waiting list) was not found to be synonymous with factors that led to residential placement, which primarily occurred in emergency situations when caregiving was no longer tenable. Two possible explanations are suggested, both of which indicate planning may be less efficacious than anticipated. Either the service system is only responsive to emergencies and allocation of resources is based on urgency rather than systematically planned for and foreseen need, or alternatively, parents turn down offers of placement, refusing to implement plans and relinquish care until absolutely necessary. This latter point suggests the importance of a focus on preparation for the transition from parental care as well as the formulation of plans.

Few writers raise questions about the appropriateness of parents formulating plans that resemble detailed blueprints for the future of their adult child with intellectual disability. However, Grant (1988) suggests that contemporary ideologies and values reflected in the service system may challenge taken-for-granted rights of parents to decide the future pattern of care. Edgerton (1994, p. 56), alternatively, does not discuss planning directly but implies its restrictiveness when he notes that:

> The lives of mentally retarded people who live with their parents or residential care providers are over determined; one might say because not only is their present day organised, arranged and regimented by other people, so is tomorrow and the future.

Attempting to identify a plan, particularly one that involves a suitable and desired residential situation for the rest of their adult child's life may not be realistic for some parents. It may be argued that it is inappropriate, particularly in view of the lack of consultation that sometimes occurs, the later life development that is yet to be experienced, and the risk of locking someone into an environment that may become inappropriate or be more restrictive than warranted.

SUMMARY

Central themes to emerge from this review of older parental carers of adults with intellectual disability and planning for the future care of their co-resident adult children are the reluctance of parents to make concrete plans, and the dilemmas and difficulties that confront parents and service providers if they do embark on the planning process. A range of suggested approaches and roles for professionals in facilitating parental planning are reviewed but the absence of a store of practice wisdom and the existence of few specialist programs mean the efficacy of these approaches is largely untested. Despite the recent focus on the critical importance of planning, its effectiveness has not been well researched. This study contributes substantially to existing knowledge of whether planning is a crucial task for parents and which types of plans are most successful in achieving the dual aims of a smooth transition from parental care and longer term security and stability for adults with intellectual disability as they age.

CHAPTER *3*

Sources of support in later life

Through choice, commitment or simply a lack of alternative options, a majority of adults with intellectual disability receive the bulk of support from informal sources and live with their parents who play a pivotal role in their lives (Beange & Taplin, 1996; Fujiura & Braddock, 1992; Seltzer & Krauss, 1994; Walmsley, 1996). The ageing of adults with intellectual disability coupled with that of their parents and life course changes of other family members inevitably bring associated changes to family relationships and informal support. Adults who are co-resident with ageing parents live in a social world dominated by family, with few friends of their own. Their support networks are typically family embedded and community insulated (Grant, 1993; Prosser & Moss, 1996). Hands-on care is primarily a mother's responsibility but siblings and other relatives provide support and companionship both to parents and the adult with intellectual disability. Parental death or incapacity will cause a major life transition, a shift to non-parental care, and mark an upheaval and re-arrangement of their informal support networks.

An understanding of the roles informal supports can fulfil and knowledge of the type of informal supports available to an individual provide important indicators of the nature of formal services that a person may require. However, knowledge about the family relationships and informal support available to older people with intellectual disability, when their parents are dead or incapacitated is extremely limited (Krauss & Erickson, 1988; Krauss et al., 1992; Seltzer & Krauss, 1994; Seltzer et al., 1993). This chapter examines the nature and significance of informal support for older people, predictors of informal support for ageing adults with intellectual disability and the limited research about their informal support networks in the post parental care phase of their lives.

CONCEPTUALISATIONS OF INFORMAL SUPPORT

Informal support is often imprecisely defined and used interchangeably with terms like informal care, social support network, social support, community care, or simply care. The importance of personal relationships is central to most conceptualisations of these phenomena.

> Informal care provided by family, friends or neighbors is care provided on the basis of affective and particularistic ties that link particular individuals. The basis may be different—common membership of a kinship system, personal affinity between friends, geographical propinquity among neighbors—but in all cases, in contrast to the other three types of care, this is provided on the basis of personal ties between individuals as individuals. (Bulmer, 1987, p. 17)

The nature of support provided informally can be far-reaching. For example, Hooyman defines informal social networks as:

> A series of linkages along which information, emotional reassurances and services flow to and from a person and his or her exchange relationships. These services may be economic, social or emotional. What distinguishes informal social networks from traditional social service delivery is that within the former, exchanges are not formalised. Instead, informal networks rely on people caring about each other and on their natural helping tendencies. (Hooyman, 1983, p. 133)

As Hooyman suggests, informal support is a multidimensional concept, broader than just the provision of direct assistance or supervision with personal care and the tasks of everyday living. It can fulfil a broad spectrum of functions from tangible direct care tasks; emotional support and companionship to indirect tasks such as care management, advocacy and intangible roles such as caring about and overseeing of wellbeing.

One of the simplest conceptions is that of Bulmer who considers that informal care has three components: physical tending, that is the most intimate kind of support; material and psychological support, that involves provision of direct services but not physical contact; and more generalised concern about the welfare of others, that may or may not lead to the other two types of help (1987). Parker (1981) suggests that care describes two kinds of involvement: care about people that includes feelings of concern or anxiety, and the actual work of looking after those who cannot do so for themselves, involving feeding, washing, protecting and comforting. Parker calls this latter type of care tending. Subsequent authors have used a similar dichotomy, although different language, to distinguish between caring for and caring about people (Dalley, 1988; Land, 1995). Seltzer and her colleagues dichotomised care into either instrumental, the provision of direct aid; or affective, the provision of emotional support (Seltzer & Krauss, 1994).

Sussman (1985) suggests that families provide direct or indirect care to older people. He conceptualises indirect care differently from either generalised caring about or affective support. His notion of indirect care is that families act as facilitators, protectors, advocates and buffers for older people in relation to bureaucracies, and provide information about service options. This idea reappears, reframed in modern language, with the suggestion that families should have a case management role and plan services on the behalf of individuals (Cantor, 1989; Seltzer, 1992b). Case management is suggested as the most important care providing function that a family can fulfil on behalf of an elderly relative (Lowy, 1985).

Many conceptualisations of informal care include a component, variously called instrumental support, direct care or tending, that meshes with the tasks performed by a primary carer or caregiver. These terms, primary carer or caregiver, are often used to refer to parents of adults with intellectual disability who live at home with them. These roles involve the provision of personal care or assistance and supervision with tasks of daily living such as housekeeping and food preparation (Greenberg et al., 1993; Roberto, 1993a).

'Care' and 'carers' have gained prominence in recent years. Twigg and Atkin suggest 'a striking element of the last decade has been the increasing reference to carers in public policy domains, carers have moved out of the shadows into the policy area' (1994, p. 1). The term 'carer' is commonly applied to the primary caregivers of a variety of groups such as children with disabilities, older people, and adults with physical, intellectual or psychiatric disabilities. However, this term is misleading, since different definitions of the extent and nature of care that has to be provided to qualify as a carer are used (Nolan et al., 1996; Schofield et al., 1998).

The shift towards a focus on carers has also been criticised as contributing to the enhancement of dependency for people with disabilities, shifting the focus from the person requiring support and confusing notions of care with support (Dalley, 1997; Swain & French, 1998). Such criticism comes particularly from the independent living movement (Morris, 1993). Further, the focus on a carer as the main provider of informal support detracts from a broader understanding of informal support and the complementary and valuable roles often played by other informal sources. The term carer is used almost exclusively in relation to people who are cared for at home (ABS, 1995) which means that the continued role of informal support for people who do not live in the community is easily overlooked using this perspective.

The focus on carers has, however, brought community attention to the enormous burdens of care borne by community members. It has unified carers of diverse groups and acted as a catalyst for advocacy, analysis of the economic costs of community care and provision of support to informal carers (Carers Association of Australia, 1995; Rosenman, 1991). The scope of this book extends beyond primary carers and encompasses a much broader notion of informal support that is firmly grounded in personal relationships and involves a range of possible components that may be provided by kin, friends or neighbours in the context of the community or supported residential accommodation.

THE SIGNIFICANCE OF INFORMAL SUPPORT

Community care, which has been a dominant theme of social policy since the 1980s, has focused much attention on the nature and importance of informal support to older people and people with disabilities (Bornat et al., 1997; d'Abbs, 1991; Graham, 1993; Twigg & Atkin, 1994). Pierce and Nankervis suggests a basic philosophical principle underpins community care policy: 'receiving care at home is infinitely better than in institutions' (1998, p. 107). The policy emphasises the deinstitutionalisation of people with intellectual and psychiatric disabilities and the avoidance of residential care for older people. These policies are underpinned by the existence of and reliance on informal sources of support which are principally the family and women: 'Community care means care by family and in practice, care by the family equals care by women' (Finch & Groves, 1980, p. 494). For example, a large scale Australian study of carers found that 79% were women (Schofield et al., 1998).

Informal care provides the bulk of services for older and disabled people (Hooyman, 1983; Chappell, 1990; Fine & Thompson, 1995; McDonald, 1997). 'It is universally recognised that members of social support networks, especially kin, play a vital role in supporting and caring for the elderly' (Jarvis, 1993, p. 2). Large-scale statistical surveys support these findings. For example, an Australian survey showed family members provided more than 80% of the assistance given to older people (McDonald, 1997). Despite the increased provision of community services in recent years, the availability of informal support, particularly by a co-resident, remains the most crucial factor enabling frail older people to remain in the community (Cantor & Little, 1985; Fine & Thompson, 1995; Horowitz, 1985; Rosenman, 1991).

Effective informal support networks are connected to psychological and physical wellbeing and lower use of formal services: 'In sum social support for older people appears to be related to higher morale, less loneliness and worry, feelings of usefulness, a sense of individual respect within the community and a zest for life' (Hooyman, 1983, p. 139).

The focus of most research has been on people living in the community; however, although the roles fulfilled may vary, informal sources of support can be equally significant for people entering long-term care (Bear, 1990; Litwak, 1985). Litwak suggests that informal sources will have important ongoing roles where primary care tasks, such as household management, are replaced by formal organisations (1985). Formal organisations routinise tasks and neglect the idiosyncratic needs of the people. Informal sources can compensate for these tendencies by supplementing services; for example, by helping with personal grooming or supplementing diets. Litwak also suggests that a formal organisation cannot take over all tasks performed by families or friends. They are unable to adequately provide emotional support or financial and personal affairs management and, if kin do not provide such services when an older person is institutionalised they may be lost.

BALANCING THE INTERESTS OF CARER AND CARE RECIPIENT

Informal support may, however, also have some negative aspects and research also refers to the possible costs of being a care recipient, the importance of achieving a balance between the interests of carers and care recipients and the potential tensions and conflicts between their respective needs (Kahana, Kahana, Johnson, Hammond & Kercher, 1995; Morris, 1993; Walmsley, 1996). Little is known about the mechanism by which informal support influences wellbeing and the link may have been exaggerated (d'Abbs, 1991).

Incongruities may exist between the perceptions of the caregiver and care recipient so that informal help may at times involve capture and control. For example, one writer suggests that many disabled people feel stifled and oppressed by the care they receive and have little control over the amount received or the manner in which it is provided: 'the care they have received is often of a custodial nature, and provided in a controlled way' (Macfarlane, 1996, cited in Swain & French, 1998, p. 81).

Grant raises similar issues and discusses the possible conflicting interests between people with intellectual disability and their families, who are often unquestioningly accepted as speaking for them, (Grant, 1986; McGrath & Grant, 1993). The nature of the caring relationships between older parental carers and adults with intellectual disability is further illuminated by Walmsley who developed a threefold typology of family relationships: 'supportive', 'dependant' and 'conflict ridden' (1996). She describes a subgroup of mutually supportive relationships, which occur when one parent has died and the surviving parent becomes physically frailer. Help is proffered from both sides with tasks such as gardening, cooking, housework and shopping undertaken by the adult with intellectual disability who often takes a pride in his or her role. However, the sometimes restrictive nature of these relationships was also noted. For example, in this study one man said, 'not being nasty, but when my mum goes I'd like to marry Isabelle' (Walmsley, 1996, p. 12). Some dependant relationships were characterised by a reversal of the expected norm, where an infirm parent was almost totally dependent on his or her offspring, whose freedom was considerably restricted. However, despite increased interdependency in later life caring relationships, Walmsley found they continued to be characterised by the parental control over key aspects of their adult child's life (1996). The norms of caring developed by parents over many years often include parental control over many aspects of the adult child's life, including mediating their contact with the community which is often labelled 'overprotective' (Shearn & Todd, 1996). It may be perceived to have jeopardised the growth and development of their offspring and provoke feelings of anger and frustration in professional staff (McCallion & Tobin, 1995; Smith & Tobin, 1993a).

PREDICTORS OF SUPPORT NETWORKS FOR OLDER ADULTS WITH INTELLECTUAL DISABILITY

The nature and extent of an individual's informal support network changes through his or her life course, determined by the interaction of a multiplicity of factors, including individual characteristics and situational factors, mediated, in particular, by gender and family ties (Antonucci & Akiyama, 1987). The nature of support networks while parents are alive, and parental centrality as primary carers and as a pivotal link to other family and friends indicates the occurrence of a significant upheaval when parents die or become incapacitated. Because most people with intellectual disability will not have married or had children (Ashman et al., 1993), in later life they will lack a spouse and children who typically provide the bulk of care to older people. Their closest relatives in the post-parental care phase will be siblings, aunts, uncles or cousins. Mainstream gerontological studies suggest that relatives such as these are much more likely to provide affective support and do not normally play significant instrumental or caregiving roles (Cicirelli, 1992; Johnson & Catalano, 1981; Wenger, 1987). Also, the nature of support from these relatives, particularly siblings, while parents are alive suggests that informal support may be limited and that replacement of parental roles, particularly in the realm of direct caregiving may be problematic.

Parental protection from a hostile community means that adults with intellectual disability may have been insulated from the community and have had few opportunities to make their own choices or to extend and build their social network. The protected lives that many adults experience makes predicting their future network characteristics and support needs difficult, since their potential for building relationships and coping in a less protective environment will not have been tested and will be largely unknown.

Theoretical propositions

Theories of informal support proposed by Litwak (1985) and Finch and Mason (1993), suggest the possible nature of informal support available to adults with intellectual disability after the death of their parents. Litwak's theory of differential primary groups suggests that, because of their different group structures, members of an informal support network cannot easily substitute for one another. Thus, it is unlikely that other kin will replace the day-to-day personal care and supervisory tasks that a parent has fulfilled, since they will not have the required characteristics (commitment, proximity, frequent contact, available resources). Replacement is only likely to occur where a network member with atypical characteristics exists, such as an unmarried sibling who lives in close proximity (Litwak, 1985). However, other close family members are likely to continue in their existing roles and may substitute for those tasks, previously fulfilled by a now absent network member, which match their characteristics. An example of this may be a task such as financial management that requires long-term commitment but not proximity. However, Litwak suggests that siblings, because they may also be elderly and have their own family commitments, may have a limited capacity to provide support and may not have the necessary resources to substitute for missing network members.

No clear rules of family obligation determine which kin will provide what support. Finch and Mason (1993) suggest that kin responsibilities to each other develop and change over time, built on and reflecting the history and nature of relationships between individuals, and that 'specific responsibilities emerge as part of a long standing relationship between the parties which have a past as well as a present and anticipate a future' (Finch & Mason, 1993, p. 28). Sets of commitments by particular family members will develop over time through a process of implicit or explicit negotiations that appear to follow certain patterns. Thus, people in similar kin positions may negotiate very different responsibilities. The structural position of people in respect to gender and genealogy will influence the commitments they negotiate but the influence will be relative to each individual biography without any logically predictable pattern. This model suggests the difficulty of predicting from kin relationships alone what kind of support will be provided. A person who lacks close family members may have other more distant kin with strong commitments towards them. This suggests the importance of understanding relationships among family members, and informal agreements, when considering the nature of informal support that may be available.

Finch and Mason's model underlines the importance that individual family dynamics play in determining the later life support networks and perhaps also the salience of parental plans and expectations. Parents often have high expectations about the role siblings will play in future care but, as they are reluctant to make plans, such expectations often remain informal or implicit (see chapter 2). Seltzer and her colleagues suggest that the current involvement of siblings is an important predictor of their expected and intended future role in provision of support to their brother or sister with intellectual disability (Seltzer et al., 1996).

Social networks are not synonymous with social support but are frameworks for the study of the provision of support. They are the vehicles through which support is exchanged, although not all network members provide support. Analysis of social networks draws attention to the structure of relationships among a set of actors, the specific exchanges that take place and the roles actors play in relation to one another (Bulmer, 1987). It provides an understanding of how the transmission of support is related to the characteristics of an individual, the ties that link network members and the network that contains those ties. By opening up for investigation supportive ties anywhere in a network, this approach avoids the assumption that social support is provided by specified social or kin categories.

The 'convoy of social support' is a model of social networks over the life course, which offers 'a global theoretical framework of interpersonal relationships over time' (Antonucci & Akiyama, 1987, p. 519). The model suggests that the history of supportive relationships is central to understanding present relationships, and that people move through life surrounded by a convoy of others with whom they exchange social support. Convoys are lifelong but dynamic, varying across time and situations.

The model is a framework to organise factors that determine the structure and functions of an individual's support network over the life course. The properties of the individual, their demographic characteristics, personality and abilities, are one set of factors. The properties of the situation, external aspects of the environment, roles occupied, place of residence, organisational membership and life events are another set. Both sets affect the structure of the convoy that is associated with size, connectedness, stability, symmetry, complexity and homogeneity. The convoy structure in turn affects its functions; the actual support given or received, or exchanges by members of the convoy. Properties of the convoy combine to determine its adequacy that is generally measured by the individual's subjective opinion and directly related to wellbeing.

The model provides a useful framework which brings together the variables that influence an individual's social support network across time. By stressing their dynamic nature it emphasises changes that occur to social networks over the life course. This has particular relevance to people with intellectual disability and notions of parental planning for future care by highlighting an awareness that support networks can alter as individuals and their convoy members age, and as a result of environmental and/or situational changes.

INFORMAL SUPPORT NETWORKS OF OLDER ADULTS IN THE POST-PARENTAL CARE PHASE

Several distinct threads are identified in the literature concerning informal support networks of older people with intellectual disability. The most dominant refers to the limited nature of networks and characterises this group as 'the familyless elderly' (Hogg et al., 1988) who unlike their 'normal' peers, may have no significant others as early as middle age because they have not married or lived in the community to develop friendships with neighbours, and carers (often parents) have died (Gibson et al., 1992). It is suggested that friends and professionals will be more important than family in support networks and that the few family members involved will be mainly siblings, nieces and nephews (Krauss & Erickson, 1988; Seltzer, 1985). Owing to their network characteristics and their perceived difficulty in replenishing any losses to their support networks, older people with intellectual disability are thought to be particularly vulnerable to social isolation (Kropf, 1994; Seltzer & Seltzer, 1985).

Related to this thread, it is often suggested that older people with intellectual disability have a high need for formal services. For example, one study noted that 'Late adult "placement" in a care facility or nursing home is the probable alternative for a disabled person who has lost his or her parents' (Walz et al., 1986, p. 626); and another suggested that 'Parents who have maintained their adult children at home are reaching ages where they must place their middle-aged children into residential settings' (Lakin et al., 1991, p. 66). Although supported accommodation is the most commonly identified service necessary in later life, other areas such as advocacy and case management have also been suggested as being important (Gibson et al., 1992). It is striking that when the loss of parents is anticipated, the continuing or additional roles that remaining informal network members may play are often ignored.

A different, more positive thread, but one for which there is little evidence, points to the intergenerational transmission of caregiving, suggesting that informal support, particularly that provided by siblings, will be important in the provision of care to older people with intellectual disability. For example, Janicki and Seltzer suggest:

> The public sector would not be able to absorb the wave of new clientele if, upon death of the parent, all adults with developmental disabilities who remained at home up to that point needed publicly-supported residences. Rather, it is the extended family, primarily the siblings, who step in as primary caregivers when the parents are no longer able to fulfil this function. (1991, p. 103)

Further, it is also suggested that:

> for aging persons with developmental disabilities, parents then siblings take on the primary responsibility of providing care. In both situations women (i.e. wives, mothers or daughters) tend to be responsible for providing day to day care for the recipient. (Roberto, 1993b, p. 16)

Similarly, much of the focus is on the replacement of the primary carer, and other more intangible roles informal sources may fulfil are largely neglected.

Network characteristics

A common characteristic of the informal support networks of older people with intellectual disability is the absence of an informal primary carer. Although Gordon and her colleagues suggest little evidence exists to test the accuracy of the assumption that parental death is a catalyst for placement in a residential facility, consistently less than a fifth of older people with intellectual disability are reported to live in a private home (Ashman et al., 1993; Bigby, 1994; Gordon et al., 1997; Hand & Reid, 1989; Hogg & Moss, 1993; Prosser & Moss, 1996). This trend is illustrated by a longitudinal study of ageing carers where three-quarters of the 21 adults with intellectual disability who had lost both their parents moved to a formal residential setting (Gordon et al., 1997). However, in sharp contrast, Edgerton's (1994) longitudinal study of ex-institutionalised older people found that all the study cohort lived in private homes in the community, most without a primary carer. This serves as a reminder that not all people with intellectual disability require such a carer.

Several qualitative studies give an indication of who, if anyone, replaces parents as informal primary carers and the frequency with which this occurs. In the absence of parents it is predominantly siblings and occasionally more distant relatives or family friends who provide informal primary care (Gordon et al., 1997; Grant et al., 1995; Heller & Factor, 1991; Prosser & Moss, 1996). For example, Gordon et al. reported that it was siblings who replaced parents as primary carers in all five instances where the continued provision of informal primary care occurred (1997). However, the limited evidence available suggests that primary carers who replace parents do so only on a short-term basis and that a period of informal non-parental primary care is often followed by a move to supported accommodation (Grant, 1988; Prosser & Moss, 1996).

The influence of family relationships

Survey data show that, with some exceptions, older people with intellectual disability are childless and unmarried (Ashman et al., 1993; Hand, 1994; Moss et al., 1989). Thus, for the majority, a sibling will be their closest relative but for the estimated 30% without siblings it will be aunts, uncles, cousins, nieces or nephews (Ashman et al., 1993). In spite of these atypical family constellations, Hogg and Moss (1993) suggest that family remain the chief providers of informal support as people with intellectual disability age. Blacher (1993) suggests that family members may be the only people with a long-term relationship to the older person and a perspective broad enough to encompass all of a person's service needs.

The proportion of older people with intellectual disability to have at least occasional contact with relatives varies considerably. For example, Hand (1994) found that 71% were in contact, and Kearney et al. (1993) found that 45% were in contact. Seltzer (1985) concluded that probably no more than one-third of ageing people with intellectual disability had contact with their siblings. However, early results from her longitudinal study suggest that when both parents are deceased, in every family siblings have some involvement and where multiple siblings exist, generally more than one has regular contact with their brother or sister with intellectual disability (Gordon et al., 1997). A study of older residents in British long stay hospitals found that just over half had no contact with family members, which is similar to findings from an Australian national survey (Ashman et al., 1993; Kearney et al., 1993). Similarly, a US study of older people in supported accommodation found that half had no living family or were never visited by them, and of the other half, 6% saw a relative weekly, 8% monthly and 35% less than monthly (Anderson et al., 1992).

Studies of institutionalised and ex-institutionalised older people suggest the salience of care background to family contact. For example, Skeie (1989) found that where institutional residents had spent much of their lives at home, siblings were more likely to replace parents as regular visitors than they were for residents who had been institutionalised most of their lives. Similarly, Edgerton (1994) suggests that family members were unimportant in the support networks of his ex-institutional cohorts. However, despite this, a very positive picture of their social networks emerged. Edgerton (1988, p. 333) suggests older individuals were 'embedded in worlds of meaningful and reciprocal relationships with other people'.

The nature of family relationships, need and parental expectations are associated with sibling roles. Indicators suggest that siblings may fulfil or exceed the expectations of their parents regarding their involvement in the life of their brother or sister with intellectual disability (Griffith & Unger, 1994). Hogg and Moss (1993) suggest that the age, functional level, or type of residence of the person with intellectual disability will not affect contact with relatives. However, their study and several others (Hand, 1994; Ashman et al., 1993) tend to indicate that place of residence may be a factor. People in institutions have the least contact with relatives and those living with family tend to have most (Hogg & Moss, 1993). This variability may, however, be due more to their residential and family history rather than simply a function of their current place of residence. Ashman et al., (1990) suggest that locations may also be a factor, in that people in rural areas are usually more involved with their relatives than people who lived in the city.

Friends and acquaintances

Studies indicate that most friendships of older people with intellectual disability are tied to a specific context and only about half those with friends have contact with them outside their place of residence or day activity (Anderson et al., 1992; Ashman et al., 1993; Hogg & Moss, 1993). For example, Ashman et al. (1993) indicate that, while 70% to 90% of people had social contact with friends or staff at work or in their place of residence, only 40% had contact with them outside these settings. Context specific friendships pose the challenge of ensuring the maintenance of friendships as people age and retire from day centres or move from house to house. It appears, however, that maintenance of friendship ties across contexts rarely occurs and that severed long-term ties with friends who have a disability are not replaced by new friendships with peers who do not have a disability (Grant et al., 1995).

With the exception of Edgerton's sample, approximately one-third of older people with intellectual disability are thought to be without friends (Grant et al., 1995). Accounts and perceptions of friendships differ among respondents. Grant and his colleagues found that most older people with intellectual disability claimed to have access to a network of social acquaintances and friends in their community. However, they suggest subtle differences exist between these two types of social relationships, and although everyone had acquaintances, friendships involving intimacy and reciprocity were rarer (Grant et al., 1995). This study highlights the significance of acquaintances in social networks and suggests that older people are more likely to lack friends than they do acquaintances. Acquaintances can provide a sense of identity or belonging to the community and at the same time place few expectations on people. Despite the existence of acquaintances in the community, older people do not appear to have strong relationships with their communities. For example, Grant et al. (1995, p. 42) conclude that individuals 'experienced degrees of physical, functional and organisational integration in their social lives but lacked personal, social and societal integration in a variety of ways'. Anderson et al. (1992) found that only 45% of older people, from a variety of residential situations, had met a neighbour. The residential mobility experienced by people with intellectual disability, especially those who have lived with parents, disrupts longstanding relationships and connections with local communities (Grant et al., 1995).

It seems that individual characteristics affect friendships more than family relationships such that more competent people are likely to have more contact with friends (Moss et al., 1989). Environmental factors also have a significant influence on friendship patterns and Nahemow (1988) suggests that older people are particularly affected by the environment in which they live. Older people with intellectual disability who live independently in the community or in group homes have consistently been shown to have more contact with friends than those living in institutions or with family (Anderson et al., 1992; Ashman et al., 1993; Hogg & Moss, 1993). The strong tendency for older people with intellectual disability to live in residential settings that are restrictive and present a poor fit between level of functional competence and environmental opportunities offered, provides some explanation for the vulnerability and limited nature of their friendship ties (Baker et al., 1977; Bigby, 1997; Seltzer et al., 1988; Seltzer et al., 1982).

THE INTERSECTION OF FORMAL AND INFORMAL SOURCES OF SUPPORT

Using a detailed network typology, Wenger demonstrates that the level and nature of formal support required by an older person is dependent on their network type. Different types of networks throw up different needs and problems. Network types may change over time. Her work links a theoretical approach to social networks with professional need assessment and intervention (Wenger, 1991, 1994, 1995). The identification of a network type is a reliable shortcut to predict the availability of informal support, the nature of reciprocal relationships, type of presenting difficulties and the effects that the passage of time or growing dependency may have, and assists in planning social intervention (Wenger, 1994).

Models of social work practice have examined more directly the interweaving of formal and informal sources of support (Biegal, 1985; Challis & Davies, 1986; Collins & Pancoast, 1976; Hooyman, 1983; Sharkey, 1989; Trevillion, 1992; Whittaker, 1986). For example, one conceptual framework for the integration of formal and informal care suggests the social worker's role should be that of a network or system consultant (Whittaker, 1986). Other claims are made for use of a network approach in social intervention:

> Network analysis may prove to be a useful means of moving towards assessments that go beyond the narrow possibilities of services provided by one agency. It may help the movement towards care planning, case management, a better partnership with other workers and with informal carers, and new imaginative forms of intervention. (Sharkey, 1989, p. 403)

As suggested earlier, a focus on carers and more generally informal sources of support is characteristic of recent changes in the pattern of welfare service delivery across many sectors, particularly aged care. This pattern is exemplified by Baldock and Evers (1991) who suggest that the traditional pattern of personal care services has changed from one based on standardised services where interaction with informal systems was implicit to a new pattern where services are flexible, interaction with informal care systems is explicit and informal and formal care are complimentary rather than substitutes for each other.

A primary role identified for formal services, in some instances, has been to support and strengthen networks of informal carers (Griffiths, 1988). This approach is derived from a perception that an untapped reservoir of informal support exists in the community that can be harnessed to meet social needs, and assumes that all relationships can be turned into caring ones (d'Abbs, 1991; Specht, 1986). The use of a network approach and promotion of the informal sector in this manner is critiqued as providing the opportunity for the state to retreat from its role as a provider of social services by shifting the balance of care towards the unpaid labor of women (d'Abbs, 1991; Baldock & Evers, 1991; Land, 1995).

The effective interweaving of formal and informal support is important to maximise outcomes for older people. Some coordination of formal organisation and primary group's activities must occur but obstacles such as the contrasting structures of these two groups make it difficult to achieve (Bulmer, 1987). The balance theory of coordination suggests a mid point exists between formal organisations and primary groups when they are close enough to coordinate tasks but distant enough to prevent a clash of structures (Dobrof & Litwak, 1977). However, Bulmer (1987) suggests that in different situations, various types of relationships exist between the two forms of support, including colonisation of the informal by the formal, competition, conflict, coexistence, collaboration, and confusion. Twigg and Atkin (1994) demonstrate that relationships between carers and formal services are affected by the professional's perception of the caring situation. Carers are perceived either as resources, co-workers, co-clients, or as having no valid role and needing to be superseded. They suggest that, where younger adults with intellectual disability are cared for, significant conflict occurs between informal and formal sources of support and the dominant model is one of superseded care. An Australian study of relationships between formal and informal care concluded that for true interweaving of support systems to occur, changes are needed to the organisation and funding of services and additional resources are required (Fine, 1994).

The intersection of informal and formal systems of support will be an important issue for older people with intellectual disability. Theories of informal support, particularly Litwak's, strongly indicate that both formal and informal sources will be required to replace services previously undertaken by parents. Though various sources of support may be complementary, the literature reviewed here suggests the balance and intersection between them may be problematic.

SUMMARY

This chapter considered empirical research and theory concerning provision of informal support and discussed its application to older people with intellectual disability. The significance and breadth of informal sources of support for older people was considered. However, the application of theories of informal support suggests, for various reasons, that people with intellectual disability may not find informal sources to replace all the care previously provided by their parents; in particular, tasks such as day-to-day supervision and household management. A review of the limited literature concerned specifically with informal relationships of older people with intellectual disability indicates that only a small proportion have informal primary carers and these are usually only short-term carers. The extent of family contact is variable and the nature of family support remains largely unexplored although the significance of siblings in parental expectations is apparent. Indications are that friendships may be tied to specific contexts and are more likely to be influenced by individual characteristics and external factors than is family support. This review suggests that formal sources of support may be very important to older people with intellectual disability. However, various propositions from the literature on social intervention suggest the intersection of formal and informal support may require specific attention and resources.

CHAPTER 4

Older people with intellectual disabilities: A diverse and hidden population?

The term 'older people with intellectual disability' encompasses a diverse group from a broad age span, with different life experiences, abilities, and service histories. Determining the demographic characteristics of this group is problematic because of a dearth of data, the differing definitions used, and the existence of a 'hidden' group who are unknown to formal service systems. This chapter reviews data on the size and characteristics of this population, highlighting its diversity. The latter part introduces the group of older people with intellectual disability who are the focus of this book.

DEFINING AN 'OLDER PERSON'

Gerontologists define old age by using chronological age, and from the perspective of functional changes that occur as a person grows older. They refer to biological ageing, psychological ageing and social ageing (Hooyman & Kiyak, 1991). Concepts such as the 'third age' and 'fourth age' or 'young old' and 'old old' are also used (Janicki, 1992; Laslett, 1989). Most commonly, however, gerontologists differentiate the 'young old' as 65-plus, the 'old old' as 75-plus and 'oldest old' as 85-plus.

There is no consistent definition of an older person with intellectual disability but, generally, a lower age than for the broader community is used. Reviewing 35 studies of older people with intellectual disability, Seltzer and Krauss (1987) found 11 different age cut-offs, ranging from 40 to 75 years; with varying terms, including 'older adults', 'aged', 'ageing' and 'elderly adults' being used. The most common age used was 55 years. More recently, definitions of older adults that have been used are 50 years in a national survey of older people with an intellectual disability in New Zealand (Hand, 1994), 50 years in an Oldham, UK survey (Hogg & Moss, 1993), 60 years in several studies in Victoria, Australia (Bigby, 1992; Community Services Victoria, 1992a) and 55 years in an Australian national survey (Ashman et al., 1993). Studies by Krauss and Erickson

(1988) and Prosser and Moss (1996) focusing on the family and informal support networks of older adults use the lower age of 40 years.

Any chronological cut-off point is arbitrary and may result in the inclusion of some individuals who, on the basis of their current physical, psychological and social abilities, would not be considered elderly in a functional sense, or in the exclusion of younger individuals who already exhibit signs of premature ageing (Seltzer & Krauss, 1987). The propensity of people with Down syndrome to experience premature ageing accounts to an extent for the low chronological ages sometimes used in definitions, although generally people with intellectual disability age in a similar way to the general population (Seltzer et al., 1994). Seltzer suggests that:

> The challenges of defining old age in this population are substantial, as a result of the atypical ageing manifested by some members of this group and because of their early life onset of functional limitations. There appears to be an emerging consensus that 55 should be used to define the onset of old age in persons with developmental disabilities. (Seltzer, 1992a, p. 594)

SIZE OF THE POPULATION OF OLDER PEOPLE WITH INTELLECTUAL DISABILITY

Population ageing has been a defining characteristic of Western nations in the later part of the twentieth century. In the 1950s approximately 8% of European, North American and Australian populations were aged over 65 years; by 1990 this had increased to 13.4%, 12.5% and 10.9% respectively (Gibson, 1998). Countries have experienced differential rates of growth, but followed a similar trend, with the over 80s age group having the highest rate of growth, increasing at approximately one and a half times the rate of the aged population generally. For example, in Australia between 1985 and 1995 the annual growth rate of the population over 65 years was 3.1%, while in the same period the annual growth rate of the population over 80 years was 5.0% (Gibson, 1998). In the UK, from 1976 to 1996 the over-75 years population increased by 23% and the over-85 years by 42% (Harris, 1998). Table 4.1 shows the proportion of the population over 65 years and over 80 years in the US, UK and Australia for 1992–93.

The absolute numbers and proportions of older people in populations will continue to increase over the next 20 years, although the rate of growth may slow (Gibson, 1998). In Australia the annual growth rate between 1995 and 2005 is forecast to be 1.4% for the over-65-year age

TABLE 4.1 **Proportions of the population over 65 years and over 80 years in the US, UK and Australia for 1992–93**

Country	Percentage of the population 65 years and over	Percentage of the population 80 years and over	Percentage of the over-65 population aged over 80 years
UK	15.8	3.8	24.3
US	12.7	3.0	23.3
Australia	11.7	2.4	20.7

group and 3.3% for the over-80-year age group. Projections are that the number of aged people will continue to increase until 2021, when those over 55 years will constitute 18% of the population. The rate of growth is expected to slow between 1992 and 2011, but then, owing to the ageing of the baby boom generation, to expand again until 2021 (Department of Health Housing & Community Services (DHHCS), 1991). In the US it is estimated that while one in nine of the population were over 60 in 1994, over the next 30 to 40 years this will increase to one in five. A lowering of infant mortality rates, longer life expectancy, falling birth rates and the ageing of the baby boom generation all account for population ageing.

Ageing is a relatively new phenomenon to confront individuals with intellectual disability. The current cohort of older people with intellectual disability is the first group to have survived into later life in any sizeable numbers. This is illustrated by the dramatic change in their life expectancy that has occurred in the past 50 years. The average age of death for people with intellectual disability who lived in institutions was 22 years in 1931, which by 1959 had increased to 59 years (Carter & Jancar, 1983). By 1993, the average age of death for all people with intellectual disability was 66.1 years and 55.8 for people with Down syndrome (Janicki et al., 1999).

Parallel to the general community, the number of older people with intellectual disability is increasing but from a much smaller base. For example, from 1982 to 1997 the proportion of clients, aged over 60 years, registered with Australia's Victorian State Government as having an intellectual disability, doubled from 3% (321) to 6.35% (1201) (Cocks & Ng, 1983; Department of Human Services (DHS), 1997). An Australian national survey in 1993 identified 2543 people with intellectual disability aged over 55 years, who represented 0.07% of the total population in that age group. Estimates suggest that there are between 200 000 to 500 000 older people with intellectual disability in the US (Parkinson & Howard, 1996). Matthew Janicki suggests the size of this group could double over the next 30 years, while for Australia it is suggested that their number will increase by 20% in the next five to ten years (Ashman et al., 1993; Janicki, 1992).

Making accurate estimates of the current and projected population of older people with intellectual disability is hampered by several factors. Large-scale population studies, such as those conducted in Australia by the ABS, use broad classifications of disability and do not treat people with lifelong intellectual disability as a separate group. Although the life span of people with intellectual disability has increased significantly in the past 50 years, this group still has higher age-specific mortality rates and shorter life expectancy than the general population (Eyman & Borthwick-Duffy, 1994). This makes it difficult to extrapolate figures from either the general population or from the population with intellectual disability. The most commonly used figure to estimate the size of this population is 0.4% of the population over 55 years, in contrast to the 1% often used in relation to younger age groups with intellectual disability.

Owing to higher age-specific mortality rates, growth of the 80-plus age group among people with intellectual disability is less significant than among older people generally. In an Australian national sample of people with intellectual disability aged over 65 years, people over 80 years comprised only 7.6% (Ashman et al., 1993). This is a much lower proportion than the estimated 20% of people aged over 65 years who are aged over 80 years in the general community (DHHCS, 1991). In Ashman's study 50% of older people with intellectual disability were aged between 55 and 65 years and 90% were between 55 and 75 years.

Similar trends are found in other studies; for example, a New Zealand national survey found that 55% of the people aged over 50 years were between 51 and 60 years, with only 2% over 80 years. A UK study reported that 5.7% of people with intellectual disability over the age of 50 were over 80 years, while 75.4% were aged between 50 and 70 years. Thus, older people with intellectual disability are predominantly the 'younger old', a trend that is likely to continue.

A further complicating factor in estimating the size of the population of older people with intellectual disability is the suggestion that a high proportion of older people remain 'hidden' in the community and are not counted in client data held by specialist services (Horne, 1989a; Jacobson et al., 1985), an issue discussed further below. Allied to this is the concern that most surveys of older people with intellectual disability have only focused on service users (Seltzer & Krauss, 1994), neglecting those who are unknown to specialist services and perhaps providing a skewed impression of this population's characteristics.

Duffy, Widaman and Eyman (1991), in a lengthy discussion of methodology, suggest that commonly, in studies of older people with intellectual disability, no systematic sampling procedure is used and samples of convenience, those in touch with disability service systems, are used. In their view, such samples are biased against people with a milder intellectual disability, as they are less likely to be in touch with services. Seltzer and Krauss (1994) suggest that virtually all studies of older people with intellectual disability are based on non-probability samples comprising service populations or volunteers meaning that findings can only be generalised to the service population. Hogg writes:

> A critical concern in such studies in the community is the fact that we know many people with mental handicap are unknown to service providers. Purely administratively based surveys, therefore, inevitably involve an underestimate of numbers and are likely in unspecified ways to result in somewhat distorted data. (Hogg, 1990, p. 462)

OVERVIEW OF CHARACTERISTICS OF OLDER PEOPLE WITH INTELLECTUAL DISABILITY

Health and physiological ageing

Most people with intellectual disability age physiologically in a manner similar to the rest of the population, although some groups, most notably people with Down syndrome, show signs of premature ageing. Changes associated with normal physiological ageing include reduced physical stamina, less efficient circulation, sensory changes such as loss of hearing and increasingly poor eyesight, muscoskeletal changes whereby bones become frailer, and increased risk of chronic disease and medical problems (Minichiello et al., 1992). It is notable, however, that despite physiological changes associated with ageing among the general community, two-thirds of older people are free from any condition that makes them dependent on assistance.

No conclusive evidence exists in regard to the relative health status of older people with intellectual disability in comparison to their younger peers. Since people with more severe disabilities have a higher mortality rate, Moss (1991) speculates that older people with intellectual disability would be healthier than their younger peers. However, studies by Sally Cooper (1997a, 1998) suggest that the effects of old age on physical health mean that older people have poorer health than their younger counterparts. In particular, incontinence, reduced mobility, hearing impairment, arthritis, hypertension and cerebrovascular disease are all more common among older than among younger people with intellectual disability. Cooper also suggests that, compared to the general population, older people with intellectual disability have higher rates of hypothyroidism, cerebrovascular disease, epilepsy and Parkinson's disease. Cooper suggests, however, that despite their increased health needs, older people are less likely to have input from health services compared to younger people with intellectual disability (1997b). Similarly, Australian research suggests that older people with intellectual disability have higher rates of untreated medical conditions (Ashman et al., 1996; Beange et al., 1995).

Functional or psychological aspects

Contrary to many of the myths, people's ability to learn is not greatly affected by age. Findings by Lifskitz demonstrate quite clearly that older people with intellectual disability have a continuing ability to learn (1998). This group follows similar trends to other older people in regard to intellectual functioning and adaptive behaviour. For example, many will continue to develop right up to their 60s and their cognitive abilities do not begin to decline until the mid 60s (Adlin, 1993; Hogg et al., 1988). However, there are indications that the memory process may be affected by advancing age, particularly short-term memory.

Older people with intellectual disability are consistently found to have superior skills compared to their younger counterparts on dimensions such as adaptive and challenging behaviour, and functional skills (Walker et al., 1995, 1996). For example, Walker, Walker and Ryan, found that 'though older people were more likely to have a physical disability or a long term illness, in other aspects of everyday living they were less dependant, than those under the age of 50 years' (1996, p. 137). Edgerton suggests that in later life people with intellectual disability are more competent than at any other stage of their life (1994). The apparent higher level of competence in later life is due to both lifelong development and the healthy survivor effect, whereby people with more severe disabilities have higher age-specific mortality rates.

Older people with intellectual disability have higher rates of psychological disturbance and mental illness compared to younger groups, although much of this may be accounted for by the high rates of Alzheimer's disease among people with Down syndrome (Cooper, 1997a). Higher rates may also be associated with personal losses such as death of parents and other relatives and friends that older people are more likely to experience than younger people.

Social attitudes and expectations

Several writers suggest that older people with intellectual disability suffer a double disadvantage, as members of two disadvantaged groups; the aged and the disabled (MacDonald & Tyson, 1988; Walker et al., 1995). Like other older people, those with intellectual disability experience ageism, the negative community stereotypes held about the aged, their skills, value and potential to contribute to society. 'Service providers and others are falling into the trap of stereotyping older people in a way they would not with younger people with intellectual disability' (Walker & Walker, 1998b, p. 140). Evidence from the UK has consistently shown that lower expectations are held in regard to older people with intellectual disability compared to younger people. As a group they experience fewer choices, less programming, decreased access to day services, lower quality programs. They are less likely to be resettled from large institutions and are at risk of being reinstitutionalised in later life (Cooper, 1997b; Walker & Walker, 1998b). A primary barrier to social inclusion may be the low expectations held by those around older people with intellectual disability, rather than any other element (Walker & Walker, 1998b, p. 141). Several writers including Wolfensberger, one of the architects of normalisation, suggest that all older people are held in low regard by the community and provided with poor quality, segregatory, congregate services.

A major age-related change, associated with social roles and expectations of older people, is retirement from active participation in the workforce. This can be accompanied by financial vulnerability and insecurity, loss of status, and disruption to social networks. It requires a change of lifestyle and replacement of lost roles and structures that regulate day-to-day activities (Encel, 1997). In its narrow conception, retirement will only affect the minority of people with intellectual disability who are in employment, but it is commonly also considered in relation to those who attend various vocational or non-vocational day activity programs. The question often posed in this regard is retirement to what?

Australian studies of older people with intellectual disability reflect trends found overseas. As a group they are the younger old, dispersed across the community (with some notable concentrations where deinstitutionalisation has occurred), experience lower levels of disability, are more likely to live in supported accommodation and less likely to attend day programs than their younger counterparts (Ashman et al., 1993; Bigby, 1994; Janicki & Seltzer, 1991).

A HIDDEN GROUP?

Reference has been made to the 'hidden' population of older people with intellectual disability, (Bigby, 1995; Horne, 1989b) and some writers estimate that as many as 60%–75% are unknown to disability services (Jacobson et al., 1985). Researchers agree that older people and those who are middle-aged living at home with older carers are more likely to be unknown to disability service system than their younger counterparts (Fullmer et al., 1997; Janicki et al., 1998; Moss et al., 1992; Seltzer & Krauss, 1987; Smith et al., 1994).

Horne (1989a) suggests that older people with intellectual disability are hidden to varying degrees, or in different ways; some just lose touch with services while others, or their families, deliberately choose to remain 'hidden'. The relative paucity of service options when the present cohort of older people were younger may explain why they are less likely than younger people to be in touch with disability services. However, it is important to remember that the definition, and therefore the extent and nature of the hidden population, will vary between different local and national administrative and service systems, and across time. For example, the study undertaken by the author demonstrated that most of those hidden from disability services were not well hidden and were known to the aged care service system. However, among those known to disability services, the use of these services decreased as they aged (Bigby, 1994).

Several comprehensive case finding studies illuminate the size of the hidden group. Horne's outreach study conducted in Oldham, UK located 90 older people, identified by various community informants, of whom 79 had an intellectual disability. Forty-six of this group, 58%, were not known to intellectual disability services (Community Mental Handicap Teams) (Horne, 1989a). The subsequent study, undertaken by Moss, Hogg and Horne, which also located older people with intellectual disability through formal channels, comprised 75% who were known to disability services and 25%, located via the outreach study, who were unknown (Moss & Hogg, 1989).

In an extensive New Zealand case finding study, 19% of people with intellectual disability over 50 years who were located had not had previous contact with disability services. Half of the older carers of adults with intellectual disability located by a series of pilot outreach projects by Area Ageing Agencies in New York State were unknown to disability services (Janicki et al., 1998). A study in New York State which sought out older carers of adults who were not using disability day services located 176 older carers whose son or daughter were using day services and 59 who were not. Of these families, 37 had never used a day service. Although non-use of day services was associated with low utilisation of disability services, these families were using aged care services either for the parent or their adult offspring (Smith et al., 1994).

The case finding exercise undertaken by the author for the study reported in this book was the first systematic attempt to establish the existence and extent of the hidden population of older people with intellectual disability in Victoria, Australia. The case finding exercise was undertaken in two administrative regions of Victoria, and identified a total of 215 older people with an intellectual disability, of whom 51 (24%) were not known to the Department of Human Services and therefore a regional disability services team. However, not all of those found by the case finding exercise met the criteria for inclusion in the main study since many had left home prior to mid-life. People with intellectual disability who are known to the Department of Human Services are those registered on their database, which is a requirement of the *Intellectually Disabled Persons Services Act 1986* for the receipt of services funded under the Act. The database includes not only all current service users but also people who are no longer in receipt of services. The database existed in a rudimentary form before the 1986 legislation and therefore includes some people who have been out of touch with the system for as long as 25 years (Ashman et al., 1993; CSV, 1992a).

These case finding studies allow the differences between the hidden and more visible group to be examined, which exemplifies the diversity of the population of older people with intellectual disability. For example, the study by Moss, Hogg and Horne demonstrated that although the characteristics of the two groups were similar, the patterns of formal service they received were quite different. Those who were not in touch with disability services relied mainly on aged care services and had lower levels of community activities and individual programming (Moss et al., 1992; Moss & Hogg, 1989).

In the Victorian study, high proportions of both groups of older people lived in aged care facilities; however, a higher proportion of those unknown to disability services (24%) lived in a private home compared to those who were known (9%). Similar to the expected trend, this study found that people who remain at home with parents until at least the age of 40 years are more likely to be out of touch with disability services in later life than those who leave home prior to the age of 40 years. Half of the older people who had lived at home until the age of 40 were known to disability services compared to 93% of those who had left home prior to the age of 40.

Some understanding of the size and nature of this 'hidden' group is vital in order to understand the service demands they may make in the future and to facilitate service planning. A concern of service providers is that many of those who have remained 'hidden' at home with family and out of touch with services will, as they get older, begin to make demands on the service system for the first time (CSV, 1988; Tippet, 1993).

A DIVERSE POPULATION

Research on older people with intellectual disability has used inconsistent definitions of old age and often failed to differentiate between various sub-categories of the population. This hampers comparison between studies, confuses life course stages and makes it difficult to identify the sources of support for older adults who have been cared for by their parents until mid-life. Ageing people with an intellectual disability are not a homogenous group; although predominantly the young old, they span the entire age range from 55 upwards, and also include those younger people with particular etiologies who experience premature ageing.

Some studies use a wide, undifferentiated age range which includes people as young as 40 years (Krauss & Erickson, 1988; Prosser & Moss, 1996; Seltzer & Krauss, 1987). The use of broad age bands, and the inclusion of people, together in one group, who are at very different stages of their life course obscures the changing sources of support and needs as they age. For example, 'older' can refer to a person in their 40s living at home with parents and to an 80-year-old whose parents died 30 years ago. Broad age spans also obscure the differing capacities of family members, particularly siblings, to provide informal support at various stages in their own life course. For example, the informal support a sibling can provide to a 45-year-old person with intellectual disability at home with elderly parents, when the sibling is aged 40, has teenage children and is a full-time member of the workforce, will be very different from what they could provide 20 years later, at which time the older person is 65 years old and their sibling is aged 60, is widowed, has no child-rearing responsibilities and is retired from the workforce.

Differentiation by age group is also important because the rate of age-related disability and chronic health problems increase quite dramatically with age, with the highest rates among the 80 plus age group. For example, in the general community 44% of people aged between 60 and 65 have one or more chronic illnesses and this proportion increases to 54% between the ages of 65 and 75 and to 66% for those aged over 75. The likelihood of experiencing dementia also increases with age; the prevalence is 1% of people aged between 65 and 75, 7% between the ages of 75 and 85 and 25% of those aged over 80 years (Australian Institute of Health and Welfare (AIHW), 1997).

The physiological ageing processes for most people with intellectual disability are similar to those without a disability (Adlin, 1993; Anderson, 1989). Particular subgroups, however, experience the physical effects of ageing very differently. People with Down syndrome experience premature ageing and increased risk of early onset Alzheimer's disease (Moss & Patel, 1997; Zigman, 1997). This group still has a considerably shorter life expectancy compared to others in the community. The average age of death for a person with Down syndrome is 55.8 years compared to 70.1 for the general population (Janicki et al., 1999). After the age of 50, people with Down syndrome have an increased risk of loss of adaptive skills and a higher risk of Alzheimer's disease compared to other groups, with about 45% developing symptoms of Alzheimer's while they are alive (Dalton et al., 1994). People with severe physical disabilities such as cerebral palsy experience marked physical decline, particularly in respect of mobility, as early as their 40s (Balandin & Morgan, 1997).

Residential history affects later life family relationships and sources of informal support. People in supported accommodation who have lived at home most of their lives and only moved to a placement in later life are often not differentiated from those who have spent most of their lives in an out-of-home placement (Ashman et al., 1993; Hand, 1994; Seltzer, 1985). Yet these two groups are likely to have experienced very different relationships with family and the community, which affects later life informal support (Antonucci & Akiyama, 1987; Skeie, 1989).

Particularly during the next 20 years, the population of older people with intellectual disability will be divided into several distinct groups based on life course history and/or linkages to formal service systems. They will comprise those who have lived a portion of their life in large institutions and have been resettled in the community during adulthood, those who remained with family but left parental care during young adulthood, and those who remained living at home with parents until they reached middle-age. Not all people with intellectual disability will be receiving day or supported living services from the state funded disability service systems as they begin to age. A minority will be working in federally funded supported or open employment schemes, and others may have remained outside the disability service system completely. Of this group, some, particularly those who remained at home with parents may still be living independently in the community, supported informally, and others may be using private supported accommodation services which in Victoria,

Australia are supported residential services. Some evidence suggests a group of older people, who were relocated from institutions prior to the major closures in the early 1990s, are resident in supported residential services and not linked in to any specialist services for people with intellectual disability (Bigby, 1992).

The cohort effect whereby each generation of older people traverses a unique social, cultural and economic context during their life course also accounts for significant differences among older people with intellectual disability. Each cohort will be different from the next and certainly the characteristics and needs of those who are older now are likely to be very different from those of the young adults today when they reach old age.

Policy and service development must address the concerns of the whole age spectrum of older people with intellectual disability and reflect the need for both third and fourth age programs. Account must also be taken of the varying degrees to which ageing people with intellectual disability are already connected to formal service systems and the individual variations associated with the ageing process. This study focused exclusively on a group of older people with intellectual disability who remained living at home with parents until their own middle age, and included those who were both known and unknown to the specialist disability services system.

A DESCRIPTION OF THE STUDY POPULATION

The rest of this chapter introduces the 62 older people with intellectual disability who made up the group for this study. Four case studies give some insights into the variety of their life experiences, relationships and use of services since they left parental care. Thirty-four were male and 28 female, they had all lived in Australia since their childhood and all but three were of Anglo background. All were born in 1939 or before, so they were all aged over 55 years. Their ages ranged from 55 to 87 years, with an average of 65 years. The average age that people left parental care was 52 years, the youngest was 40 years and the oldest was 73 years. At the time of the study, on average people had been living away from their parents for 12 years, although this varied from one to 46 years. The average age of their parents when they relinquished care was 86 years.

All of the group were regarded by both family and service providers as having mild to moderate intellectual disability but their skills and limitations varied. What they had in common were limited intellectual functioning and adaptive skills which resulted in poor numeracy and literacy skills and a requirement for direct assistance or supervision with at least some activities of daily living. Hence, who or what services provided the primary care they required was a crucial issue for this group.

The families of each person had acknowledged their intellectual disability since childhood. For many this meant they had led sheltered lives with very limited expectations of achievement and participation in the community. Most received only a few years of schooling and few had ever been in paid employment. Many primary informants remarked upon the lost opportunities of these older people and the changes that have occurred in social attitudes and expectations towards people with intellectual disability since their childhood. Reference was often made to how different their lives would have been had they had been born at another time.

Clearly, as for all people with an intellectual impairment, disability was a result both of impairment and their experiences within society and social organisation (Oliver, 1990). However, for some of these older people, age-related health problems further complicated the picture. Four of the six people who had Down syndrome, were diagnosed as having Alzheimer's disease. In all, 25% of the group had major health problems that restricted their mobility and affected their functional abilities. A further 25% had minor age-related health problems, such as sensory loss.

Most of these people had an informal social network of family and friends whom they saw at least twice a year. On average, their networks comprised six people, although the size varied from 0–20 people. Family members dominated most informal networks; 33% of the group still had a parent alive and 79% had a sibling. No one had children but two people were married to each other and another was separated from his wife. While most people had informal acquaintances, 33% could not name a friend.

As table 4.2 shows, the majority of the group lived in an aged care facility. Only 10% lived in specialist disability accommodation and 25% lived in a private home, several of whom received domiciliary support services.

The nature of people's accommodation had changed considerably since their transition from parental care. Over 75% of the group had moved house at the time of transition or later. On average, each person had moved twice although the number ranged from one to six moves. The majority of the group relied on an aged or disability support pension as their only source of income, although several had inherited substantial sums from parents or other relatives. Most people did not manage their own financial affairs, although only a few people had a formally appointed administrator.

Most people did not participate in structured day activities although some attended aged persons' day centres, clubs or social groups on a casual

TABLE 4.2 **Type of accommodation at time of study**

Type of accommodation	Number	%
Supported residential service	8	13%
Aged persons' hostel	21	34%
Nursing home	11	18%
(Total aged care facilities)	(40)	(65%)
Home with relatives	7	11%
Home alone or with friends	9	14%
(Total private home)	(16)	(25%)
Disability hostel	4	7%
Group home	2	3%
(Total disability accommodation)	(6)	(10%)
Total	**62**	**100%**

or part-time basis. One person was still working in the job he had held for many years and two worked in a sheltered workshop. The nine people who attended a disability day centre on a full- or part-time basis had done so for more than ten years, some for as many as 40 years.

Just over 50% of the sample, 33 people, were known to a regional disability services team, although less than this used disability services. Only five people had a general service plan prepared by a regional team and even fewer had a case manager. Eighty-five per cent of the group used aged care services, which included home help services, case management programs, aged care residential facilities and day centres.

The average age of people who were not known to regional disability services was marginally higher and this group left home at a slightly older age than those known to disability services. A higher proportion of people unknown to disability services lived in aged care accommodation and in private homes. However, similar to Horne's (1989a) sample, the characteristics of those people who were unknown to disability services did not differ significantly from those who were known. However, people who used disability services were distinguished by their receipt of structured skill development or maintenance programs that are generally not available to those who only use generic aged services.

CASE VIGNETTES

This study examines various dimensions of the life experiences of the group, including parental planning, the outcome of plans, transition experiences, further changes experienced in later life, the nature of primary

TABLE 4.3 **Sources of primary care and strength of informal support network of study population**

Source of primary care	Strength of informal support network	
	Strong	**Weak**
Formal services only	19	6
Informal and formal services	16	11
Informal support only	10	0
Total	**45**	**17**

care provision, informal relationships, and formal sources of support. The following vignettes give some indication of the patterns of these dimensions in the lives of individuals. For this purpose, the study population is classified along two dimensions, the means by which primary care had been provided since transition from parental care, and the strength of their informal support at the time of the study. This classification is demonstrated in table 4.3; the vignettes are drawn from the four largest categories.

Bruce Cooke

Since the transition from parental care, Bruce Cooke has received primary care from informal and formal sources but his life has had very stable elements with a strong supportive informal network. He is an example of a person who has never used specialist disability services and first came into contact with aged care services in later life. His experience illustrates a gradual process of transition from parental care, preceded by informal planning. Bruce, his sister Edith and the hostel supervisor were interviewed.

> Bruce is 78 years old and his transition from parental care was a gradual process that began when he was 72 years old. He now lives in a modern aged persons' hostel five minutes drive from his sister's home. He is frail but still mobile, sometimes incontinent and needs assistance with personal care tasks. Although his sister understands him very well, others have difficulty comprehending what he says. The only contact Bruce has ever had with disability services was when his mother refused the offer of a place at a day centre when he was a young adult.
>
> Bruce lived with both parents until his father died when he was 58. He and his mother then moved to live with his sister Edith and her husband. They lived in a unit attached to Edith's house that his mother financed. His mother died, aged 89 years, after a long illness, during which Edith nursed her. During her mother's illness Edith gradually took over supervision of Bruce's personal care and assured

her mother that she would never abandon Bruce. Bruce still becomes very upset when his mother is mentioned.

For most of Bruce's life, his mother was very protective of him. When they lived with Edith, his main activities were 'doing the messages' for an elderly lady next door, walking around the neighbourhood and accompanying his mother and sister to church meetings. Consequently, Bruce was well known by local residents and shopkeepers. Some time after his mother's death, his sister had to seek care for Bruce while she went into hospital, and was put in touch with an aged care complex. After a period of respite care, Bruce began to attend an elderly persons' day centre once a week. He enjoyed the social events and interaction with other people there.

Edith had several painful spinal operations and in addition her husband developed heart problems and cancer. With her own poor health, she found it increasingly difficult to care for Bruce as well as her husband. Out of necessity rather than choice Edith arranged for Bruce to move into the hostel in the same complex where he attended the day centre.

Bruce moved into the hostel when he was 76. He joins in some organised activities there, and goes for walks around the block. He chats with the other residents but could not name any particular friends. His sister visits him every other day, bringing cake and other tasty food to keep in a tin in case he is hungry and cannot make himself understood. Edith rings the hostel on the days she does not visit. She manages his finances, arranges medical appointments, liaises with the hostel and monitors his care. Although she thinks Bruce is happy there she worries about him. She often brings Bruce home to see his brother-in-law. Edith's daughter, Sonya, visits Bruce at least once a month, bringing her two young children. Four members of the church congregation visit Bruce approximately every three months.

Bruce has three other siblings but it has always been Edith who had the closest relationship with him and his parents. Two of the siblings live interstate, and the other in the country. Neither Bruce nor Edith has had any contact with them since their mother's death, following a dispute about Edith receiving an unfair share of her mother's estate.

Beatrice Rowley

This vignette is of Beatrice Rowley who has received primary care only from formal services. Beatrice received care first in the form of domiciliary support provided by a disability service and then through residence in an aged care facility. Although her informal network is small, it is a very important source of support for Beatrice. She was one of the very few people whom formal service providers assisted in managing the transition from parental care. However, her case illustrates the difficulties and frustrations often experienced in relationships between informal and formal sources of support and the need for consistent reliable support if people with disabilities are to be supported to remain in the family home after the death of their parents. Beatrice's case is also an example of someone whose use of disability services has diminished as she has aged. Beatrice, her niece Karen and the supported residential service proprietor were interviewed.

> Beatrice is 67 years old. She left parental care when she was 51. Now she lives in a supported residential service where most residents are much older than she. She is a petite woman who is quite fit but has eye problems that require an operation. She communicates well and manages her personal care. She is not able to read or write and is aware of her intellectual limitations.
>
> She is registered with a regional disability services team and attended a disability day centre for several years as a young adult. For a few years following her mother's death she received substantial support from disability services, but has not had any contact or services from them for the past six years.
>
> Beatrice's parents separated during her childhood and she lived with her mother. Her mother died, aged 88 years, when Beatrice was 51. Only informal plans had been made for her future, whereby Karen, her niece, was expected to take responsibility for Beatrice. At the time of Beatrice's mother's death, Karen, her closest relative, was aged 37; she lived across the city and had a young child. Karen's mother had died when she was young and she had spent much of her early life living with her grandmother and Aunt Beatrice and established a close relationship with Beatrice. In later years, Karen had not got on with her grandmother but had maintained contact, visiting every couple of weeks. Karen owned the house in which Beatrice and her grandmother lived, having inherited it from her mother.
>
> During her mother's illness, an aged care service provider referred Beatrice to the regional disability services team. In Karen's view the regional team worker took charge of Beatrice after her mother's death, only superficially involving her in plans as next of kin and owner of the house in which Beatrice lived. Karen felt that very few options were considered for Beatrice. The disability worker arranged for Beatrice to remain in her family home and share it with a woman who had previously lived in a state institution for people with intellectual disability. General supervision, help with household management, personal care and social participation were to be provided by a disability outreach support service, whose workers visited regularly.
>
> This arrangement worked extremely well for the first year until the level of support became more unpredictable. In Karen's view, the support workers provided inadequate supervision and guidance with things such as meal planning, personal care and budgeting. Support workers changed frequently and later ones often took a less direct-

ive role and did not have the same commitment as those who had originally devised the plan. The health and fitness of Beatrice and her co-resident declined. They gradually went out less and their relationship deteriorated. Although Karen monitored the situation and was often contacted by concerned neighbours she was unable to supervise their daily lives. At times she had felt overwhelmed by the problems and frustrated in her attempts to negotiate increased support from the regional disability services team.

Despite these concerns, Beatrice and her co-resident managed to live together for ten years until, finally, the co-resident's health problems became critical. A regional team worker arranged for Beatrice to move to a nearby supported residential service and the team has not been in touch with her since.

In the supported residential service, Beatrice shares a room with another woman. She has recently been given a cat. Beatrice likes living there and gets on well with the other residents, some of whom mother her. She regularly attends senior citizens' activities at two local community centres. She enjoys going to these activities and walks there with several other residents. Beatrice participates in more activities now than when she lived with her mother but Karen is concerned that she has too few opportunities, being surrounded by inactive elderly women.

Karen works full time but stays in regular contact by phone and visits in the school holidays. Karen manages Beatrice's affairs, subsidises her living expenses, liaises with the proprietors and organises and takes Beatrice to medical appointments. Beatrice spoke warmly of Karen but also mentioned how busy she was. When discussing friends, Beatrice spoke of a previous support worker whom she no longer sees and did not name any current friends other than the proprietor of the supported residential service.

Lloyd Simpson

This vignette is of Lloyd who, like Bruce, has received primary care from informal sources and then later from formal services. For him, the passage of time and death of his parents and then closest siblings has weakened his informal support network and he is increasingly reliant on formal services to oversee his wellbeing as well as provide primary care. Lloyd is another example of someone who spent his younger years without the support of disability services and has only come into contact with services in later life. His case demonstrates that planning for future care cannot be regarded as a once off task for parents but is a continuing requirement as people age, and their families and social contexts change. Lloyd, his niece and the hostel supervisor were interviewed, from whom a clear picture of his biography emerged, though some fine details remain hazy.

Lloyd is 73 years old. He made the transition from parental care when his father died when he was aged 40. Lloyd now lives in an aged persons' hostel that is part of a large church-run aged care facility where several other older people with intellectual disability live. His health is good apart from a skin complaint affecting his legs. Lloyd talks with much enjoyment about his early life and his family and showed the interviewer many old photo albums. He has never had any contact with specialist disability services.

Lloyd's family lived in the country. He had seven brothers and a twin sister. When both his parents died, Lloyd went to live with his favourite brother John. He enjoyed helping John breed bees, collect honey, and distil Eucalyptus oil. Several years later, John died and soon after his wife died also. Lloyd went to live with another brother George, and stayed with his brother Jim for holidays each year. Lloyd had nothing to do and this arrangement did not work out too well. After a family meeting, it was decided to find an alternative place for him. His twin sister lived in the city and was very involved in the church. She found Lloyd the place in the aged persons' hostel that was near her home. He moved there when he was 59.

When Lloyd first moved to the hostel, his brothers, particularly George and Jim, visited him regularly and he always went to stay with one of them for Christmas. His sister managed his affairs and visited or took him out every week. But his sister died in 1991 and only three of his brothers are still alive. In the last couple of years they have had health problems and are now much less involved in his life than previously. They see him, at most, once a year. George, the eldest, has a power of attorney but all Lloyd's financial affairs are managed by the hostel.

Lloyd rings all three brothers every couple of months. Now and again one of his many nieces or nephews calls in but none are regular visitors. His niece Sally, his sister's daughter, lives nearby and though she saw much of Lloyd when her mother was alive, she does not have a close relationship with him or feel any obligation to him. She is very preoccupied providing care for her sister (another of Lloyd's nieces) who has intellectual disability and Parkinson's disease.

Sally ensures that someone visits Lloyd at Christmas and on his birthday. Her husband's parents live in the same aged persons' complex as Lloyd and they invite him for afternoon tea once a week. Lloyd mentioned three friends, a couple in the country whom he has not seen for years and a woman who works in the laundry at the hostel. A range of organised activities is available at the hostel that Lloyd could join in, but he chooses to help in the laundry most days.

Barbara Flynn

The final vignette is of Barbara Flynn who has only experienced primary care from informal sources and whose informal support network is very strong. Her case illustrates a smooth planned transition from parental care and the development of new skills, interests and friendships in later life. Barbara is one of the very few people who has began to use adult disability services after the transition from parental care, although she has not been formally assessed or registered with a regional disability services team. Barbara, her eldest sister Connie and the coordinator of a neighbourhood house for people with disabilities were interviewed.

> Barbara is 57 years old. Her father died when she was 38 and her mother seven years later when Barbara was 45. She now lives in her own unit next door to her eldest sister Connie and her family. Barbara has good health. She manages her own domestic tasks on a daily basis, but requires assistance with shopping, banking and travelling. She knows her way around the local neighbourhood but never goes further afield on her own. Her unit is spotlessly clean, decorated with family photos and sculptures from her pottery classes. Barbara has three married sisters, ten nieces and nephews and eight great nieces and nephews.
>
> Barbara began attending a day program for adults with disabilities several years ago. This is the first adult disability service she has used, although respite care was offered to her sister by a hospital social worker several years ago.
>
> Her parents left their estate to Barbara, with her two eldest sisters as trustees. It had always been accepted that her sisters would care for Barbara when her parents died. After her mother's death, Barbara stayed with her younger sister Henny. During this time, the proceeds from the sale of their parents' house were used to build a unit next to her sister Connie's home. Two years later she moved into the unit where she has now lived for the past 11 years. She cooks and manages by herself. Her sister, who is not in paid employment and still has one of her children at school, checks on Barbara every morning and they generally have afternoon tea together.
>
> They are a close family and all four sisters meet weekly at Connie's place. Barbara goes out shopping with Connie once a week and sometimes visits or goes out with her other sisters. Last year she went on holiday with one of them. Although Connie supervises Barbara's affairs and day-to-day life, they all discuss major decisions. Barbara sees all her more distant relatives at least several times a year, some more often. She has a special relationship with her nephew Will, Connie's son. He is named in Connie's will as the person to take over responsibility for Barbara.
>
> While living with her parents, Barbara's life was very sheltered and restricted. She attended a special development school until she was 18 and then stayed at home. She managed the house, only ever went out with her parents and had no friends. After her parents' death her sisters decided that broadening her horizon was important and

since then her life has really changed. Through the local council they found the day program that she attends two days a week. Here she has tried many activities, among which her favourite is pottery. She has made many acquaintances and four friends. She regularly goes out with her friends over the weekend to the movies or shopping. Barbara is well known around the neighbourhood where she walks her dog. She also participates in a church social club for people with disabilities that arranges outings once a month.

Connie sees little change occurring in the future but can see the possibility of Barbara going to a nursing home if her health deteriorates and she can no longer look after herself.

SUMMARY

This chapter has reviewed the main characteristics of the diverse group included in the population of 'older' people with intellectual disability. The size of this population and the extent of the hidden population are discussed. The latter part of the chapter provided a descriptive introduction to the characteristics of the sample and some of the findings of the study. It provides a backdrop for the following chapters that present a more analytical approach to the types of planning undertaken by parents, the transition from parental care, and the lives of this group of older people with intellectual disability as they aged.

PART TWO

THE NATURE AND SUCCESS OF PARENTAL PLANNING

CHAPTER 5

Key person succession plans

Concern about the future care of their adult child with intellectual disability is a major issue for all parents. Many parents express a wish that their adult child should die before they do. However, parental attitudes towards making plans and the ability of plans to allay anxieties vary quite considerably. This chapter analyses the types of plans for the future made by parents for their adult children with intellectual disability. Most studies of parental planning and expectations of the future are prospective, with the parents as the informants. This study is retrospective. Informants are not parents but those with a stake in the implementation of plans, such as the person with intellectual disability, their siblings and other relatives. The memories of these people, their perceptions and interpretations are relied upon to describe the nature of planning undertaken by parents. Formal documents, such as wills, trusts and family trees supplement memories but mainly, the data reflects the perception by others of parental intentions.

'THE WORRY OF THEIR LIFE'

Many parents recognised the difficulties inherent in making plans. For example, Hilda's brother recalled his parents' concerns about the future care of his sister:

> 'The big worry in father's mind was, "what happens when mother and I go". Worry is a significant word. They (parents) were continually worried about her. It was the worry of their life. You couldn't plan in those days and you couldn't plan if you were on the salary of a Presbyterian minister with a view to a very poor retirement. What plans could they make?'

Constructing plans was perceived by some parents to reduce concerns about the future. The life course stage that their other children had reached was an important factor in the feasibility of some parental plans and promoted a reduction of their anxiety about the future. For example, Allen's mother had planned for his sisters to provide care for him and one of them said:

'Mother always used to say, "I hope he goes before me". That was her main [concern]. Like all the mothers [that] you speak to this is the thing: they'd like for the child to die before them. And we (sisters) always used to say, "Don't worry about him", but she did. That was the natural thing for her. She was much more worried when we (the sisters) had young children because she knew that it was hard if you've got a young child. As our children grew up and were married and left home it sort of became easier. I think she was more relaxed with the thought that taking him in to our home won't be quite so bad.'

The development of services was central to some parents' plans and their anxieties were reduced when these came to fruition. Some, like Doreen's parents, were involved in these developments. Her sister said:

'There had been a certain amount of talk and dad supported the day centre with the establishment of a hostel and he expected Doreen to live there. Once the hostel was opened, he had peace. I think he had an inbuilt hope that I would maintain close contact and that both (other sister also) of us would.'

Some parents had been unwilling to discuss or make very detailed plans. Vera's niece, for example, said that Vera's mother had:

'...always refused to contemplate any planning. She wanted both herself and Vera to remain and die at home. Mention of planning with aunt was a taboo subject.'

For some parents, the satisfaction they gained from caring may explain their reluctance to take planning seriously. Lucas's mother, who was forced to give up caring for him because of her ill health, said:

'I'd rather have him at home. It goes against my grain to have somebody else doing what I would like to be doing. I don't think I'd be doing any more [planning] than I did. I'd just go on happily from day to day. We were quite happy. We had nothing to complain about.'

THE NATURE OF PLANS

Most parents undertook some form of planning, and this ranged from vague expectations to comprehensive blueprints. Plans are either explicit or implicit. Explicit plans are any arrangements concerning the future care of their adult child with intellectual disability made by parents before the circumstances that demanded them. Explicit plans relate to a future time when parents have died, are incapacitated or chose to cease being the primary carer. They contain ideas that have been written or discussed regarding future financial support, supervision, or residential and care

TABLE 5.1 **Combinations of parental plans**

Planning combination	Number of parents	
	Number	%
Implicit key person succession only	15	24%
Explicit key person succession only	1	2%
Financial only	4	6%
Residential only	4	6%
Explicit key person succession and residential	3	5%
Explicit key person succession and financial	15	24%
Residential and financial	3	5%
Explicit key person succession, residential and financial	9	15%
No plans	3	5%
No information available	5	8%
Total	**62**	**100%**

arrangements for their adult child with intellectual disability. Arrangements made at short notice, as a response to immediate or impending circumstances, by either a parent or another person, are differentiated from plans. Such arrangements are conceptualised as transition management issues and are dealt with in the discussion of transitions.

Implicit plans are expectations held by parents about the future care of their adult child with intellectual disability of which others are strongly aware but which have not been discussed. Hopes that a child would die before their parent are not included as plans.

Within this broad conceptualisation of plans, three types are identified, 'key person succession plans' (explicit or implicit), financial plans, and residential plans. A majority of parents (69%) made a key person succession plan. Although this was often in conjunction with another type of plan, very few had planned comprehensively by combining the three types of plans. Table 5.1 demonstrates the popularity of key person succession plans and the various ways they were combined with other plans.

Key person succession plans

Key person succession plans are characterised by the planned transfer of responsibility for overseeing the wellbeing of the person with intellectual disability to some other nominated person or persons. The roles specified for these people vary from being highly prescribed to vague and open ended. When roles are specified, tasks such as supervision of the person with intellectual disability, oversight and monitoring of service provision and administration of financial affairs are more common than the direct provision of care.

Siblings were nominated to take responsibility in the majority of key person succession plans. In cases where a person with intellectual disability had more than one sibling, particular expectations were often placed on each. Sometimes, however, particularly where a will was involved, siblings were expected to share roles. An example is Godfrey who had three brothers. One of them said:

> 'Mother had talked to our older brother. He was his (Godfrey's) guardian for a long time. Mum used to talk to him about the way to go. But it's up to us (all three brothers). She left us the money.'

It was not only siblings who were nominated as the responsible people in plans. Where a person did not have a sibling or poor family relationships existed, someone else was named. Non-siblings nominated in key person succession plans included an aunt, friends of the family and cousins. The common feature was the existence of a long-term relationship between those nominated and the family of the person with intellectual disability. For example, Ada was an only child and her maiden aunt, who had lived next door for many years, was expected to take responsibility for Ada. The plan Rod's mother made is a good example of where siblings had a poor relationship. Rod's plan involved a minister who was a friend of the family, who said:

> 'They (parents) asked me to be the executor of the will and they charged me as it were to keep a roof over Rod's head, and then when he died that the property be given to his brothers or his brothers' children.'

Implicit key person succession plans

Implicit key person succession plans had not been discussed and were the unspoken expectations that parents held of others about the roles they would assume in the future. These expected roles were usually vague but focused on overseeing wellbeing. This type of plan, however, involved more than just hope. The nominated person was usually strongly aware of parental expectations and had implicitly accepted them. In one sense, these plans were minimal but, in another, were open ended and had enormous scope. When an implicit key person succession plan was made, it was generally the only sort of plan a parent had formulated.

Nadia and Ada are good examples of people for whom implicit key person succession plans had been made:

Nadia's sister Julie said that her mother hadn't needed to talk to her or plan [for the future]. It had just been accepted that the family and she in particular would provide care for Nadia. There were no formal agreements and it had not even been talked about. Nadia herself said that her mother had never talked to her about what would happen when she died but she thought that her mother may have had a talk to Julie, her sister, about keeping an eye on her.

Ada's aunt, in reply to the question of whether Ada's mother had planned for the future, said:

> 'No. I think she realised that I would take over. We never spoke about it. I think she just took it. We are Christians, you know. We believe in God and the Lord Jesus Christ and I think she just knew the Lord would look after her and that I would fill in. We just more or less took it for granted, I think.'

Explicit key person succession plans

Explicit key person succession plans had a similar defining characteristic: the nomination of another person to take responsibility to oversee the wellbeing of the person with intellectual disability. But, unlike implicit plans, they had been discussed with the nominated person or written into a formal document such as a will and were frequently made in conjunction with residential or financial plans. An example of an explicit key person succession plan made in conjunction with a financial plan is that made in respect of Nora, whose brother said:

> 'Dad certainly talked to me about that (future plans for Nora). We (brother and sister-in-law) would be responsible for her. He never expected us to take her into our own home. There was no doubt whatsoever, when dad died the will was written that things would come to us that I would be responsible. It was written [in the will] "your love and attention will be given to Nora during her lifetime".'

The type of care that parents hoped would be provided in the future had sometimes been discussed, but rather than being formulated into a detailed plan, it was more often expressed as a general direction for the nominated person to follow. Harry's is a good example of a plan that contained few details for implementation. His sister said:

> 'Mother always had this thing that you couldn't take Harry to live with you—that it was important to keep him in his own home. Mother's wishes regarding what would happen to Harry were made clear but no plans were made for putting this into operation.'

In contrast, several plans were far more detailed and specified roles that were to be played by a number of people. For example, Madge's parents made an explicit key person succession plan, in conjunction with a residential and financial plan, all of which were very specific. Her brother said, regarding his parent's plans for Madge:

> 'Part of the deal was that I had a whole of life situation in the family home on the understanding that when they were no longer able to look after her that I would look after Madge. That was with Mutual Trustees. Just to look after her wellbeing and to oversee. That was done in conjunction with an aunt of mine. My parents built and supplied a house for them for that purpose. Part of the deal that my parents made with my aunt and uncle was that they would be co-trustees for Madge. In return for that, my parents gave the land and the money to build a house next door to the house that they (parents) built. I would live next door (on the other side) to Madge and supervise Madge and the co-resident.'

Residential plans

Thirty per cent of parents had made a residential plan. These were more concrete and detailed than key person succession plans and usually made in conjunction with another type of plan. Residential plans involved placing the person's name on a waiting list, organising their move to supported accommodation or arranging for them to continue living in the community. Preferences for future living situations expressed in these plans fell fairly equally between aged care services, disability services and informal support in the community.

Six parents planned for their adult child to live in disability accommodation. All of them had been involved in voluntary parent associations that had built or planned residential accommodation such as hostels or small group homes. Seven parents planned for the person to live in an aged care facility such as an aged persons' hostel or retirement complex. Two of these parents had also planned a move for themselves on the understanding that the adult child could remain there after their death. The plan by Jim's mother is a good example of a residential plan combined with financial arrangements.

> Neither Jim nor his mother had a close relationship with his two siblings. Jim's mother negotiated with a church organisation to build a house on an empty block of land in a retirement complex and left the house and her estate to the church. In return the church would ensure that Jim was provided with a place to live and support for the rest of his life.

Six parents planned for their adult child to live in a private home with either a sibling, a second cousin or with a co-resident. For example, Madge's plan, mentioned previously, involved a co-resident moving into the family home. One of the most complex residential plans was that prepared by Jack's father. It included a financial and key person succession plan as well, and was one of the few cases where all three types of plans had been made.

> Jack's sister is a nun and his brother is deceased. When his mother died, Maud, his second cousin, who had spent much of her childhood with Jack's family, was asked to return to care for Jack and his father. Jack's father did not discuss plans for Jack's future care with Maud but made plans in his will. The will left small sums of money to Jack's sister and Maud, and a legacy of ten pounds a week to Jack. It stated that as long as Jack was boarding with Maud she would be allowed to live in the house for a rent of two pounds ten shillings a week. The residue of the estate was left to the children of Jack's brother, who would also receive the proceeds from the sale of the house at the time that Jack ceased to board there with Maud.

Financial plans

Half the parents had made a financial plan, usually in conjunction with another sort of plan. These were generally fairly simple and mainly comprised wills that left all or part of the estate to the adult with intellectual disability, sometimes with a family member as a trustee. Alternatively, the estate might be left to siblings with the expectation that they would use part of it for the benefit of their brother or sister. For example, the plans made by Amy's father included a financial, residential and key person succession plan.

> Amy has a brother and two sisters. One of them, Gayle, has always had a close relationship with both Amy and her parents and, according to her daughter, it was always accepted that she would look after Amy in the future. While he was still fit, Amy's father paid for an extension to be built onto Gayle's house to provide an extra bedroom and bathroom for Amy to use in the future. In his will Amy's father left Gayle more than her expected share of his estate, some of which was to be held in trust by her for Amy.

Timelines for implementation

The majority of parents had wanted to continue to care for their adult child as long as possible. They envisaged that plans for future care would not be implemented before their death or inability to continue caring. Several informants suggested that the reason for this was the deep bond between parents and their adult child and the interdependence developed between them in later life. As parents aged, the degree of support they provided was often matched by support received from their adult child, leading to a finely balanced reciprocal care situation. One example is Lenny, whose mother's health had deteriorated in the years before her death and she had relied on him to do much of the shopping and other domestic tasks. Lenny's sister in answer to the question of whether her mother had made any plans said, 'Not for while she was alive. She needed him'. George's brother referred to the interdependence between his mother and George by saying, 'She was as dependant on George as he was on her. It was a knife edge situation.' Talking about when he lived with his mother, George himself said:

> 'I couldn't have been able to come to functions here or at the church. If I went to the cricket all day Saturday I'd come home and find mum on the floor and she wouldn't be able to get any help, she wouldn't be able to ring up. I just couldn't go away and leave her on her own. I'd have to stay in with my mum, I couldn't do the things which I would like to do.'

Nevertheless a small minority of parents (10%) did make and implement a residential plan for future care before their death or incapacity. One example of this is that of Jim, above, who moved with his mother into the house she had built in a retirement complex.

FACTORS ASSOCIATED WITH PLANNING

Being known to the disability services system alone was not associated with the propensity of parents to plan or the type of plans they made. However, the use of a disability day service was associated with the type of plans parents had made and appeared to have encouraged parental planning. A higher proportion of parents whose adult child attended a day service while they lived at home had made an explicit key person succession plan, and more had made all three types of plans, than parents whose child had not attended such a service.

Family constellation and relationships were associated with the type of plans made by parents. Table 5.2 shows some of these trends. More families with siblings had made plans than those without siblings. Over three quarters of families with siblings had made a key person succession plan, compared to families without siblings where less than half had made this type of plan. A higher proportion of parents who had a close relative living next door had only made an implicit key person succession plan compared with parents who did not have a close relative nearby.

TABLE 5.2 **Family characteristics and type of planning**

Type of plan	Family characteristics					
	With siblings		Without siblings		Total	
Implicit key person succession	16	32%	1	15%	17	30%
Explicit key person succession	24	48%	2	28%	26	46%
No key person succession	10	20%	4	57%	14	24%
Any sort of plan	48	96%	6	86%	54	95%
No plan at all	2	4%	1	14%	3	5%

The figures are too small to use statistical tests but a trend was evident. Where a successor to the parent was clearly apparent (i.e. where a close relative was living nearby or there was a sibling), parents were more likely to plan implicitly. When no obvious successor to the parent was apparent, parents were less likely to have planned but, if they did so, their plans were likely to be explicit.

Since only three parents had not made any type of plan, drawing any conclusions about their characteristics by contrasting them with parents who had made plans is difficult. A common feature of families that did not plan was the absence of an apparent successor to the parent. In one family there were no siblings, in the second the sibling predeceased the parent and in the third the sibling was estranged from his mother's cohabitee and had lived interstate for many years. However, this factor did not differentiate families who planned from those who did not, since similar circumstances were found among families across both groups. In such cases, people other than siblings had been nominated in key person succession plans. A possible determining factor may have been that families without siblings, who did not plan, lacked sufficiently strong ties with a friend or more distant family members to include them in a key person succession plan. Alternatively, parental reluctance to confront the issue of planning as described at the beginning of this chapter may also be an explanation.

INVOLVEMENT IN PLANNING

The parents of many of the study population had been widowed and it was the surviving parents who were primarily involved in making plans. As demographic trends would suggest, women had generally outlived their husbands and, thus plans were most often formulated by mothers.

The voluntary parent associations, which established many of the disability day centres, and the staff of these centres, played a key role in planning. They had raised planning for the future as an issue for parents by providing information and encouraging consideration of the future. For example, lawyers specialising in wills and estate planning had been invited to address parent meetings and staff had sometimes actively encouraged parents to place their adult child's name on a residential waiting list or drawn vacancies to their attention. Some associations had also initiated the building of hostels or group homes, thus ensuring that parents had concrete options for which to plan. For example, Norman's sister said:

> 'My mother worked very hard with the other mothers at the time to get the hostel going. Because I was single and my brothers were married and she could see the burden would be left to me, she felt there must be a hostel for these people to go to. They didn't have any government support.'

The actions of staff and members of voluntary associations help explain the association between attendance at day services and the greater propensity for parents to plan. The involvement and interest of siblings had also been an important factor, since it was often they who had raised the issue of the future with their parents and encouraged them to make plans or assured them that their implicit plans would be realised. Bruce's sister talked about her mother's concerns for the future:

> 'Mother always used to say, "Whatever's going to happen to Bruce" and I used to say, "Well mum, you know that I've looked after you all this time. I'm not going to abandon him when you go. I'll look after him".'

The people with intellectual disability who were the subjects of plans were rarely mentioned as having been included in planning for their future. Nevertheless, the conclusion cannot be drawn that they were not involved, as informants may not have been aware of discussions between parents and their adult child with intellectual disability. However, older people with intellectual disability, when interviewed, spoke very little about parental planning. Three people still living at home with their mothers were interviewed but did not form part of the main sample. They had all discussed the future with parents and were aware of the plans made for them.

PLANNING FOR 'CARE ABOUT' RATHER THAN 'CARE FOR'

Parents clearly had strong anxieties about the future and felt responsible for securing the care of their adult child with intellectual disability. Most parents had made some form of plan, but few had made the comprehensive concrete plans suggested in the literature as being necessary (Heller

& Factor, 1991; Smith et al., 1995). Many of the findings—including the development of a greater number of financial than residential plans, an emphasis on informal arrangements, the association between the propensity to make plans and use of disability services and a desire not to implement plans until absolutely necessary—are similar to those reported in the literature discussed in chapter 2. However, a much smaller proportion of parents in this study (10%) had planned for direct care to be provided by family members than has been reported by other studies (Card, 1983; Griffith & Unger, 1994). Legislation in the Australian state of Victoria, where the study was conducted, precludes parents from making formal guardianship plans before the necessity for the appointment of a guardian arises, so direct comparison with the international studies cannot be made. However, many key person succession plans resembled informal guardianship arrangements and the proportion of parents who made such plans far exceeded those reported to make guardianship plans in overseas studies (Heller & Factor, 1988a).

The most common type of plan, a key person succession plan, reflected similar intentions to the designation of a 'vice president' that most families in the study by Krauss were reported to have made (1990). However, few details of the expected function of the 'vice president', other than to take responsibility for the overall wellbeing of the adult with intellectual disability and, exceptionally, to provide direct care are reported by Krauss.

The core element of key person succession plans was the transfer of responsibility for the person's overall wellbeing to one or more people in their informal support network. Expected roles and tasks were often left open-ended and unspecified but, where details had been discussed, the primary tasks envisaged for those assuming responsibility were supervisory and managerial rather than the direct provision of care. The emphasis was on indirect care, ensuring that someone took overall responsibility for the person with intellectual disability. How direct care and assistance with the tasks of everyday living would be provided and by whom was less often addressed.

Key person succession plans envisaged that people nominated in plans would provide care for the person with intellectual disability similar to that conceptualised as 'indirect', or 'caring about', rather than 'caring for' (Dalley, 1988; Sussman, 1985). The focus on caring about and the low level of detailed or residential planning meant that informal support was the type most often directly mentioned in parental plans. Only a small minority of plans explicitly involved reliance on formal services for future support. This may be due, however, to omission rather than a reflection of intent since two-thirds of the residential plans that were made expected to utilise formal accommodation services. This suggests a dichotomy of expectations about future care comprising general supervision by informal network members and direct provision of care by formal services.

Key person succession plans embodied the explicit agreements, or implicit understandings, that parents had negotiated with others. Normally those nominated in key person succession plans were close relatives. Expectations were based on the reality of the parent's informal networks rather than on kin ties alone. Parents did not plan to rely on people with whom they did not have a strong relationship. Thus, parents nominated other relatives or friends in plans rather than siblings where a poor relationship between a sibling and their parent or between the sibling and the person with intellectual disability existed. However, where this occurred expectations were often made very clear through the use of explicit, rather than implicit plans. The reflection of the reality of relationships in plans was also demonstrated where parents nominated a particular sibling to assume a more central role than the others, as in the case of Nadia described earlier.

The types of tasks envisaged for those nominated in key person succession plans often matched their group characteristics, which is a central element of the differential theory of primary groups (Litwak, 1985). Assumption of responsibility for overall wellbeing, management of affairs, and overseeing receipt of services requires a long-term commitment which the relatives or friends nominated possessed. They did not generally have the characteristics of close proximity or frequent face-to-face contact required to provide direct care and this was not the kind of task most parents expected of them.

Where more detailed residential plans were made, they did not foresee the developmental potential or portray a vision of future achievements by the person with intellectual disability. Instead, as reported in the literature, plans were concerned with security and stability and most sought out permanent arrangements in sheltered residential environments (Gold, 1987; Griffin & Bennett, 1994).

CONCLUSION

This chapter has documented the nature of plans made by the parents of the study population. Informal care of an indirect nature figured prominently in parental plans, the majority of which centred around agreements or understanding about the transfer of responsibility for overseeing the wellbeing of the person with intellectual disability to a close member of their informal support network. Expectations that parents held of others had often been negotiated and a match existed between the tasks people were expected to do and characteristics needed to fulfil them.

The conservatism of parental plans and the apparently limited involvement of people with intellectual disability in their construction raises issues about the legitimacy of parents making future plans for the rest of their middle-aged child's life. The relatively low level of concrete or comprehensive plans and parental preference to continue caring and not implement plans until absolutely necessary raise questions about the effectiveness of parental planning, the feasibility of implementation and their role in the process of transition from parental care. These questions can only be answered after an examination of the transition process and later life developments of adults with intellectual disability, which are dealt with in subsequent chapters.

CHAPTER 6

The transition from parental care

Rather than being a sudden event, the transition from parental care was, for most people, a gradual process managed informally by family, without crisis or recourse to formal services. This chapter describes and analyses the process of transition and the resulting changes that occurred for adults with intellectual disability. In particular, the implementation and contribution of parental plans to a smooth transition are examined. The process of transition from parental care has two dimensions that do not always occur simultaneously. The defining dimension is the parent ceasing to provide primary care for the adult with intellectual disability. The second dimension is parental relinquishment of responsibility for overseeing their child's wellbeing and major decisions in their life.

REASONS FOR TRANSITION

The average age of parents when they ceased to be primary carers was 86 years. Transition occurred in the majority of cases because of parental death, incapacity or a move by parents to supported accommodation. A pre-planned residential move from parental care while their parent was in good health accounted for only 10% of transitions, and family disputes caused the remaining 3%. At the time of their transition, half the adults had at least one parent alive.

Most of the study population were middle-aged when they left parental care; the average age was 52 years. Because of the criteria used in this study, 40 years was the youngest age at which a person had left home, while the oldest age was 73 years. At the time of transition just over 50% of the adults were younger than 55 years and 75% were younger than 60 years.

CHANGES AT THE TIME OF TRANSITION

Because a change of primary carer was the defining feature of the transition from parental care, at the time of transition everyone experienced at least this one significant change in his or her daily life. Additionally, just over half the study population moved house as well. Table 6.1 shows

TABLE 6.1 **Living situation straight after transition, and nature of residential move**

Type of transition	Number	%		
No move; remained in home and lived:	(28)		(45%)	
• alone		10		16%
• with already co-resident sibling		13		21%
• with already co-resident other relative		3		5%
• with unrelated co-resident		2		3%
Moved within the locality and lived:	(7)		(11%)	
• with siblings		6		10%
• in supported residential service		1		1%
Moved locality and lived:	(27)		(44%)	
• with siblings		4		7%
• in supported residential service		2		3%
• in aged persons' hostel		9		15%
• in nursing home		1		1%
• in disability accommodation		11		18%
Total	**(62)**	**62**	**(100%)**	**100%**

the diversity of people's living situation straight after transition and the nature of residential moves they had made.

Just over half either did not move house, or if they did, remained in their local area. For most of these people, a close family member replaced their parent as primary carer. The rest of the population changed both locality and residence at the time of transition but nevertheless retained considerable elements of stability. Several went to live with a close sibling, and all of those who moved into disability accommodation and two who moved to an aged care facility continued to attend the disability day centre they had attended for many years. Most people who moved into disability accommodation already knew some of the residents, who were people from their day program. Over three-quarters of adults who moved had regular contact with a parent and several spent their weekends at home with their parent for the first few years after transition.

Table 6.2 summarises their residential situations straight after transition. Over 50% continued to live in a private home, 21% moved to an aged care facility and 18% to disability accommodation. Forty-two per cent of people lived with a sibling, another relative or a friend who acted as their primary carer directly after the transition. However, some of those who lived alone also had a relative or friend nearby who became their primary carer. Thus, more than half the study population had an informal primary carer, usually a sibling, directly after the transition from parental care.

TABLE 6.2 **Living situations straight after transition from parental care**

Living situation	Number	%
Private home alone	10	16%
Private home with sibling	23	37%
Private home with other relative	3	5%
Private home with co-resident	2	3%
(Total private home)	(38)	(61%)
Aged persons' hostel	9	15%
Supported residential service	3	5%
Nursing home	1	1%
(Total aged care facility)	(13)	(21%)
Disability hostel	7	12%
Group home	4	6%
(Total disability accommodation)	(11)	(18%)
Total	62	100%

A characteristic of the transition process was the division of two functions that had hitherto been performed by parents; the provision of primary care and the responsibility for overall wellbeing of the adult with intellectual disability*. After transition, these functions were split between two different people or agencies for almost half the adults. For all except very few adults, an existing informal network member became a 'key person' in their life and took responsibility for overseeing their wellbeing. These people, who were an important element of stability in the adults' lives directly after the transition from parental care, were usually a close relative or friend and in a few cases, for a while, remained a parent.

Group differences

Following transition, a higher proportion of adults who were unknown to disability services remained in private homes with informal primary carers, 79% compared to the group who were known to disability services,

---

* Assuming responsibility for overseeing the wellbeing of the adult with intellectual disability was often an undefined expectation of key person succession plans. However, when this term is used in the text and does not refer directly to plans, it is defined as undertaking three or more of the following instrumental tasks for the person with intellectual disability: decision making, financial management, legal tasks, mediation, monitoring, primary care, supervision, service coordination, backing up other informal carers, and skill development. These tasks are discussed further in chapter 10. Primary care is defined as providing direct or supervisory assistance with two or more activities of daily living.

of whom only 41% remained in a private home. An even lower proportion of those who attended a disability day centre remained in a private home. The proportion of adults who moved to an aged care facility was similar across all groups and did not vary with use of disability services. Contrary to expectations from anecdotal evidence, very few adults came into contact for the first time with disability services at the time of their transition and none of those previously unknown to services moved into disability accommodation.

Transferring the responsibility for care

For the majority of people, the process of transition was gradual rather than sudden. Typically, it involved someone else, usually a sibling, slowly assuming responsibility for the wellbeing of the person with intellectual disability and either taking over their direct care or organising alternative care. This process often occurred in parallel with increased support to the primary carer by the same person, since, by this stage, the primary carer was usually a widowed mother whose health had begun to deteriorate.

The gradual nature of transition was most evident for the 30% of adults who, prior to transition, either lived near or with other family members as well as their parents. Bruce, who was introduced in one the vignettes in chapter 4, is an example of someone who experienced a gradual transition.

> Bruce lived with both parents until his father died when he was 58 and he and his mother moved to live with his sister Edith and her husband. They lived in a unit attached to Edith's house that his mother financed. His mother died, aged 89 years, after a long illness during which she was nursed by Edith. During her mother's illness Edith had gradually taken over supervision of Bruce's personal care and assured her mother that she would never abandon Bruce. After their mother's death, Bruce continued living with Edith for a further six years.

Humphrey is another example where a daughter provided care for her mother and gradually took on more care of her brother. Humphrey's brother talked about the relationship between his sister and Humphrey as their mother aged:

> 'In later years she (sister) spent a lot of time looking after mum. She'd be up there five or six days a week looking after her. This was probably when she came so much closer to Humphrey because she had to look after Humphrey as well as mum. Mum was so relieved when my sister got Humphrey into here (aged persons' hostel).'

As part of the transition process, responsibility for organising services and taking major decisions for the adult with intellectual disability was gradually assumed by someone else. For example, Vera continued to live with her mother but, both before and while her mother was hospitalised, her sister slowly took over responsibility for managing her affairs.

> For several years, despite her own limited mobility and failing health, Vera's widowed mother continued to provide day-to-day care for her. Vera's sister, Jane, provided support to her mother, took over care of the garden, and assumed responsibility for the management of Vera's affairs with the external world, such as her financial and medical needs. Vera's niece said, 'Jane was there two or three times a week. She was always there at her (mother's) beck and call. There was never a thank you, just duty. Jane was looking after her mother and Vera.' Vera broke her leg and was hospitalised for almost a year, during which time her mother fell several times and was taken to hospital. However, she refused to contemplate a move to supported accommodation and discharged herself. Despite her mother's protestations, Jane felt that her mother would be unable to care for Vera when she was ready to leave hospital. Jane investigated alternatives and arranged for Vera to move into an aged persons' hostel. Her mother died very soon after Vera moved.

Another example is Barry, whose sister Rita gradually replaced her mother as Barry's primary carer and took over responsibility for organising formal services to provide alternative long-term primary care for him.

> Barry and his mother had lived next door to his sister Rita and her family for many years. As her mother got frailer, Rita supported her and Barry to remain at home. She did the shopping and domestic tasks for her mother and took over the personal care tasks with which Barry needed assistance. Rita commented that, 'Mum and Barry couldn't have remained at home if we hadn't been living here'. Her mother had put her own name on a waiting list for a local aged person's complex but had not made any residential plans for Barry. Her mother was ambivalent and agonised about moving to a hostel, not wanting to break up Barry's home. Rita felt that her mother was tired and would enjoy the social life at the hostel. Rita began to investigate supported accommodation for Barry. She said, 'Unbeknownst to my mother I went round and had a look at nursing homes for him. I didn't want to be sneaky but I didn't want to upset her by [letting her] worry about it. The best thing was quietly to have a look.' When her mother was offered a place in the hostel, Rita encouraged her to take it and offered to have Barry stay with her until a place in a nursing home became available for him.

In Brendan's case, his sister took a similar proactive role in organising alternative care by a formal service without the full knowledge or support of her mother.

> Brendan and his mother moved to live near his sister Lois after his father's death. In the years that followed, his mother's health deteriorated and she began to lose her sight. Lois gradually became more involved in managing their (mother and Brendan's) household and providing care for Brendan. Lois wanted her mother to live with her but knew she would be unable to cope with Brendan as well. She said, 'She (mother) would not leave her house while Brendan was there. So I made appointments to see (a disability service). My mother didn't know. I started the ball rolling and eventually they found him a place. I had to put him there (disability hostel). My mother wouldn't do it. She was most upset.'

Periods of deteriorating parental health made the inevitability of transition more apparent to both the parent and other family members. During this period, the time and opportunity were available to arrange for the future care of the person with intellectual disability or implement plans established by parents.

Sudden transitions

A few transitions (8%) occurred quite suddenly, allowing less time to make arrangements. Although the process of transition was hurried, it was still generally managed by family members. For example, when her father was taken to hospital Nora's brother realised that she urgently needed alternative accommodation.

> Nora lived with her widowed father in the city. Her brother John, who lived several hours drive away, visited them every weekend. When her father was hospitalised, John had to find alternative accommodation for Nora. He and his wife searched their local area. He said, 'We were absolutely desperate, I knocked on the door at (disability hostel), and told them the story. It must have been a good story. Nora stayed for 17 years.'

Brian's sister was also confronted with the task of finding alternative accommodation for him at very short notice but for different reasons.

> Brian had always had a close relationship with his sister Sheila. His mother had remarried and Sheila felt that they (mother and stepfather) had sometimes neglected Brian's health and treated him badly. Once she had stepped in to ensure he got proper medical treatment. After a row between Brian and his stepfather, his mother decided that Brian would have to leave. She rang Sheila and told her to find somewhere for Brian. Sheila said, 'Mum just couldn't cope. She just said, "He has got to go" and she meant it. I had to find something for him'. Through Sheila's church connections, she obtained a place for Brian in a church-sponsored aged persons' hostel.

Sudden transitions did not always involve the use of formal services. Support was arranged for some adults so they could remain at home. For example, Rod's mother had asked a minister who was a family friend to be the executor of her will and ensure that Rod always had a roof over his head.

> The friend explained, 'When Rod's mother died that meant Rod was left on his own, and I didn't know how we were going to care for him because he wasn't capable of caring for himself. So I got a family to live in the house and gave them free board in return for them looking after Rod.'

Partial transitions

Ten per cent of adults moved into a residential placement before their parents' incapacity. Their names had been on a waiting list and they moved when they were offered a vacancy but often only after considerable deliberation. The transition for these people was, at first, only partial. Parents had relinquished direct care but retained overall responsibility for their adult child's wellbeing and had considerable involvement in their lives for a longer period. Godfrey is an example of where this occurred.

> Godfrey attended a specialist day centre. His mother had been very involved in fundraising and supporting the centre to build a hostel. When it was built, Godfrey moved in. His mother, however, kept in close contact with the centre and was involved in all decisions about Godfrey's care. Godfrey went home to stay with his mother every fortnight and for six weeks every year, during the holidays.

TRANSITION MANAGEMENT

For a few people, including Bruce (see above), the transition from parental care was so gradual that it was almost imperceptible. However, for the majority, as exemplified by Barry, Vera and Brendan, the process was more apparent and was actively managed, quite often by someone other than a parent. Transition management involved investigating the availability of other forms of support and organising alternative care when it was considered necessary. It also involved making major decisions on behalf of the adult with intellectual disability, such as where they should live and when a residential move should occur.

An informal network member managed the transition for most people. Sixty-three per cent were siblings, 16% were parents and the others were more distant relatives, family friends or professional service providers.

Predominantly, however, it was siblings, nominated in key person succession plans, who managed the transition. Adults with more than one sibling usually had a closer relationship with one of them, and it was the closest sibling who took responsibility for managing the transition (see chapter 8 for further discussion of sibling relationships). This sibling who, for clarity is described as the prime sibling, was more likely to be a sister than a brother and was usually the child most involved in caring for their parents in later life. In cases where a brother was the prime sibling in preference to a sister, the adult with intellectual disability had a strong relationship with their sister-in-law as well. Exceptionally, in two families, several sisters had a close relationship with the adult with intellectual disability and the responsibility for managing transition was shared. In most families, the wife or husband of a sibling shared in some tasks involved in managing transition. However, sisters-in-law were usually more involved than brothers-in-law.

Where adults did not have a sibling or had a poor relationship with them, some parents had made a key person succession or residential plan that nominated someone else or a service to take responsibility for overseeing the wellbeing of their adult child. Where such a plan had been made, the person or service nominated took responsibility for the management of transition.

The role of formal services in transition management

Formal services only managed the transition process of three people in the study group, but played a role in the transition of almost a quarter of cases. Service providers such as hospital social workers and staff of disability day centres provided advice, assistance and encouragement to the person who was managing the transition. Only three families had a formal case manager from a regional disability team at the time of transition. A good example of support provided by formal services is that provided by hospital social work staff to Lewis's brother.

> Since his mother's death, Lewis and his father had lived alone. Despite the help offered by his brother Ray, the condition of the house deteriorated and his father neglected both his own and Lewis's health. Lewis ended up in hospital with an ulcerated leg. The doctor suggested that Lewis should not return home, since his father was not really up to looking after him. Ray's wife praised the assistance the hospital social worker had given her and Ray. She said, 'She (the social worker) was absolutely brilliant. She spoke to us and gave us a list of nursing homes.'

Another example is the support and encouragement given by disability day centre staff to Doug's parents.

> Doug moved to a hostel attached to the day centre, which he had attended for many years. He goes home to his parents, who are in their 80s, at the weekends. His parents oversaw Doug's move from home but they felt that the day centre staff had initiated it. Doug's father said, 'It wasn't our decision. It was Laura's (staff person at the centre). Oh well, it's easier. I think they (staff at the centre) worked out that it was the right decision. I think they realised that we were due for a bit of a let up.'

Only one person, Bertha, had her transition managed in an emergency by a worker from the regional disability services team. Bertha's mother had not planned for her future. Bertha initiated her own transition, which was sudden and occurred in the context of a personal crisis.

> Bertha lived with her mother who was beginning to suffer from dementia. Her mother's de facto, Stuart, also shared the house. Bertha felt that he didn't like her. Bertha had a good relationship with her brother who lived in Western Australia. But he had never got on with Stuart, who had excluded him from the family home. Bertha attended a specialist day centre several days a week. She told one of the staff at the day centre that Stuart had raped her. The coordinator contacted both the police and the regional disability services team who arranged for Bertha to be placed immediately in a special accommodation house.

The other two people whose transition was managed by a formal service already knew the professional worker involved and their transitions were not as sudden as Bertha's.

Involvement of the person with intellectual disability in transition decisions

The process of transition was characterised by others taking over responsibility, control and making decisions for the adult with intellectual disability. Very little evidence suggested that their thoughts, feelings, skills and preferences were taken into consideration during the transition process.

PROCESSES OF TRANSITION

Siblings often remarked, with some perplexity, that their brother or sister with intellectual disability had seemed unmoved by the death of their parents. Perhaps it was because of this perceived insensitivity to loss that attention was not paid to the feelings of grief arising from the death of their parents or the loss of their home. Nora's brother described her reaction to her father's death:

> 'When we went to tell her that dad had died she said, "Oh" and then said, that she had been to see the *Sound of Music* yesterday and that it was a lovely film. Not another word was said. Same thing happened when mum died.'

Another example is that of Mary, to whom no one had explained that she would not be going back home.

> The decision to leave home and move from the care of her mother had never been discussed with Mary by her mother or sister. At the time of the study, Mary had lived in a supported residential service for six years. She suffered from a degenerative disease and said very clearly that she thought she could go home when she was better.

In contrast, some evidence suggests that others may have been aware of the person's feelings and the enormity of their loss but had felt powerless to do anything to ameliorate them. The remarks of Lenny's sister, who, directly after her mother died, brought him to live with her in the city from the small country town he had lived in all his life, are a good example: 'I locked up the house. I put him in the car. That was that: the end of his little life.'

In several exceptional cases, the preferences of the person with intellectual disability were clearly taken into account in the transition process. For example, Rachel was very involved in church activities and knew her way around the local area very well. Her brother said:

> 'When mother died she (Rachel) didn't want to come down to where we lived in Bromley. She wanted to stay with the church. She had a strong bond with Grantham. She'd lived there for 40 years. They (sister-in-law and church social worker) chased around and found this place (special accommodation house).'

Walter also took an active role in choosing where he would live after transition.

> Walter had two sisters and a brother. Over the years, he developed a strong relationship with his sister-in-law, Jacquie. Walter worked in the family business until it was sold after his father died. Jacquie then persuaded his mother to let Walter attend a disability day centre. Walter loved the centre and made many friends. One of his friends had moved to an aged care complex with his mother. Walter's mother's health deteriorated and she began to need a lot of support from family members. During this time, Walter explained to his sister-in-law that

the complex, where his friend lived, was where he wanted to live when he couldn't live with his mother any more. Jacquie investigated and put his name on the waiting list. When a place came up, Walter chose to move there although Jacquie had told him he could live with her and his brother.

A remarkable example of a sensitive and gradual transition process was Allen's. His sisters took it in turns to live with him and their mother for the last six years of his mother's life, and then continued to do this for several years after she died. One of his sisters said:

'We'd (sisters) been going over there (family home) so long that we were part of his family again. The fact that there was someone living there all the time before mum died [meant] it wasn't as bad. We were there, and then after mum died, instead of whizzing him out of the house that he'd always lived in all his life, we stayed on. We didn't sell the house for about 18 months to two years. We slowly kept doing the same things that we were doing when mum was there so it wasn't [a major break] and he got used to just us.'

LOSSES INVOLVED IN THE TRANSITION

Given the distance of many informants, it was difficult to gain a clear picture of the emotional impact that transition had on members of the study population. However, a growing literature clearly demonstrates that people with intellectual disability suffer emotionally from their experiences of loss, need preparation for changes and the chance to grieve (Harper & Wadsworth, 1993; Kloeppel & Hollins, 1989; Sinason, 1992; Wadsworth & Harper, 1991). Many of the informants who had been involved in the adult's transition from parental care did not acknowledge these emotional processes and, as a result, many adults with intellectual disability were excluded from the normal rituals surrounding change, loss or death.

The changes and losses experienced during transition included loss of home and locality, loss of contact with some informal network members, change of primary carer, and the death of parents (these issues are discussed more fully in chapter 8). But as has been considered, for most people the transition from parental care was a gradual managed process during which not everyone experienced multiple losses. For many, losses were balanced by elements of stability and continuity. Indeed, as will be explored in subsequent chapters, for those people who continued to have contact with a parent or did not have to leave their home, the transition from parental care appeared to be a less traumatic change than other changes they experienced later in their lives.

PARENTAL PLANNING AND THE PROCESS OF TRANSITION

The expectations encapsulated in parental plans were reflected in both the process and outcome of the transition from parental care. The overwhelming reasons for transition, parental death or incapacity, suggest that most parents realised their ambition to provide care for their adult child for as long as they were able. In the short term, most plans were successfully implemented; what parents had envisaged in their plans usually coincided with what actually happened directly after transition. Although, the criteria for success was difficult to judge since many key person succession plans were vague and open-ended.

Where a key person succession plan had been made, and a parent did not oversee the transition, people nominated in the plan stepped in and took responsibility for managing the transition from parental care in all cases except one. As the case examples illustrate, the detailed planning and organisation of the transition are effected informally, usually by those nominated in plans. Typically, those nominated in plans made arrangements when they were needed and filled in as necessary the details of the framework laid out by parents. They often foresaw the necessity for transition and by investigating options and organising alternative care they facilitated the process of transition and successfully averted any crisis and inappropriate short-term placements occurring.

Financial and residential plans were also successfully implemented, each with one exception. These plans often provided a blueprint for those nominated in key person succession plans that made their task easier and more specific. Where residential plans had been made, people with intellectual disability had gained access to supported accommodation either before they needed it urgently or at the time that they did.

Plans not implemented

Not all key person succession plans had been implemented at the time of the study. Some parents managed the transition and retained responsibility for overseeing the wellbeing of their adult child for several years after relinquishing primary care. Financial plans were mainly contained in wills and some had not been implemented on transition or by the time of the study, as parents were still alive.

One residential plan was not implemented. It had been prepared for George by his mother who had planned for him to live with his brother, Stephen.

> When George's mother's failing health forced her into a nursing home, Stephen felt unable to go ahead with his mother's plan for George to live with him. Insufficient funds were available to build a granny flat to give George independent space. Stephen and his wife had two teenage sons. He worked full-time and his wife part-time. His wife was providing substantial support to her mother who was in a nursing home. They felt the strain on the family's resources would be too great if George came to live with them. The staff at the day centre George had attended for many years discussed plans with Stephen and supported his decision. They helped to arrange for George to have the respite bed in the hostel attached to the centre, where, at the time of the study, he had lived for over a year.

This case exemplifies reasons, suggested in the theory of task specificity discussed earlier, why other kin may not be suited to fulfilling the task of primary care provision for an adult with intellectual disability and the costs involved in doing so.

The financial plan not implemented was that contained in the will prepared by Ted's parents. Ted's parents had left their entire estate to him. His brother contested his parents' will and was awarded a share of their estate.

The role of planning in facilitating transition

A link between the existence and implementation of a plan per se and facilitation of transition was not easy to establish in all cases. It was not clear, for instance, whether people nominated in key person succession plans who managed transition would have done so regardless of the existence of a plan because of their close relationship to the adult with intellectual disability. For example, a cousin and a social worker, both of whom had a long-standing relationship with the parent, stepped in to manage the transition of two of three people for whom parents had not made any plans. Marie's cousin was one person who did this.

> When Marie's mother became ill, her aunt Harriet rang her cousin Anne who explained, 'I went over and she (Marie's mother) was admitted to hospital. Marie couldn't stay by herself. I think her mother had probably been ill from the day before and Marie was meant to be going to the centre. She hadn't even known to get herself ready to go and Libby (mother) was sitting in the chair. I rang Cindy (centre administrator). I had got to know her a fair bit and they had a house where she (Marie) could stay. I took her down. I did it because there was nobody else to do it.'

However, it did appear that key person succession plans forewarned and prepared the nominated person for their expected role in transition. Those nominated in plans did not leave their intervention until the last minute, as Marie's cousin had done, but appeared to be more willing to step in and take preventive steps instead of waiting until a crisis developed.

Only 20% of parents had made a residential plan that involved supported accommodation but during the transition process almost twice as many people moved to such accommodation. Adults, like Marie, who had needed alternative accommodation, obtained what was sought without too much delay. No one was forced to take what was considered by the person managing his or her transition as inappropriate accommodation. However, appropriateness depends on the criteria being used and it is debatable whether some placements, particularly those in aged care facilities, were appropriate for those who moved into them. For example, 50% of those who moved into an aged care facility at the time of transition were in their early 50s; their average age was 57 years compared with an average age of 80 years for all residents of such facilities (Ronalds, 1989). None had Down syndrome, which is a predictor of premature ageing. This issue is examined more fully in relation to current living situations in chapter 9.

Most parents had made some type of plan, the bulk were key person succession plans, which in many cases were unspecific and remained informal. However, the nature of transition experienced by the study population suggests the efficacy of this type of plan, at least in the short term. The dire consequences of a lack of concrete planning suggested in the literature (Smith et al., 1995) did not eventuate. Despite parents continuing to care until the last minute and only 15% having made comprehensive plans (i.e. all three types of plans), the sudden crisis transition and urgent requests to services for assistance and placements that figure so often in discussions and anecdotes of transitions occurred rarely. Nor, as had been suggested, did transition result in people who had been out of touch with disability services contacting services for the first time to seek their assistance.

SOURCES OF SUPPORT IN THE PROCESS AND OUTCOME OF TRANSITION

The transition for the majority of adults was managed informally. Although not conclusive, it seems that key person succession plans helped to ensure, where it was necessary, that a member of the adult's informal support network took responsibility for managing their transition from parental care. These plans represented a negotiated commitment of siblings or more distant informal network members to manage the transition and oversee the wellbeing of adults with intellectual disability. They provided a mechanism or the means, in the form of a key person, whereby the transition from parental care could be flexibly managed and arrangements made at an appropriate time. This mechanism, typically, compensated for the lack of a detailed residential plan and obviated the need for more detailed plans. It also allowed parents to avoid dealing with or confronting many issues involved in the transition of their adult child from their care.

People nominated in key person succession plans, in addition to their involvement in the transition process, retained an important role in the life of the person with intellectual disability by overseeing their wellbeing. This role is examined in more detail in later chapters. Over the longer term, this continuing role differentiated those nominated in plans from people who had stepped in to manage the transition without having been nominated.

The number of adults with an informal primary carer directly after transition exceeded the 10% expected from the examination of plans in chapter 5. It is also much higher than would be expected from the literature discussed in chapter 2. However, the studies by Prosser and Grant and the theory of task specificity suggest provision of informal care by kin other than parents is not a long-term arrangement because of the high costs incurred by other kin (Grant, 1988; Litwak, 1985; Prosser & Moss, 1996). The next chapter examines this issue, analysing the characteristics of kin who provided informal primary care and the length of time they sustained it.

A characteristic of the transition process was the split of the two functions hitherto performed by parents: the provision of primary care and the responsibility for overall wellbeing of the adult with intellectual disability. During the process of transition these functions were often split between a parent and the person nominated in the key person succession plan. Later the functions were more commonly split between the key person and a formal service. Many plans had envisaged this split, expecting informal network members to take a management role and formal services to provide direct care. This differentiation of tasks by group was apparent to some extent after transition; responsibility for overall wellbeing of the person with intellectual disability was almost exclusively the domain of informal network members and, in comparison, formal services provided direct care for almost half the adults.

When the study population was grouped according to the members' connection with disability services, a link between this characteristic and type of residence straight after transition was suggested. The high proportion of adults attending disability day services who moved into disability supported accommodation suggests that families who are already part of the disability service system have advantageous access to specialist services compared to those outside the system. An explanation of this trend may lie in the history and nature of disability services in Victoria. Most day centres were established by voluntary parent associations and, until 1986, associations financed and managed services with little government control or support. Many associations developed accommodation options and a sense of obligation to meet parental needs because of the substantial voluntary input parents had made.

Nevertheless, at the time of transition, access to disability services was not an issue for families outside the service system. There was no evidence to suggest that those unknown to the system had difficulty gaining access. Disability services had been responsive when approached, albeit by very few families. Most families outside the disability system had relied on informal sources of support to both manage the process of transition and to provide primary care. Few had sought assistance from formal service systems. Why this was so and whether choice, lack of knowledge or mistrust of specialist services was the reason was not always clear.

Almost three-quarters of families had managed the transition process without the support of formal services. Support that was provided generally came from hospital social workers or staff from disability day centres rather than regional disability teams. This may be explained by historic factors. The study population made the transition between one and 46 years ago whereas regional disability teams have only been established for the last 15 years. However, no evidence indicated that adults who had made the transition more recently had been more likely to receive assistance from regional teams.

For those families involved in day centres, strong support with both the planning and management of transition was provided by the tight-knit communities of parents that surrounded disability day services and staff. This support from a peer group and specialist staff, aware of the issues, who knew the adult with intellectual disability well, was not available to families outside these services. Thus, involvement with a disability day centre supported families in both dealing with the transition and in gaining access to disability residential services. It also secured considerable stability and security for the adults with intellectual disability, who, after transition continued to attend the centre and moved into accommodation attached to centres where they knew most of the residents.

CONCLUSIONS: PARENTAL PLANNING AND CONTINUING TRANSITIONS

The managed nature of the transition from parental care and the successful implementation of parental plans have been described. Where plans were informal and lacked detail, those nominated in key person succession plans compensated by organising access to services and making other arrangements when they were necessary. Formal services played a limited role in managing the transition and provided primary care to just under half the study population after transition, less than expected either in the literature or parental plans. The experience of transition had elements of stability as well as change for most of the adults with intellectual disability.

At the time of their transition, only a few adults were 'old' or met the definition of an older person used in aged care policy. Just under half were aged over 55 years and met the younger definition of 'older' that is commonly used in respect of people with intellectual disability. Their need for a primary carer and support was not age related and did not stem from loss of functional abilities or poor health. They needed support because their parent had ceased to provide primary care and because of their intellectual disability.

The first part of this chapter described a snapshot of adults with intellectual disability directly after transition. However, life course, family, and policy changes affected their lives and their social networks in the years following the transition from parental care. Thus, for some people the picture was very different at the time of the study. At this time they were all older people and some arrangements foreseen by parental plans and implemented at the time of transition had gone awry, the balance between informal and formal care had shifted and the ease of access to disability services had changed dramatically. As they had aged, many adults had experienced further transitions, resulting in more extensive losses than they experienced during the transition from parental care.

Therefore, answers to questions about the importance of parental planning to the security and stability of adults with intellectual disability, the success of plans and who or what replaces parents as primary carers are susceptible to change over time. The role of planning, the patterns of support for older people with intellectual disability and the reasons behind these patterns can be more fully understood by charting their lives, tracing changes and mapping networks of support in the years following transition from parental care. The challenge of this task is taken up in the next three chapters.

CHAPTER 7

The post-parental care phase

This group of adults with intellectual disability made the transition from parental care in their middle-aged years and, like any other group of middle-aged adults, their lives did not remain static. The years that followed were marked by many other life changes, some of which widened their horizons and brought new opportunities for development while others reflected the group's vulnerability to loss of informal support and enforced mobility as they aged. Characteristically, these developments were unplanned and unpredictable. Mapping the changes since their transition from parental care provides insights into the nature of the mid- and later life of adults with intellectual disability and provides a broader picture of their support needs than is possible by simply taking a snapshot of their situation at the time of the study.

This chapter overviews the changes adults with an intellectual disability experienced as they aged during the post-parental phase of their lives, and identifies the reasons underlying these changes. Primarily the focus is on situational factors such as shifts in place of residence and primary carer, which are easily quantified and can be tracked with a degree of specificity. Other changes such as a person's level of independence, their degree of autonomy and extent of community participation are harder to quantify and greater reliance is placed on qualitative data and informant's impressions. The impact of these later life changes on social networks is discussed in more detail in the following three chapters.

RESIDENTIAL CHANGES

As demonstrated in the previous chapter, the transition from parental care and a residential move do not always occur simultaneously. Just under half of the study group did not move house at the time of transition. However, by the time of the study, which ranged from one to 47 years later, only nine people had not moved house at all. Half the group had moved more than once, one person as many as six times. Fifty-three adults of the group of 62 had undergone 109 residential moves, of which only 34 occurred at the time of transition. Table 7.1 summarises these residential moves,

TABLE 7.1 **Summary of living situations adults moved from and into**

Living situation at time of move	Moved to	Moved from	Net movement	No move at all
Parental home at time of transition	—	34	−34	—
Private home with relatives	21	29	−8	4
Private home alone	3	8	−5	5
Private home with friend	3	2	+1	—
Aged persons' hostel	23	2	+21	—
Supported residential service	20	12	+8	—
Nursing home	14	3	+11	—
Disability hostel	10	6	+4	—
Group home	9	8	+1	—
Disability respite	3	2	+1	—
Hospital respite	2	2	0	—
Psychiatric hospital	1	1	0	—
Total	**109**	**109**		**9**

Note: This table summaries the living situations that adults moved from and into that involved a residential move. At times their living situation changed without a change of accommodation, which is why living with a co-resident is not included. When people ceased to live with a co-resident they did not move but moved later. This meant they moved from a situation where they had been living alone.

showing the types of accommodation people moved from and into. As it demonstrates, more adults moved *from* living with relatives or alone than moved *to* these living situations, and aged care facilities had the largest net influx of people.

Tables A1–A7 in appendix 3 provide more detail, summarising where adults moved to and from for each residential move. These tables demonstrate trends in residential movements, showing movements from private homes to supported accommodation, and movement into, but then out of, disability accommodation. Table 7.2 provides a snapshot of accommodation type at two points in time, directly after transition and at the time of the study, and clearly shows that the proportion of adults living in both private homes or disability accommodation declined in the period following transition, while those in aged care facilities increased substantially.

Reasons for residential changes

Residential moves were often fraught with conflict and dissatisfaction. Over half were associated with contextual factors, such as changed circumstances of their carer or problems with services, rather than the characteristics of the older person. The reasons why residential moves occurred are summarised in table 7.3.

TABLE 7.2 **Type of accommodation straight after transition from parental care and at the time of the study**

Living situation	Straight after transition Number	%	At time of the study Number	%
Private home alone	10	16%	7	11%
Private home with sibling	23	37%	5	8%
Private home with other relative	3	5%	2	3%
Private home with co-resident	2	3%	—	—
Private home with friend	—	—	2	3%
(Total private home)	(38)	(61%)	(16)	(25%)
Aged persons' hostel	9	15%	21	34%
Supported residential service	3	5%	8	13%
Nursing home	1	1%	11	18%
(Total aged care facility)	(13)	(21%)	(40)	(65%)
Disability hostel	7	12%	4	6%
Group home	4	6%	2	2%
(Total disability accommodation)	(11)	(18%)	(6)	(8%)
Total	62	100%	(62)	(98%)

Note: Due to rounding, some figures do not add up to 100.

TABLE 7.3 **Reasons for and frequency of moves from different living situations**

Living situation moved from	Inability of carer to continue	Pressure from service	Increased support needs	Quality of service	Choice arranged
Parental home					
Home with relative	19		6		4
Home alone		2	5		1
Home with friend					2
Aged persons' hostel			2		
Supported residential service		3	1	8	
Nursing home				3	
Disability hostel		5	1		
Disability respite					2
Group home		6	2		
Hospital respite					2
Psychiatric hospital					1
Total	19	16	17	11	12

Inability of carer to continue

The most common reason for residential moves was the inability of an informal primary carer, who had replaced a parent, to continue in that role owing to death, poor health, competing family commitments or unwillingness. The inability of a primary carer to continue was the most common reason for a move out of a private home. Several residential changes experienced by Lloyd, whose case vignette appeared in chapter 4, occurred for this reason. Another example is Amy, whose sister had to decide between caring for her husband or Amy.

> As her father had planned, Amy went to live with her sister Gayle and her family when her father moved into a nursing home. They lived together for about five years and Amy began to attend a disability day centre. However, towards the end of this time, Gayle's husband developed an illness that affected his personality. He found it more difficult to tolerate Amy's somewhat eccentric behaviour, particularly her eating habits. Gayle found it very stressful caring for both her husband and Amy and eventually arranged for Amy to move to the hostel attached to the day centre. Gayle's daughter Janet explained, 'I just remember the anguish that mother (Gayle) had. Dad was sick and Amy was starting to distress him. Mum had the dilemma of putting Amy into (hostel) or getting her in somewhere. She was torn between the stress it was causing dad and the feeling that she was getting rid of Amy.'

The reasons informal primary carers did not continue to provide care are considered further in the section on changes of primary carer later in this chapter.

Inflexibility, inadequacy and pressure from services

Pressure from service providers was the most common reason that people moved out of disability accommodation. These moves were contentious and unsupported family members were angry at the way things were handled and felt that their views were disregarded. The pressure from service providers for people to move arose for two reasons. The first was because of the implementation of existing or new organisational policies that resulted in service providers deciding their services were no longer appropriate to the individual's needs. When this occurred, the adults concerned were encouraged to move to a more appropriate setting. For example, Godfrey's move from the disability hostel, described in a vignette later in this chapter, occurred because of a change of policy. Another example is Dave, who had to move from a group home because when he retired he no longer met the requirements laid down by the policy of the service provider.

> Dave experienced several moves after transition from parental care. The last occurred when he was living in a community residential unit and he decided to retire from the sheltered workshop. When Dave retired, aged 59 years, he no longer complied with the organisation's policy that residents must have a full-time day placement. Although his physical support needs remained similar, alternative accommodation in an aged care facility was organised for him.

Changes in an individual's health or functional capacity and consequent difficulties encountered by staff in managing behaviour was another reason that service providers applied pressure to move. Staff perceived that their service could no longer adequately meet the needs of the person with intellectual disability because of such changes. This view was often disputed by family members who felt the poor quality of services, excessive staff turnover, inflexibility and refusal to attempt to meet the changed needs of the person were the major contributory factors to moves rather than the health or behavioural changes of the service user.

The case of Beatrice, vignetted in chapter 4, illustrates a residential move that occurred for these reasons. Beatrice's niece considered that the breakdown of the co-resident arrangement and her subsequent move to supported accommodation resulted from numerous changes in staff, their misguided philosophies and lack of commitment and understanding of her aunt's needs. Another example is that of Madge. Although her parents had planned comprehensively for her future, arrangements had not worked out as they envisaged. Her brother arranged for her to move to a disability hostel from which she was later forced to move when her behaviour put too great a strain on staff resources.

> After her mother's death Madge remained at home with a co-resident. Her brother, who lived next door, supervised Madge on a daily basis. Madge was an incessant talker and co-residents found her very difficult to live with. When a place became vacant at the hostel attached to the disability day centre she attended, her brother decided she should move there, despite his aunt's concern that this was not what Madge's mother had wanted or planned. In retrospect, her brother felt that the move was the best decision he had ever made. Madge remained at the hostel for 12 years, spending some weekends with her brother. Towards the end of this time Madge developed some obsessive behaviour that led to medical problems and posed management problems for hostel staff.
>
> After a period in hospital she went back to the hostel but staff found it harder to supervise her. She began to get up in the night and,

at times, was unsteady on her feet. Her brother's offer to pay for additional supervisory staff was rejected. Staff suggested she move to a nursing home. Without her brother's knowledge, staff arranged for Madge to be assessed by an aged care assessment team who considered a nursing home was inappropriate. Twelve months elapsed, during which time, hostel staff continued to press for her transfer elsewhere. Eventually, she was reassessed as barely eligible for nursing home care and her brother moved her to a private hospital to give him some time to look around for a suitable nursing home. He was still not convinced that she needed nursing home care but could not find any other appropriate alternative. Three years before the study, at the age of 58, Madge finally moved to a nursing home.

Increased support needs

The need for an increased level of support was indisputably the reason for 17 residential moves that occurred for people in a variety of accommodation types. Emma is an example of someone who experienced a move for this reason.

Emma was 61 when her mother died. She continued to live with her sister Sylvia who was 55 and still working in the city. They hired a home help to assist with domestic tasks and either a paid companion or the neighbour kept Emma company during the day. Emma's physical disabilities increased with age and she gradually began to need help with personal care tasks and became unsteady on her feet. Despite this, they regularly attended a croquet club and after Sylvia retired they drove to Queensland together to visit other relatives. Eighteen years after her mother's death, Emma had major surgery on her stomach and Sylvia, by then 73, was advised that she probably could not cope with Emma at home. Emma moved to a special accommodation house but didn't like it so returned home for a while. She then moved to a private hospital and from there to a geriatric centre until a place was available at a nursing home.

Quality of service

Concerns about the quality of a residential service led to 11 moves from nursing homes and special accommodation homes. Nobody moved from an aged persons' hostel or disability accommodation because of quality issues. Concerns about quality resulted from a lack of private space, poor food and care, inconvenient location and changes of ownership. The vignette of Hilda, described later in this chapter, illustrates several moves because of concerns with quality. Another example is Ted and Brendan who lived in a special accommodation house that was subsequently closed by the Department of Health. Ted said:

> 'There was a lot of violence and a lot of argument. They (staff) wouldn't let me go out. [I was] getting the same sort of food every day. You couldn't go back for a second serve if you wanted to.'

Choice

Twelve people who moved to short-term respite accommodation either chose to move or had planned to remain where they were for only a short period. Such moves were generally part of a planned process and did not occur because the accommodation was inappropriate. A good example of such a move was described in the vignette of Barbara Flynn in chapter 4, who went to live with one of her sisters while a unit was being built next door to another sister. Another example is Isobel.

> After her mother died, Isobel lived with her sister until she met Rod through an introduction agency. Isobel later married Rod and moved across town to live in his home.

FACTORS ASSOCIATED WITH RESIDENTIAL CHANGES

The major trends of residential movement were from informal to formal living situations, from formal to formal living situations, and from disability-specific to aged care facilities. Particular types of accommodation were associated with specific reasons for moving. Moves occurred from private homes and the care of relatives to formal services because relatives could not continue to care or because adults with intellectual disability needed more support. Moves occurred from disability accommodation or from private homes with outreach support because these services considered they could no longer provide appropriate care as a result of organisational policies or changed support needs. Moves occurred from special accommodation houses and nursing homes because of dissatisfaction with quality.

Half the group experienced multiple changes of accommodation and, as table 7.3 demonstrates, some types of accommodation had higher movement rates than others. People who lived in private homes, special accommodation houses and disability accommodation were more likely to experience moves than those in other types of accommodation. Therefore, experience of multiple moves may be associated with the quality and flexibility of services or characteristics of informal carers rather than individual characteristics.

Characteristics such as age, contact with disability services and remaining in informal care rather than moving to formal care did not differentiate movers from non-movers and were not associated with the number of moves. A higher proportion of adults with major health problems than those without experienced multiple changes of accommodation. However, difference between the two groups was not statistically significant. The time elapsed since transition from parental care was significantly associated with the number of residential moves people had made. Adults who had been away from parental care for more than ten years were more likely to have moved more than once compared to those who had been away for less than ten years.

Significantly, parental residential planning was not associated with stability of accommodation or the number of residential moves. Although all but one of the 19 residential plans were successfully implemented at the time of transition, in the years that followed arrangements envisaged in a third of these plans were substantially altered. Such changes are illustrated by the case of Madge above and that of Godfrey which is vignetted later in this chapter.

MANAGEMENT OF ACCOMMODATION CHANGES

The majority of residential moves after transition, like those at the time of transition from parental care, were organised and managed informally by the people nominated in key person succession plans. However, fewer later moves were handled solely by informal network members, and formal services played a greater role. Disability services staff from regional offices and day centres organised and managed accommodation changes for eight people and provided assistance to six others. In the case of three people, in the absence of an informal network member willing to oversee their wellbeing, a guardian was appointed by the Guardianship and Administration Board with the power to make accommodation decisions. The functions of formally appointed guardians were limited in both scope and time.

As some examples, such as Madge and Godfrey's cases illustrate, most of the moves from disability services occurred after pressure was applied by service providers and in a context of conflict between staff and family members. In several instances, moves were initiated and managed by disability service staff against the wishes of family members. Later residential moves contrasted sharply with those made at the time of transition, which had rarely been contentious and where relationships between formal and informal support systems had been positive.

Advice and assistance with residential moves were generally received from either the disability or the aged care services system, with very few people receiving help from both systems. In this respect, little evidence of collaboration between the two service systems was found, an issue that is examined in detail in chapter 9. Possible reasons for a lack of collaboration are a lack of knowledge or perceived problems of accessibility by staff of either system in relation to the other.

Group differences

Considerable differences, similar to those found directly after transition from parental care, still exist between the place of residence of the study population when they are grouped according to their contact with disability services. A much higher proportion of adults attending disability day centres still lives in disability accommodation than any other group. The proportion of people living in aged care facilities has increased but remains similar across both groups. A higher proportion of adults unknown to disability services continues to live in private homes compared with all other groups.

CHANGES OF PRIMARY CARER

All of the study population experienced a change of primary carer on transition and two-thirds had at least one further change of primary carer. Later changes of primary carer were generally also associated with a change of accommodation. Therefore, the number of primary carers usually coincided with the number of residential moves but sometimes exceeded them. Dot, whose case is vignetted later in this chapter, is an example. When her sister died, Dot remained in the flat she had shared with her sister but her primary carers changed to staff of a domiciliary care service. Gerry is another example.

> When Gerry left the disability hostel, he lived in rented accommodation and moved flat several times but continued to receive primary care from the same outreach service.

Where primary care was provided by a formal service, staffing and roster alterations meant primary carers changed more frequently than accommodation changes indicate. An example is Beatrice, whose vignette was considered in chapter 4. She lived at home supported by outreach staff for ten years but in this period had at least 12 changes of support workers.

TABLE 7.4 **Primary carers straight after transition and at time of the study**

Primary carer	After transition Number	%	At time of study Number	%
Sibling	26	42%	7	11%
Cousin	1	1%	1	1%
Aunt	2	3%	1	1%
Church member, friend or co-resident	4	7%	3	5%
(Total informal)	(33)	(53%)	(12)	(19%)
Domiciliary services	2	3%	1	1%
Residential staff, disability	11	18%	6	10%
Residential staff, aged care	13	21%	40	65%
Senior citizens' centre social worker	1	1%	—	—
Disability outreach	1	1%	3	5%
Not known	1	1%	—	—
(Total formal)	(29)	(47%)	(50)	(81%)
Total	**62**	**100%**	**62**	**100%**

Note: Figures have been rounded.

Despite considerable imprecision regarding the number of actual changes of primary carer, the reasons they occurred and the trends they followed are similar to those found in relation to accommodation changes; from informal to formal, formal to formal and from specialist disability to aged care. Table 7.4 contrasts the source of primary care straight after transition with the source at the time of the study. The biggest change was the increased (45% to 81%) proportion of people who received primary care from formal sources and the increase from 21% to 65% of those who received primary care from an aged care facility.

Decline of informal primary carers

In the years that followed the transition from parental care, the proportions of people who had an informal primary carer declined from just over half directly after transition to one-fifth by the time of study. During this period, 41 informal carers provided primary care for a total of 33 people, 29 had ceased to do so and 12 were still doing so. Table 7.5 summarises the reasons that informal primary carers discontinued provision of care. The predominant reasons stemmed from the carers' characteristics, their inability or unwillingness to continue, rather than a change in the charac-

TABLE 7.5 **Reasons informal primary carers discontinued in this role**

Reason for ceasing primary care	First primary carer	Subsequent carers	Total
Carer unwilling to continue, problems unrelated to health	7	3	10
Ill health of carer or spouse	4	—	4
Death of carer	6	3	9
Short-term arrangement only and planned moves not related to problems between older person and carer	3	1	4
Increased care required by older person	1	1	2
Total ceased	**21**	**8**	**29**

teristics of the person who was cared for. In the post-parental care phase, the average length of time that informal primary care was provided was 6.3 years but ranged from a few weeks to 21 years.

CHANGES OF LOCALITY, DAY PLACEMENT AND HEALTH

Twenty-seven people changed locality at the time of transition from parental care and a further 19 moved locality later. Therefore, at the time of the study, almost three-quarters had moved from their original locality, which often resulted in a loss of community ties, and acquaintances. Informants spoke warmly of how well known the adult with intellectual disability had been in their local area because they had 'done the messages'. For example, Bruce's sister said:

> 'The only thing he (Bruce) did was the messages for the lady next door. He would always go over to the shops for milk. If you gave him a note and the money in his purse he'd go and get whatever you wanted from the shops over there. He interacted with the neighbours in the street. They all knew Bruce, everyone knew him and all the shopkeepers knew him and they all liked him.'

Allen had lived in the same street with his parents since he was born until he moved into his sister's house when he was 56. His sister said:

> 'He knew the boys in the street. He had a close relationship with them. He then used to go down and see them almost every night when he came home and talk about the football. He knew them from when they were a lot younger.'

Social contact with neighbours was generally lost when people moved out of home, although Godfrey always called in to see an old neighbour when he visited his brother who lived near to where his parental home had been.

At the time of transition from parental care, only two people ceased attending a disability day centre but, as they aged, eight more ceased attending. At the time of study, only nine older adults were attending a disability day program, two of whom had started attending after the transition.

The study population experienced the physiological processes of ageing, which, for some, meant some deterioration of their health and loss of physical and adaptive functions. These losses were particularly marked for four of six people with Down syndrome, who experienced the early onset of Alzheimer's, and those in the over-65 age group. A quarter of the group developed major health problems, limited mobility or became very frail in the period after their transition from parental care.

CASE VIGNETTES

Three short case vignettes illustrate the diversity of changes that occurred in the lives of the study population, the reasons for these changes and the positive as well as negative effects of change. They are drawn from the two major groups defined in chapter 5 which were those who had received primary care from formal services only, or from both informal and formal sources. The case of Dot is illustrative of those who experienced a change of key informal network member. A representative case of the group who had relied only on informal primary care is not included since this group experienced fewer changes of residence or primary carer than other groups, and Barbara, whose case is vignetted in chapter 4 is illustrative of this group.

Dot Brown

No data was available about plans Dot's parents had made for her future care. In the years after her parents died, Dot moved twice but experienced more changes of primary carer than this. Her reliance on formal services gradually increased and, although informal sources were still significant, these too had changed. The primary informant for Dot was Ethel, the president of the senior citizens' club, who had known Dot for more than 20 years.

> Dot was 41 years old when her mother died. Dot remained at home with her co-resident brother who took over as her primary carer. After neighbours had contacted the local government Community Services Department about the state of their house and her brother's ability

to provide care for her, Dot began to attend the local senior citizens' centre every day for lunch. At the centre she acted as a volunteer, laying all the tables and clearing away. She lived with her brother for about 17 years, until he died. After his death she stayed in the house alone and her sister, who lived in the next suburb, supervised aspects of Dot's daily life and domestic management. The family home had become very run down and her sister found it difficult to provide support to Dot. Eventually Dot moved to live with her sister, who died a year or so later. Dot remained in her sister's flat alone with intensive domiciliary support from a local government aged care program funded by HACC.

Ethel, the president of the senior citizen's club, which she has attended for many years, took a close interest in Dot and when her sister died took a major role in managing Dot's affairs and organising services for her. Ethel tried unsuccessfully to get assistance for Dot from a regional disability services team, arranged for her sister's burial and organised for the church to sponsor her move to a flat in a new aged persons' complex in her original suburb. While going through Dot's papers, Ethel discovered Dot had a brother in the country whom she had not seen for 20 years. Ethel arranged for the police to contact him but he was in his 80s, in poor health, and did not want to play any role in Dot's life. Ethel continues to oversee Dot's affairs for her. Dot is now aged 62. She gets regular assistance with domestic tasks from local government domiciliary services. Ethel helps her with financial and other affairs and Dot continues to attend the senior citizen's club every day for lunch.

Godfrey Allen

Godfrey's mother had planned comprehensively for his future care. He would move into the hostel attached to the disability day centre, his eldest brother would be his guardian, and her estate would be left to her three sons to manage for him. Although his mother oversaw Godfrey's move to the hostel, Godfrey experienced two further residential changes. His living situation at the time of the study, four and a half years after her death, was very different from the one she had envisaged.

> Godfrey moved into a hostel when he was 40 and returned home every weekend and for holidays. His mother died 11 years later and, within several months of her death, Godfrey was moved out of the hostel to an independence-training house. Six months later he moved to a rented flat shared with Gerry, another ex-resident of the hostel. Godfrey is now 56 and has lived with Gerry for the past four years. They receive support with household and financial management from a disability outreach service and domestic assistance through the local government's HACC program. Godfrey ceased attending the disability

day centre and moved to a sheltered workshop that was nearer his home. Two of Godfrey's brothers live in Queensland, including his eldest who is in poor health. Another brother lives in the suburb next to Godfrey and has taken over the role of 'guardian', that his mother envisaged the elder brother would play.

Godfrey's brothers thought that they had not been consulted about Godfrey's move out of the hostel. In their view he had been forced to move and their mother's wishes had not been respected. As Godfrey had led such a sheltered life, they thought that he was not ready for so much independence. One of his brothers said, 'It was her (mother's) wish that he stay there (hostel). They (the government) started all these new social reforms. It's not up to us. We're not [his] guardian. They tell you what they are going to do. They don't ask you. He'd never had money in his life. He'd never bought groceries. They (regional disability services) had been talking about this before mum died, moving people out and they wouldn't do it while she was alive.'

Godfrey now had much more freedom and independence than he had ever had. Despite his misgivings about the process, one of his brothers considered that Godfrey's life had been very regulated at the hostel and he was coping all right in the flat, went to some interesting places and could now get all round the city on public transport.

Hilda Parkes

Hilda's history illustrates a case of someone who, like Dot, progressed towards more formal sources of care, but for whom some changes of accommodation arose from the poor quality of care provided. Hilda's aunt Dolly, who had a physical disability, had lived with Hilda and her parents all her life. Her parents had not discussed Hilda's future care with any of her brothers but their will left the estate in trust for her. The trustee was one of her three brothers, Roderick, who had the closest relationship with both his parents and Hilda.

> Hilda's father died first and then, after a long illness, her mother died when Hilda was 42. For several months, Hilda and her aunt stayed on in the family home but as both had quite substantial disabilities they found it difficult to manage the house and look after themselves. Roderick arranged for Hilda to move to a special accommodation house. She lived in three different special accommodation houses over the next 14 years. She left the first because of the poor quality of care. The second had provided a much higher standard of care but this had deteriorated when it was taken over by another proprietor. After her second move, Roderick began to investigate a place for her at the church-sponsored nursing home where his mother had been. He felt this would offer more permanent high quality care for Hilda. He said,

'We were worried what the future would be. If we got her into (the nursing home) there would be ongoing care, as long as she lived. We couldn't see the standard of care in those accommodation houses [as being] very much as a person got on in life.' Hilda moved to the nursing home when she was 56 and has lived there for the past 11 years. Several years ago an enthusiastic staff member had referred Hilda to a regional disability services team to see if a more appropriate service was available. However, Roderick did not want her to move and nothing came of this referral. He is very satisfied with the care she receives and said, 'I believe that Hilda has a busier life visiting and doing things now than she has in her past times, even when father was alive'.

PERSONAL DEVELOPMENT IN LATE LIFE

Many members of the study population experienced considerable personal development following their transition from parental care. This topic was raised quite spontaneously by many informants who drew attention to increased personal autonomy and independence, expansion of social and domestic activities, development of new skills and personal relationships experienced by members of the study population. These developments are hard to quantify as they are relative to each individual's previous experiences and the evidence stems from informants' impressions rather than systematic measurement and comparison pre- and post-parental transition.

A defining feature of many later life developments was their unplanned and unexpected nature. For example, Vera was quite frail at the time of the study and following a long period of hospitalisation had moved to an aged persons' hostel. Her nieces said:

> 'Vera has become more independent. Now she copes really well. She just does things that she would never have dreamt of doing once upon a time.'

Rod and Isobel are also good examples of people whose life developed in a totally unexpected way following transition from parental care.

> Rod and Isabel married when they were in their 50s, several years after their respective parents had died. They lived together independently in the community for about 24 years, supported informally by members of their church community. The family friend who managed Rod's affairs since his parents died said, 'Of course they (his parents) never expected Rod to marry. That's the last thing in the world they ever imagined. Rod advertised for a wife and he met a woman who fortunately was a church woman and also she was mentally retarded the same as Rod. Despite his rude ways to her, she (Isobel) loved Rod very much.'

Despite the limited control members of the study population had exercised over the process of transition from parental care, post transition some experienced greater control over their everyday lives. Three people married. Sixteen lived for some period, either with a friend or alone, in a private home in the community (albeit with varying levels of domiciliary support). Remarkably, those who moved into supported accommodation, as well as those who remained in the community, experienced increased autonomy. According to his sister-in-law, Walter, who had chosen to live in the same aged persons' hostel as one of his friends, developed into his own person after he left parental care. She said, 'The biggest change has been now (moving into an aged persons' hostel). Because now, he's totally a person. Now he can just please himself.'

Following transition, some people began to participate in a range of new activities, develop new skills and move around the community to a much greater extent than they had done previously. Lucas's mother contrasted the expectations that staff at the group home had of him compared with when he had lived at home. She said, 'He never went out on his own (at home), but he does now. They send him to the bank on his own.'

Amy moved to a disability hostel after living with her sister for some time. Her niece described her as really blossoming since the move. She said:

> 'Her life has changed dramatically for the better because she was doing things that she had never done in her life before and social occasions (sic). I can remember mum (Amy's sister) being floored the first time Amy came home and said she needed bathers because they were going swimming. I don't think Amy had ever had a pair of bathers in her life. And going to the football and going for counter meals, outings and to the pictures and shopping and things like that. Her life is just wonderful now; she is as happy as Larry.'

Godfrey, whose vignette was considered above, is another example of someone who experienced more independence in later life. One of his brothers said:

> 'Godfrey can go anywhere: travels on his own to work. Mother let him out very seldom. She let him go down to the shops in (the suburb). Now he gets all round Melbourne.'

Use of public transport was a skill that many of the study population developed in later life that facilitated their movement around the community. Other skills developed were banking, shopping, literacy, housekeeping, cooking and use of the phone. For example, since her mother died Gina has lived on her own with support from the local church community. Her church elder said:

> 'She certainly has become far more independent and able to undertake more things for herself now than she was able to do in the past. I got a feeling of real growth and development. We are quite proud of her and think she has come along remarkably.'

Participation in new social activities often coincided with more opportunities to make friends and acquaintances, which, in turn, fostered the development of social skills and competence. Barbara, whose case was vignetted in chapter 4, began attending a disability day centre after she left parental care, where she developed a network of friends. Her sisters actively encouraged her social development. One of them said:

> 'When she was living with mum and dad she (Barbara) just stayed in the home. I wish they could see what she's been doing. You know, she's marvellous at pottery. She'd never done anything like that before. She should have done [things like this] before. That's what my sister and I decided: to get her involved with other people.'

Several people formed a close relationship with a non-family member for the first time in their lives, which gave them great pleasure. The marriage between Isobel and Rod mentioned above is one illustration. Another case is that of Nadia who lived alone after her mother died, and formed a close relationship with a widower who lived in a nearby flat.

> Nadia's sister thought that he was probably the first real friend she had ever had. When Nadia showed me a picture of her friend she said, 'This is my boy. I'm very proud of him.'

Later life developments did not always follow an upward trend. The expansion of some people's horizons was followed by a decline. The onset of health problems and associated residential moves often resulted in reduced opportunities and ability to participate in activities and social interactions. However, this affected at most only a quarter of the study population. An example of someone in this situation is Morris, whose experience is presented as a vignette in chapter 9.

Explanations of late life development

Attention was drawn to parental attitudes that had restricted developmental and social opportunities for the person with intellectual disability. For example, talking about her mother, Bronwyn said, 'She wouldn't let me go out. She didn't think I was as old as I am. She wouldn't let me be friends with anybody. She wouldn't even let me talk to anybody.' Neil's sister-in-law, talking about his life at home, said, 'He didn't have a life of his own. He was always a child to mum and dad, and told what to do.'

References to these protective parental attitudes were not judgmental or blaming and often drew attention to the historical context and attitudes held about people with intellectual disability. Informants noted the dramatic changes to services and attitudes towards people with intellectual disability. They pondered opportunities members of the study population had lost and what their life could have been like had they been born at a different time. For example, Philip now lives with his brother, who said:

> 'Philip's her (his mother's) little boy and that's it. We have problems because his mother was too dominant and did too much for him. She's done a marvellous job, looked after him very well. But only when you get him away from her do you realise she has made it extremely difficult for anybody else. You can't criticise her for the care she gave him. He would have had a much happier life with her than going into one of those homes. Things that are available now weren't available then when he was at a receptive age where they could have helped.'

Amy's niece said:

> 'It just makes you realise, that had things been available for Amy as they are now, the potential that could have been realised.'

Opportunities presented by new residential environments, the attitudes of new primary carers or those who took responsibility for their wellbeing all contributed to later life developments. For example, talking about Humphrey's move to an aged persons' hostel, his brother, who lives in the same hostel, said:

> 'Humphrey's had more opportunities to travel here. Normally we do two or three trips a year away from the village. Had dad been still alive he (Humphrey) probably wouldn't have had the opportunity.'

People who replaced parents as primary carers or took responsibility for overseeing wellbeing often had a different perspective from that of parents. Some of them, like Barbara's sisters, took definite steps to encourage skill development, seek out opportunities for social contact and broaden the horizons of the person with intellectual disability. Another example is Ada's aunt, who, though she was from the same generation as Ada's mother, had a different perspective. She said:

> 'Ada's mother and I were very fond of one another so when I say this I'm not condemning her. She (Ada) was so precious: she lived a very sheltered life with her parents who doted on her and protected her. To me that is three-quarters of the problem. She knows her money now and goes to the bank and gets her own. I've got to get her used to doing things like that.'

Bruce, the subject of a vignette presented in chapter 4, also illustrates a case of a primary carer who fostered social development. His sister said:

> 'I used to let him go to the village one day a week for just social events, interacting with other people. This was after mum went. Mum would never let him out of her sight. Mum wouldn't let him go anywhere. I've always felt it was better for him to mix because he was very good with people.'

Another factor that may be associated with this late life development is the cessation of caring responsibilities and an interdependent relationship with aged parents. The transition from parental care freed adults with intellectual disability from obligations to parents and the restricted opportunities that may have resulted from living with aged parents. Middle-aged adults with intellectual disability had often shared the aged lifestyle of their parents well before their health warranted such restrictions. George pointed out how being at home with his elderly mother had restricted his freedom to pursue his own interests. At the time of the study, he was living in a disability hostel and said:

> 'If mum and I had stayed in the house together, I would have been housebound. I wouldn't have been able to do the things that I am able to do now. I couldn't. If I went to the Melbourne Cricket Ground all day Saturday, I'd come home and find mum on the floor. I just couldn't go away and leave her on her own.'

In a similar vein, Bronwyn, who has lived alone since her mother died, said:

> 'I didn't get out then (when her mother was alive) like I do now to different places, I couldn't go and leave her.'

THE CONTINUING PROCESSES OF PLANNING

The average age of the study population was 65 years. Some of these people still had many years of life ahead of them. The parents of three people continued to play a key role in their lives. For these three, parental plans were yet to be fully implemented. For most, however, someone else had replaced the parent as the key person in their life. These key people, though less anxious than parents, were concerned about the future. They foresaw changes to care arrangements and had made quite similar plans to those of parents. Like parents, the most common plan made by key people was a key person succession plan. All such plans were explicit and, unlike many parental plans, nominated people from a younger generation than the person with intellectual disability. Children of key people, such as the nieces and nephews of the person with intellectual disability, were usually nominated in plans. This remained the case when the key person was a sibling and other siblings were still alive. Like parental key person succession plans, those made by subsequent key people were open-ended, referred to supervision of wellbeing and were often tied to financial arrangements. Nora's brother explained his plan for Nora's future care:

> 'I've no doubt in my mind that all the kids will rally behind Nora should I predecease her. We've said to our children, if anything ever happens to us, that unit will be sold and you children will use that money to look after Nora. But that won't go in the will because it's just something they understand, that part of our estate is set aside for Nora.'

Several key people considered they had secured the future by making residential plans or arrangements. Diane's sister who had organised for Diane to live with her in an aged care facility said:

> 'She's OK here (aged care facility). She'll be looked after and that's a big thing. It's one of the biggest things in life when you've got a member of the family who's not capable of looking after herself or hasn't got the initiative to go in and do anything. She's here now and can be looked after and that's a big load off people's minds.'

However, key people involved in disability residential services had seen many changes of policy and were concerned about the impact of future policy changes. For example, Doreen's sister said:

> 'I do wonder about the future. I'm not worried that she won't have any money but I'm worried about the structures. I don't think she will go well in a group home, if the hostel should close. It should be closed now. They (the voluntary association) had to say they would move residents out into community residential units. Doreen needs a lot of support in a community. Like it is seems just right for her.'

A few key people had handed, or intended to hand, over responsibility for financial affairs of the adult with intellectual disability to a specialist trust fund, solicitor or to disability services. However, in only two cases did key people plan to hand over to formal services responsibility for overseeing the person's wellbeing.

CONCLUSIONS: MID- AND LATER-LIFE CHANGES

This chapter has considered the changes that characterised the study population following their transition from parental care. For many, more change occurred following transition than had occurred at the time of transition. For example, at the time of the study when all the study population were over 55 years and therefore 'older adults', 86% had moved out of the home they had previously lived in with their parents compared with 55% at the time of transition from parental care. Seventy-four per cent had moved out of their locality compared with 56% at the time of transition, and 73% had lost both their parents compared with 47% at the time of transition. Half the group had experienced two or more changes of primary carer and 63% of those who attended a disability day centre had left since the time of transition. These changes affected people's social and community networks. For example, residential moves resulted in loss of contact with neighbours and local community members who had provided a sense of identity and opportunities for social contact. Cessation of attendance at a disability day centre meant loss of contact with longstanding friends and acquaintances. The impact of these changes is considered further when the nature of social networks is examined in the following chapters.

In the years following transition from parental care, the balance between formal and informal sources of care shifted towards a greater reliance on formal sources, particularly for primary care. Almost three-quarters of informal primary carers who replaced parents subsequently relinquished that role, mostly because they were unwilling or unable to continue. The provision of informal primary care as a short-term arrangement in the post-parental phase has been noted in other studies (Grant, 1988; Prosser & Moss, 1996). The reasons that informal carers relinquished primary care are similar to those factors suggested by Litwak's (1985) theory of task specificity and are also suggested as obstacles to the provision of primary care to an adult with intellectual disability by other kin. These include the costs and stress involved and physical limitations of aged peers.

In this period, a differentiation of task by group became more apparent, as 81% of older adults received primary care from formal services. In contrast, as examined in the next chapter, overseeing wellbeing remained the domain of informal sources. In a few instances, this function had been replaced by a formally appointed guardian but with limited scope and time commitment. At the time of the study, no one had a formally appointed guardian. The following chapters will focus on this key person role in greater depth and discuss the extent to which formal services can fulfil this role and the problems they may have in doing so.

Similar trends of residential movement and primary care changes, from informal to formal sources, were found as have been reported by other studies that consistently report only small proportions of older people with intellectual disability live in private homes (Ashman et al., 1993; Hand,

1994; Horne, 1989b; Jacobson et al., 1985; Seltzer & Krauss, 1987). However, it is often suggested that the shift from informal to formal care occurs at the time of the transition from parental care (Gibson et al., 1992; Lakin et al., 1991; Walz et al., 1986). The indications in this study are that more people experience a residential move after than at the time of the transition from parental care and that the movement to formal care is accentuated in later moves.

The movement into and out of disability services following the transition from parental care has not been reported previously and suggests these services lack the capacity to respond flexibly to age-related changes. This movement indicates that opportunities do not exist for older people with intellectual disability to age in place, in the disability accommodation that has become their home. This is an issue of concern, since ageing in place is a central plank of Australian aged care policy. It also raises questions about the capacity of disability services to provide stability and security and the viability of parental residential plans that rely on disability services.

A similar high propensity for residential mobility and enforced moves among older people with intellectual disability is reported by other studies (Ashman et al., 1993; Moss et al., 1989). However, other studies have included institutional and ex-institutional populations in their samples and used deinstitutionalisation and loss of parents to account for the high rate of residential movement. The findings of this study, limited to people who had remained home till mid life, suggest the explanation of movement may be more complex. Contextual factors such as inflexibility of disability services, poor quality of aged care facilities, and the inability of informal carers who replace parents to sustain that role, as well as individual characteristics such as increased needs for support, are contributory factors in residential moves. This suggests that the high rate of mobility is more amenable to amelioration and intervention than other studies indicate.

This chapter has demonstrated that the transition from parental care marks the first of many changes in the lives of middle-aged and older adults with intellectual disability. The involvement of formal services in management and organisation of transitions increased in the years following transition, as did the need for the formal provision of primary care. This took varied forms such as disability or aged care accommodation or specialist or generic domiciliary support. Most changes that occurred in the lives of the study population after the transition from parental care were unplanned and unexpected. This was especially so in regard to the very positive later life personal development that occurred for many of the study population. The impossibility of predicting or planning is one reason for lack of association between parental residential plans and residential stability. Anxieties about the future were a continuing concern of those who succeeded parents as key people in the lives of older adults with intellectual disability. Planning for the future was a task to be undertaken in the post-parental care phase and was confronted not only by parents but also their successors. This raises questions about the efficacy of residential planning that will be considered with other planning issues when the nature of later life informal support and the outcomes of key person planning have been fully considered in the following chapters.

PART THREE

SOURCES OF SUPPORT IN LATER LIFE FOR PEOPLE WITH INTELLECTUAL DISABILITIES

CHAPTER *8*

Informal support networks of older people with intellectual disability

Previous chapters have analysed the processes of transition from parental care and subsequent life changes experienced by middle-aged adults with intellectual disability as they begin to age. Primarily, the focus has been on the management of transitions and provision of basic needs; that is, living situations and sources of primary care. In this chapter and the next, the focus is more clearly on older people with intellectual disability, and the nature and sources of their broader kinds of support are examined. This chapter describes the informal support networks of older people with intellectual disability. Understanding the nature of a person's informal network provides important clues about its potential for support, gaps that need to be bridged and maintenance action that may be required to ensure support continues.

DIMENSIONS OF INFORMAL SUPPORT

Chapter 3 considered the varied ways in which informal support has been conceptualised. Measuring the extent and nature of an individual's informal support network presents a major challenge, particularly if, as Kahn and Antonucci suggest, supportiveness is part of a continuum and cannot be measured using the dichotomy of presence or absence (1980). Detailed descriptions about relationships between study members and others in their social world were collected in interviews with informants. Four dimensions are used to analyse the nature of each person's social relationships and informal support network. These dimensions are: frequency of contact, nature of interaction, type of support provided and strength, duration and reason for the relationship.

Everyone identified as having a relationship with an older person who was in contact with them at least twice a year is included as part of their informal social network. Paid staff are excluded and considered as part of formal support networks. Contact is categorised as frequent when it is at least monthly and fairly frequent when it occurs at least twice a year but less than monthly. Young children, such as grand nieces and nephews, are not counted as network members, as they do not have independent contact with the older person.

The interactional dimension is what people do when they make contact and how and by whom contact is initiated. Contact is usually face to face but, for several people, phone calls and letters are important. Contact with network members involves some form of shared activity, such as going shopping, out for lunch, visiting a relative's home, walking together or participating in a social event such as a family celebration. It is rarely just passive visiting. Contact is initiated by the older person or a network member as either a deliberate action or one that occurs incidentally when people have network members in common with each other.

The type of support provided by network members is dichotomised into affective and instrumental support. Affective support revolves around expressing interest and concern about a person, valuing them as an individual and thereby assisting in the establishment of their self-esteem and identity. It is distinguished by the absence of any form of direct help or advocacy on someone's behalf. Affective support is expressed through the provision of companionship and opportunities for social interaction, by being available to listen when someone is upset or to discuss matters of concern, remembering and marking significant personal occasions, such as birthdays, and inclusion in family and/or social activities.

Instrumental support is more tangible and easily specified. It is the provision of some form of direct assistance to the older person or advocacy on their behalf. Ten types of instrumental support are identified:

- Decision making—regarding major life decisions such as place of residence, care or treatment received or services provided.
- Financial management—having control or supervision of financial affairs or control of major expenditure or additional discretionary sums.
- Adoption of formal or legal roles—including formal appointment as a guardian or administrator, holding power of attorney, being regarded as next of kin or the contact person for formal services.
- Mediating—negotiation and advocacy with formal service systems about the provision of services.
- Monitoring—oversight of the nature and quality of services received.
- Provision of primary care—direct assistance with activities of daily living or supervision of these activities.
- Management and supervision of medical needs—monitoring health and arranging for medical needs to be met.
- Coordination—organising support from and contact with other relatives and friends in the older person's informal support network.

- Provision of back-up support—providing support to another member of the older person's network or the short-term provision of more intensive roles as replacement for another network member temporarily absent.
- Skills development—assisting in the development of domestic and community living skills such as use of public transport, shopping or cooking.

The fourth dimension is the strength, duration and reason for the relationship. Strength of relationships varies from a high degree of attachment and closeness to ill feelings, antagonism or ambivalence. This dimension uncovers the chief underlying reason for the relationship; whether it is, for example, love and affection, obligation or duty. Judgments about the strength of relationships are based on the comments and perceptions of informants.

Network members were initially divided into family and friends; however, three further important categories were identified: 'key people', 'informal primary carers' and 'church connections'. The resulting five categories of informal network members are not, however, exclusive. For example, key people are also family members or friends. These categories, which are defined and considered in detail in later parts of this chapter, are summarised in table 8.1. The informal support network of each older person is mapped using these broad dimensions and categories and common features of network structure and composition are examined. Each person's network reflects his or her unique individual and family history, other social relationships and current circumstances (Antonucci & Akiyama, 1987).

STRUCTURE OF INFORMAL NETWORKS

A striking feature of most informal networks is the existence of a key person who proactively oversees the wellbeing of the older person with intellectual disability. This key person combines frequent contact, strong attachment, a high level of commitment and fulfilment of a wide range of instrumental tasks.

Networks are small and vary in size from 0–20 members, with an average of six. No one has children and only three people have a spouse, so for most people siblings are their closest kin. Family members dominate most peoples' networks, comprising the entire network of a third of the group, over 75% of the network for half the group, and more than 50% of the network for almost three-quarters of the group.

Only five people have no family members in their network compared to 21 who have no friends. The absence, or a small number, of family is not compensated by an increased number of friends, thus the average network size of those with a low proportion of family members is smaller than the network size of those who have a high proportion. Table A.8, in appendix 3, summaries network characteristics. Although the most common type of support provided by network members is affective, over three-quarters of the group receive some form of instrumental support, but generally only from one network member who is a relative.

Networks are generally dense, as most network members know each other. Friends are often drawn from people who attend the same day centre, live in the same neighbourhood or supported accommodation, or are part of the same church community. Density also results from an older adult sharing network members with parents or siblings. Most network members are from the same generation as the older person. Where network members from a younger generation do exist they tend to be less involved and have less frequent contact than those from a similar or older generation.

Relationships with network members usually go back many years, reflecting the predominance of family members with lifelong relationships with the older person. Friends are evenly split between those who are longstanding and more recent relationships made in the years since the death of parents. Longstanding friends are often also friends or neighbours of parents or co-participants in a disability day centre.

The average size and composition of networks varies between living situations. People living with relatives or in disability accommodation have slightly larger networks than those in other types of accommodation. The networks of people living with relatives and in aged care facilities contain fewer friends and are more often family dominated than the networks of those living in other types of accommodation. People living at home alone have networks with a greater proportion of friends and the smallest proportions of family members. Adults who attend disability day services have the largest networks. For details see table A.9 in appendix 3.

COMPOSITION OF INFORMAL NETWORKS

As noted earlier, networks comprise five main categories of members: key people, informal primary carers, family, friends and church connections. The roles and characteristics of these different categories are described and analysed in the following sections. Table 8.1 provides a summary overview.

Role of key informal network members

Three-quarters of the group have a key person. This role is illustrated by the sisters of Norman, Doreen and Nadia in the vignettes at the end of this chapter. The term 'key person' is applied to people who take responsibility for overseeing the wellbeing of an adult with intellectual disability. They are people who are informally associated and fulfil three or more of the instrumental tasks described at the beginning of this chapter. In summary, these are: decision making, financial management, formal or legal roles, mediation, monitoring, providing primary care, managing or supervising health needs, coordinating, providing back-up support and developing skills.

Assumption of a key person role only occurs when parents die or their health deteriorates and usually takes place during the process of transition from parental care. This was illustrated in chapter 6 where the informal management of transition by those nominated in parental key person succession plans was considered. For example, Brendan's sister, who organised his move to a disability hostel, said:

> 'Brendan can be warm, loving and affectionate. Obviously his attention has diverted from mum as she got older, to me. I was the mother figure by this stage. I was the one that he leant on, and that's been like that for many years.'

Some informants drew attention to the similarities between the role of key people and parental roles. For example Madge's brother said, 'I've taken over the role of my parents since they were unable to do that'. Nora's brother said, 'When dad died Nora looked upon me as dad. We've always provided everything she's needed.'

However, unlike parents had done, key people do not always provide primary care and many have a less intense and less protective relationship with the adult with intellectual disability. Overseeing wellbeing is the defining element of the key person role but their degree of involvement in the day-to-day life of the older person varies. For some, such as Norman's sister in the case study at the end of this chapter, it is extensive. Others are less involved in people's daily lives, assuming a more hands-off managerial approach.

A key person who is less involved in day-to-day affairs but who manages his brother's affairs, monitors service quality and mediates service provision is George's brother, Stephen. George's sister-in-law talked about the role that Stephen and herself play in organising services for George.

> 'If Stephen and I were not around I don't know who would do that. What do others do who don't have access to the kind of care we are able to provide?—Not the physical washing but its all that working through the paperwork, that minefield of institutions and organisations.'

Who are key people?

Most key people were nominated by parents in key person succession plans and have managed the transition from parental care and subsequent

TABLE 8.1 Major categories of informal support for the study population, their roles, characteristics and frequency

Category	Roles	Relationship	Characteristics	Frequency*
Key person	• *Overseeing wellbeing*: three or more instrumental tasks: decision making, financial management, formal or legal roles, mediation, monitoring, primary care provision, managing medical needs, coordinating, skill development, back up other network members. • *Regular contact* • *Affective and social contact*	Predominantly siblings (36), parents (3) distant relatives (4) church members or friends (4)	Close long-term relationship. Strong emotional bond. Often a negotiated commitment via a key person succession plan. Role usually assumed during transition, but sometimes later as partial replacement for parental functions. No automatic succession to role based on family ties. Stable, unaffected by mobility.	47–76%
Informal primary carer	• *Primary care*: direct assistance or supervision with two or more activities of daily living. • *Daily contact*	Sibling (7), distant relatives (2), church member or friend (3)	Close long-term relationship, usually combined with key person role and co-resident, more likely to be single, female, co-resident or close to adult prior to transition. Not a long-term role, average 6.3 years.	12–19%

Family members	• *Affective support and social contact:* visiting, shared activities, social events. • *Instrumental tasks:* acting as next of kin and power of attorney, back-up support for key person. • *Contact* varied. Average two times a year with four family members (including family members who are key people).	Siblings (47), parents (18), distant relatives (aunts, uncles, nieces, nephews, 32), siblings in-law (47)	Incidental contact with older person rather than a proactive role. Pattern of contact a reflection of longer-term family relationships. An adult child of sibling key person may have a closer relationship and be nominated as key person successor. Dominated networks more than 50% of network for 72% of sample.	57–92%
Friends	• *Affective support and social contact* • *Contact* varied. Average contact monthly with two friends and twice a year with four friends.	Co-residents, co-participants, neighbours, unnamed acquaintances	Situation specific, shared with other network members, half long-term and half more recent. Varied with type of residence. Often assumed by informants not to exist. Mobility is liable to disrupt.	48–77%
Church members	• *Affective support, social acceptance, valued roles* • *Instrumental support* (several acted as key people or primary carers see above). • *Contact* frequent, regular.	Members of church congregation, ministers, elders	Longstanding involvement of older person and their parent in the church community. Sometimes combined with informal primary carer role.	13–21%

* Frequency relates to the number and proportion of the sample who had this category of network member. Categories are not exclusive

changes in the life of the adult with intellectual disability. Some key people have, however, succeeded the key person nominated in a parental plan and are the second or third key person since the transition from parental care. As would be expected from key person succession plans, the majority of key people are siblings. However, kin ties alone do not determine who takes on the role of a key person. The nature of the relationship between the key person and the person with intellectual disability or their parents, and nomination in a key person succession plan are as important as formal kin ties in defining who, if anyone, becomes a key person. Eleven people have a non-sibling key person despite seven of these people having siblings. Non sibling key people comprise parents, friends or church members, nieces, aunts and cousins.

Key siblings

If an older person has more than one sibling, one usually assumes the role of a key person, although often in consultation with other siblings. Comparison of the characteristics of the key siblings with other siblings for those people who have more than one sibling alive gives some clues to the defining characteristics of key siblings. If a parent had reached an implicit or explicit understanding by means of a key person succession plan with a particular sibling about the role they would play, it is usually this sibling who takes on the key person role. Someone other than the nominated person had assumed the role of a key person in only one instance. This happened to Pauline, whose younger sister was co-resident with Pauline and her mother when their mother died. The younger sister took on the key person role instead of an elder sister who had been nominated to do so in the plan formulated by her father. Another exception is Godfrey whose younger brother, because of his elder brother's ill health, took over the role expected of and previously fulfilled by that older brother.

Where siblings are different genders, more sisters than brothers become key people. A brother is only preferred to a sister when the older person with intellectual disability is male and the relationship between the sister-in-law and the older person is very strong. Key siblings are usually the siblings who have been closest to the older person since childhood and have been the sibling most involved in providing care for their elderly parents.

Thus, being a sister, the existence of a strong relationship between the older person and a sister-in-law, playing a prime role in the provision of care to parents in late life and having a strong relationship with the older person are all characteristics of key siblings. Factors such as proximity, not being in paid employment and co-residence are occasionally associated with key person status but not consistently. For example, Lewis has five siblings. His brother Ron is his key person.

> Contrary to the traditions of Lewis's family, his brother Ron rather than his older brother Fred managed Lewis's affairs. Ron's wife said, 'Fred, the eldest brother, just handed over to Ron, as he and Pop (Lewis's father) started fighting. The old school was the eldest was in charge. If anything was to be done you had to see Fred. He just didn't have the fighting power to keep going. He didn't have Pop's respect, whereas Pop respects Ron and knows he can rely on him. We (Ron and his wife) used to go over every fortnight and give Pop and Lewis their lunch. Ron is the only one who can handle him (Lewis). Very rarely they (other siblings) went over and said hello to dad and [they] didn't bother to see what he (Lewis) was doing. We've always done it. I don't know why. Mum (Lewis's mother) relied on us to clean the house through once a year. Pop still won't let others do things except me.'

The lack of automatic succession to the key person role by other siblings when a key sibling dies demonstrates the importance of the history and nature of the relationship in determining who fulfils the role of a key person. If a key sibling dies and a surviving sibling has a close relationship to the older person they succeed to the key person role. However, succession does not occur if surviving siblings do not have a close relationship to the older person. Two examples of continuing key person successions are Lloyd and Dot who are the subjects of vignettes in chapters 4 and 7. The importance of the relationship and not just the kin tie is also exemplified in the future plans made by key siblings, discussed in the previous chapter. Key people often plan for one of their children to replace them rather than one of their siblings.

Key people who are not siblings

The parents who, at first, only partially relinquish care and continue to oversee their adult child's wellbeing fulfil a key person role. There is a unique explanation for each relationship between an older person and other non-sibling key people. However, common threads are the existence of a close long-term relationship between key people and the older person and, if they are original rather than successor key people, the foreshadowing of their role in a parental key person succession plan.

Distant relatives who are key people all have atypical relationships with the older person. For example, the relationship between Beatrice and her niece Karen, a case study in chapter 4. Beatrice's sister, Karen's mother, died when Karen was a child and Karen grew up with her aunt Beatrice and her grandmother, Beatrice's mother. Another example is Ada's aunt.

> Ada and her parents had lived next door to her aunt since Ada was a child. Ada established a close relationship with her aunt who was single and had no children of her own.

As illustrated in chapter 5, Rod's mother nominated a minister who was a family friend in her key person succession plan. He has acted as Rod's key person and oversaw his welfare for 27 years. Another example is Jack, whose parents' plan was illustrated in chapter 5. Jack is 87 and his second cousin Maud, who spent much of her childhood with Jack's family was nominated in his father's plans. She has been Jack's key person and primary carer for 30 years since his father died.

Changes of key person

Key people are one of the most stable elements in the lives of older people with intellectual disability. Over three-quarters of the group have retained the same key person since their transition. The remaining quarter have lost their key person due to death or a deterioration of the relationship. In nine of these 13 cases their key person has been replaced by someone else. There is less chance, however, of gaining a second or third replacement key person. Five of those who gained a replacement subsequently lost them and only one person, Dot, found a second replacement. Consequently, as people age they are less likely to have a key person, leaving their support network with a major deficit and presenting a serious issue for service providers to grapple with.

There is no hierarchy of succession to the key person role based on family ties. Rather, succession to this role is associated with the existence of a relative or friend who has a close relationship with the older person and a strong commitment to them, which has often been negotiated beforehand. The proportion of key people who are siblings declined and the proportion of non-family members or distant family members increased as people have aged, following the transition from parental care.

Relationships with key informal network members

All key people have frequent contact with the older person. The nature of contact depends on people's circumstances and has often changed over the years. Contact generally provides opportunities for shared social activities rather than just passive visiting. An example is Hilda who lives in a nursing home and is the subject of a case study in chapter 7. Her brother Roderick visits at least once a fortnight. He said:

> 'I find it most inadequate visiting Hilda out at the nursing home. It's not much chop [very satisfactory] to go out there and sit in a chair and try and talk to her. Before, we (Roderick and his wife) would go over to the nursing home and would go for a good long walk. But of course she doesn't walk as well now. The routine we've got her down to now over the last year or so is that I ring up and pick her up and take her to (a neighbouring suburb). I buy a packet of nails and we walk up and down and look at the shops. She really enjoys it, having a good look at the shops and things. After a while she will say, 'Are you feeling thirsty?' and we look for one of the little places and we have a cup of coffee and biscuits. Then we drop her back, so we have about a two hour run.'

Madge lives in a nursing home and suffers from Alzheimer's disease. Her brother said:

> 'Now that Madge's not aware of what's happening, I call in two or three times a week and walk Madge around the place. Just to keep her mobility there.'

Most key people have a longstanding strong emotional bond with the older person and, for many, relationships appear unconditional and motivated by love and affection. For example, Michael had lived with his sister Mandy for many years, until just recently. Mandy said:

> 'Oh yes I love Michael dearly, that's why I feel a little bit guilty about it (putting him in a nursing home); you think could I do more? But when I saw him yesterday I knew it would be impossible, absolutely impossible.'

Lenny's sister talked about her relationship with him and said:

> 'He's a darling. I love him dearly. He is good company. You can sit and watch TV and have a cup of tea. He is a gentle person. His needs are very minute. He's no trouble. He just sort of sits. He used to do vegetables. You have got to program him—he's a lovely fellow.'

For others, the relationship is more ambivalent. George's brother described the relationship that he and his wife have with George.

> 'No, we are not close. There's very little we share. It's not like brothers. It's more like a carer and a client. George hangs everything on family names. We do tend to think that he is our responsibility. There isn't anyone else to do things. And, right or wrong I do feel that one of my duties, and I don't see it as a burden, is to take on each other's families. Each of us (brother and sister-in-law) will be there for each other's families.'

Feelings of attachment that the key person has for the older person usually appear to be reciprocated by them. However, two of the older people clearly do not reciprocate the feelings expressed by the key person or resent the involvement the key person has in their lives. For example, Gerry, who had lived with his sister after his parents' death, then moved to a hostel and later to a flat in the community, hated the protective, domineering attitude of his sister. His sister said:

> 'He's my brother and I feel sorry for him that things have happened to him'. Referring to his sister, Gerry said, 'She's all the time trying to run your life. I just couldn't cope with it there (at his sister's house). None of the family could cope with it the way she was trying to run everybody's' life. She's all right, but she still criticises everything that I do. She's still trying to run your life. She didn't like Donna (flatmate) at all. When I was living with her, she used to come over and pester us all the time.'

Ted's brother took on the role of a key person after his parents died, made major decisions for Ted and managed his affairs. His actions might not have been in Ted's best interest and Ted is now trying to exclude his brother from involvement in his life, an action that is respected by his case manager. Although Ted's brother is not now regarded as his key person, he had been previously and the way he had exercised this role illustrates some very important issues.

> Ted is 59. He lives in a special accommodation house that is remote from any amenities or public transport. His brother visits every three months or so but Ted says that he doesn't get on with him and he is always asking for money. They do not have a close relationship and his brother successfully disputed their parents' will that had left their entire estate to Ted. When Ted's parents died, Ted remained at home for a short period, after which his brother moved him to a special accommodation home in an outer suburb. For 10 years Ted lived in this home whose residents were mainly brain-damaged alcoholics and where conditions of food, hygiene and personal care were appalling. The home was investigated and subsequently closed by the Health Department. Just before its closure Ted's brother arranged for him to move. During the investigation, Ted was referred to a regional disability services team and, with the assistance of a case manager, Ted hopes to move to an independent living situation. He does not want to tell his brother about these plans.

Ted's case not only illustrates the power key people exercise over the lives of older adults with intellectual disability but also raises questions about the legitimacy of the key person role, its recognition and acknowledgment by others. Both Ted and Gerry's cases demonstrate that a key person may not be accepted by the older person or act in their best interests. These exceptional cases raise the broader question of who has the right to make decisions on behalf of a person with intellectual disability and who has the responsibility to question and challenge informal arrangements such as these. These issues are discussed in chapters 9 and 10.

Networks with no informal key network member

At the time of transition, three people did not have a key informal network member. At that time, formal services adopted major elements of the key person role for them on a short-term basis. In the years following transition, formal services also stepped in and fulfilled tasks associated with a key informal network member for several other people. However, the commitment and involvement of formal services to such tasks, unlike that of key informal network members, did not extend over a long period of time (the role of formal services is discussed in the following chapter). The exception is a church organisation which, through a parental plan, was requested to take responsibility for Jim's wellbeing. In this case, although the key person role is technically fulfilled by the organisation, for many years this role has been delegated to a member of the congregation who has established a close relationship with Jim and acts in an advisory capacity to organisational staff.

At the time of the study, a quarter of the group does not have a key informal network member. All except one of these older people has family members or friends but relationships with them are weaker and these network members are not heavily involved in people's lives. Although informal network members and staff of formal services fulfil some tasks of a key informal network member for these older people, no one takes responsibility for overseeing and ensuring their wellbeing across the entirety of their lives. They lack someone who can monitor service quality, advocate for them and look towards their future. They are reliant on the formal service system to fulfil many of the tasks normally undertaken by a key informal network member. Alex, whose case is considered at the end of this chapter, and Lloyd, one of the case studies in chapter 4, are both illustrative of people without a key informal network member. The theoretical and practical reasons why the formal system cannot fulfil these functions are discussed in chapter 10.

Informal primary carers

As considered in the previous chapter, the number of people with informal primary carers diminished significantly, from 53% to 20%, since the initial transition from parental care. In later life, only 20% of the group have a person in their informal network who provides regular direct assistance with activities of daily living or supervises and monitors these. These informal primary carers are predominantly family members and mainly siblings. They are all from the same or an older generation as the older adult with intellectual disability. Most informal primary carers combine their role with that of a key person. However, several, who are friends or church members and not family, do not do so. Non-family informal primary carers all have a longstanding relationship with the older person or their parents. Where a church member is the informal primary carer, this person coordinates the provision of primary care by several members of the community and liaises with the person's key network member. Common characteristics of both current and previous informal primary carers are: having lived with or close to the parent and the person with intellectual disability prior to transition, having cared for the parent of the adult with intellectual disability, having a close long-term relationship with the parents and the person with intellectual disability, being single, widowed or divorced, being female and being a sibling.

FAMILY NETWORK MEMBERS

Parents and spouses

A third of the group have one parent alive and one person has both parents alive. The majority of parents, although most have poor health and live in supported accommodation, are still members of the older person's informal network. They maintain regular contact and, in the main, provide affective support. Several of the more active parents still act as their adult child's key person.

Three of the study population married after the death of their parents. One man is now separated from his wife, who lives interstate; and although they correspond he has not seen her for over a year. The other two, Rod and Isobel, are married to each other. After living in the community for many years, they were forced to move to an aged persons' hostel because of Isobel's poor health and frailty. They share a double room and gain enormous emotional support and companionship from each other.

Siblings

Over 90% of the group had siblings but only 79% still have one or more siblings alive. The vast majority (96%) of older people with siblings see at least one of them at least twice a year. When all the siblings of the group are included, 82% have contact with their brother or sister with

TABLE 8.2 **Type of relationship between older people and all their siblings**

Type of relationship	Sibling characteristic						
	Sole or closest	2nd	3rd	4th	5th	All	
Key person	36	—	—	—	—	36	34%
Instrumental	2	5	2	1	—	10	9%
Friendly	8	19	10	3	1	41	38%
Indifferent	1	—	—	—	—	1	1%
Not in network	2	4	7	5	1	19	18%
Total	49	28	19	9	2	107	100%

intellectual disability at least twice a year. Table 8.2 summaries the nature of relationships between older people with intellectual disability and their siblings.

The dominant relationship with sole, or closest, siblings is that of a key person. Several sole or closest siblings, while they do not fulfil the role of a key person, do perform some instrumental tasks. These tasks are formal, such as acting as next of kin or holding power of attorney, and do not extend to regular involvement in the affairs of the older person. An example of this type of relationship between an older person and their sole or closest sibling is given in the case study of Lloyd in chapter 4. Lloyd's eldest brother, George, holds a power of attorney for Lloyd, and hostel staff refer to him regarding major decisions about Lloyd but he does not take a proactive interest in overseeing Lloyd's wellbeing or affairs.

At least monthly social visits or contact at family functions typifies friendly sibling relationships. This type of contact is not always initiated by a sibling and is often incidental and occurs at the same time as contact with other family members. An example is the relationship between Lucas and his brother. Lucas's mother lives in a unit adjacent to her other son's house. She said, 'Lucas is coming here for lunch next Saturday and he sees them (his brother and sister-in-law) then of course'.

Siblings with friendly relationships are important members of the older person's social network and provide companionship, a sense of family belonging and sometimes act as confidantes. An example is the relationship between Bertha and her brother Jake, who lives in Queensland. The supervisor of the supported accommodation where Bertha lives said:

> 'Jake writes to her twice or three times a month. Bertha writes to him once a week. If Bertha's got a gripe or a problem, that's it: she'll put it on paper and send it off. And also Jake comes down at Christmas time for quite a lengthy time and takes Bertha out. He sends gifts down for birthday, Christmas and Easter.'

Friendly relationships are warm without having a strong sense of duty or obligation. The social limitation of the older person and the unbalanced nature of relationships are often referred to by informants as restrictive factors. Some of these relationships have an element of constructed distance or controlled involvement established in the past by parents. For example, the supervisor of the community residential unit where Jenny lives talked about the relationship between Jenny and her brother, Tony. She said:

> 'They (brother and sister-in-law) come and take her out or to their place and she gets very animated about seeing the nephews. Belinda (Jenny's mother) is of the belief that she didn't think that Tony's life should be hampered in any way by his sister. He has his own life and own family. She doesn't doubt that Tony loves Jenny but he needs time with his family and kids as well.'

Seventeen per cent of the group has one or more siblings who are not included in their informal support network as they have contact less than twice a year. Siblings who have such infrequent contact have also, in their adult life, not maintained a close relationship with their other siblings or their parents. An example of this type of relationship is described by Jim's friend, Nettie, who lives in the same retirement complex as Jim and his mother. Jim had only seen his sister several times in the last 12 years and those visits had been encouraged by Nettie, who said:

> 'I can't remember the daughter (Jim's sister) visiting (when his mother was alive). When his mother died, she (sister) came to clean out the house. I didn't know she had a daughter. She cleaned out the house and took all the beautiful crystal, everything.'

An exceptional sibling relationship is that between Ted and his brother, which was described earlier in this chapter. This relationship is indifferent; although Ted sees his sibling fairly frequently, they have a poor relationship and Ted does not like his brother.

Siblings-in-law

Older people see their siblings-in-law less frequently than siblings. Relationships with brothers-in-law are usually friendly but only occur incidentally in the context of visits by siblings or at family functions. In contrast, older people have closer relationships with sisters-in-law, particularly the wives of key brothers, who often share instrumental tasks with their husbands. Clothes shopping and unravelling bureaucratic red tape are often seen as the province of these women. The relationship with sisters-in-law is illustrated by Hilda's brother who said:

'Hilda is terribly fond of Monica (sister-in-law) too and of course Monica is the one that fills in with things that I cannot do. [She] buys her clothes; Monica knows whether she needs that jumper or that extra nightie. Monica fills in there. Monica is a tremendous sister to Hilda.'

The attitude of the sibling-in-law towards the older person with intellectual disability is important in determining the sibling's relationship. For example, Norman's sister talked about how the attitude of her brothers' wives affected the relationship between Norman and his brothers. She said:

'A lot depends on the wives you know. They've loved Norman and they've been very good up to a point. But Linda, Chris's wife, more so than Anne (other brother's wife). Anne is a very self-centred lady, as long as it (being involved with Norman) fitted into her plans.'

Some in-law relationships have withstood the death of a sibling and several widowed sisters-in-law maintain social contact. However, no examples are found where a spouse has succeeded a key sibling. When key people talk about their replacements, they usually nominate their children rather than spouses.

Distant relatives

Several older people have an unusually close relationship with a more distant relative who acts as their key person. These relatives are aunts, cousins and nieces and are discussed in the section on non-sibling key people, above.

Although most of the older people have distant relatives, only half saw an aunt, uncle, cousin, niece or nephew on a regular or frequent enough basis for them to be included in their support network. Nieces and nephews are more likely to be seen regularly than other distant relatives. Relationships with more distant relatives are generally affective and contact is often incidental or mediated by other relatives, occurring at family functions, or key times, such as birthdays and Christmas. An example is Jack, who lives with his cousin. She sums up the incidental contact with relatives when she says, 'They (distant relatives) don't really come to visit him (Jack) but he sees them each week [when they come to see me]'. Amy's niece talked about the contact her brother had with Amy, and said, 'He wouldn't make a special trip but he would see Amy if she was home'.

The social worker who had overseen Beth's transition from parental care when her mother's health deteriorated, commented on the role of her only relative, a cousin:

'I got the impression they (cousin and husband) didn't want to be too involved. I think they will call on Beth's birthday or very occasionally they will call and take her out to tea. I think Jean (cousin) was very fond of her aunt but that was as far as it went.' Beth said that her cousin took her out now and again but that she was not close to her.

The regular contact that older people with intellectual disability have with distant relatives reflects their family's traditions. It had not been initiated after parental death or in later life. Vera is a good example.

Vera is part of a large, extended family that has always maintained contact by sharing Christmas together and having regular family gatherings. Her aunt is now too frail to visit her but two of her cousins visit her every three months.

Children of key siblings usually have more frequent, closer and more independent relationships with their aunt or uncle with intellectual disability than children of other siblings. Because of the high level of their parent's involvement, these children have often had a great deal of contact with the adult with intellectual disability. A common role for these nieces and nephews is to provide support to their parents and act as back-up visitors and managers when they are on holiday or unwell. As suggested previously, key siblings often nominate their children to succeed them. For several older people, a niece or nephew is slowly stepping into this role in place of their parents. For example, Amy's sister was sick at the time of the study. Her daughter, Amy's niece, agreed to be an informant and said:

'When mother (Amy's sister) dies, I will continue to have her (Amy) for family occasions. I probably left the telephoning to mum (Amy's sister) because mum's been there. I would assume telephone contact on a more regular basis than I do. I probably only ring now because mum's out of action. I like Amy but I suppose it is more of an obligation to make sure that somebody's looking after Amy. I couldn't think of a special day that didn't include Amy. If it was someone's birthday, Christmas or anything like that, if it was my birthday, of course I would include Amy.'

Unless they are nominated in key person succession plans, or there is a history of an unusually close relationship, distant relatives, such as Beth's cousin, do not step in as a key person in the informal support network when they are the only remaining family members. Several distant relatives had stepped in and managed the transition from parental care but their assumption of a key role was time limited and did not extend to ongoing involvement in the management of the person's affairs. In subsequent years the relationship reverted to a social one, ensuring that the person receives visits on important occasions. The role of Marie's cousin in managing her transition was considered in chapter 6 and illustrates this short-term key role. Commenting on her present relationship with Marie, she said:

> 'She's flesh and blood and I really feel that there is nobody else to go and see her. I go on all the occasions, Christmases and Easters, anything of that sort. In between, time seems to get away a bit. She (Marie) gets very excited when we go over. If I haven't been able to go I've got my daughter to go so we always cover the situation, so that we are always there because I don't want her to feel that she's you know . . . [neglected?].'

Relatives not in the support network

Relationships with distant relatives are highly valued by the older people with intellectual disability even though they may not have regular contact with them. This is particularly so for nieces and nephews and their children. Many older people have photos of all these relatives, know all their names and talk about them with great warmth. Such feelings do not appear one-sided either; family informants often say that they keep other relatives who are not in direct contact with the older person up-to-date with what is happening to them and that they always ask after the older person. A typical comment was that of Morris's sister-in-law. When she was asked about his contact with more distant relatives, she said, 'No [he doesn't see them] but, when we talk to them they always ask after Morris'.

FRIENDS AND ACQUAINTANCES

Quantifying the friendships of older people with intellectual disability is more difficult than for relatives. Friendship is not an easily specified concept and what constitutes a friend is subject to different interpretations and perceptions. In this study, a friend is taken to be any person who is perceived as such by an informant. However, instead of naming friends, reference is often made to a group of people from a particular social group, club or location that the older person knows. For example, Roger goes into the city most days to have lunch at the canteen of a large retail store. When he was asked about his friends, he said that he knew lots of people there and that they all knew him.

Unnamed groups of friends are termed acquaintances and, though they cannot be quantified, are important components of some people's networks. A third of the group have no named friends but fewer have neither friends nor acquaintances. These people are in poor health and have previously had friends. On average, older people have two friends and, as shown in table A.9, those living in nursing homes average the least number of friends (none) while those living at home alone, or with a friend, have the most (four).

Informants often consider that the older people do not have any friends of their own because of their lack of social skills or that they had always shared their parents' friends. For example, Gina's church elder said:

> 'All her (Gina's) friends were friends of her mother. She generally went everywhere with her and participated in her mother's activities.'

Doreen's sister, Hilary, illustrated in one of the vignettes at the end of this chapter, also held this view. Informants underestimate the older person's friendship network because they are unaware of people's friendships at day centres or discount peer friendships. For example, Lucas's mother said:

> 'He's never had a friend, no. He is friendly with all his pals that he sees at [the centre].'

When friendships are discussed directly with the older person, however, friends are often named whom other informants are unaware of or have discounted, as illustrated in Doreen's case (one of the case studies at the end of this chapter). Significantly, some people who have shared friends with their parents maintain a relationship with those friends after their parents' death. Gina's friendships illustrated this.

> When Gina's mother died, she continued to attend many social groups they had attended together, particularly those around the church. She regularly rang a number of her mother's old friends, whom she addressed as auntie, and sought their advice.

Relationships with friends and acquaintances are more often affective than instrumental, providing companionship and opportunities for social interaction. Several friends fulfil key person roles and several more provide primary care for the older person. These relationships are discussed in the sections on non-key siblings and informal primary carers above. Friends are evenly divided between those who are longstanding and those made in recent years. Recent friendships are those made with other day activity participants or supported accommodation residents.

Two main characteristics of friendships are that they had in the past been, or are currently, shared with other network members and are highly situation specific. Contact with friends from day or residential services is often confined to that context and does not occur outside it. Very few people whose friends are co-participants see their friends out of hours. Older people who cease attending a day program or leave a residential service rarely continue to see friends, some of whom they may have known for more than 20 years. The case study of Norman, at the end of this chapter, illustrates this type of situation specific friendship.

Older people who attend aged care day centres, such as elderly citizens' clubs, refer to other participants as their friends but cannot name individual people and do not see them out of context of the club or centre. For example, Bronwyn said:

> 'I see a lot of nice women down at the senior citizens' centre. I go down there Tuesday and Friday and go for a drive with Miriam (organiser) on a Friday morning. It's been real good. I've met nice people, nice women. I've met a couple of chaps that come with us. I do mix with men. You can't help mixing with men.'

Older people who live in supported accommodation often have a friend in the room next door or with whom they share a dining table. Such friendships never extend to shared activities outside their place of residence. Ted, who lives in a special accommodation house, talked about his friends and said:

> 'I have the cook and a couple of other people, a chappie at my dinner table and a couple of lady friends that I get the papers for. They are all too old here, I think, for me. I'd like to be somewhere they are my own age.'

Several people are exceptional and go out with friends from their disability day centre after hours. However, these activities are supported and encouraged by either staff or a key person.

Neighbours

As suggested in chapter 6, neighbours and people living in the local area are very important members of people's social networks when they are living at home with their parents. When people move out of their parental home, social contact with neighbours is usually lost. However, two people retain contact with past neighbours. Godfrey still calls in to see an old neighbour when he visits his brother who lives nearby, and an elderly neighbour sends Vera a card every Christmas.

The people who stay on in their family home or move within the local area retain local friendships and acquaintances after the death of their parents. For them, one or more neighbours are an important source of support and are regarded as friends. Support from neighbours varies from purely social to instrumental. An example is Harry who lives in the family home on his own. His sister said:

'He used to know a lot of neighbours but there has been a great change over the years. The lady down the road was a good friend of mum. She is good to him and brings his meals on wheels in every day.'

Bronwyn, who also remains in the family home alone, said:

'I've got a lot of friends, the next-door neighbours, the one over the road, Jill. She's a good friend. The people next door. It's a husband and wife. Jody down the street [I see her but] not very often, and Mrs Mulldoon, she's down the street. I'm lucky I've got such good neighbours.'

Two people who share a flat have a different local network from older people who still live in their family home. They have a local friendship network of other people with intellectual disability, who have used the same disability outreach support service, rather than contact with neighbours. These friendships with neighbours, or people in the local area, explain why people in private homes generally have larger networks than those in congregate care. Older people who live in congregate care have contact with co-residents but are no longer part of the neighbourhood.

Church connections

Church acquaintances and friends form a significant part of the support network of 20% of the group. Support from the church community has been sufficiently reliable, flexible, consistent and strong that it has enabled several older adults with intellectual disability to remain in their own homes for a number of years. More usually, however, the support from a church community is less instrumental. It provides older people with an accepting community of acquaintances and the opportunity to play valued social roles such as managing the church car parking, putting up hymn numbers and sending cards on occasions like births and birthdays to members of the congregation. Roger's life provides a good illustration of the role played by the church community.

Roger lives on his own. He gets picked up and taken to church every Sunday and joins in a range of church social events. He often drops in on various church members or telephones them for advice. The minister said that no one in particular was friends with him or kept an eye on him. Nevertheless, many members of the congregation knew him and if he wasn't around it would be noticed. She commented, 'He is part of the church furniture and his company is tolerated out of Christian duty'.

VIGNETTES

These four vignettes are broadly illustrative of different network types and their component features. The proportion of family in a support network varied from 100% to 0%; a vignette is drawn from each of the four quartiles into which the proportion of family members in support networks could be divided.

Norman Richards

Norman's informal support network comprises all family members. In total, his network has seven people, of whom he sees three at least monthly. He has another nine family members, not in his network, whom he sees less than twice a year. His sister Wendy is his key person, providing various types of instrumental support, and everyone else provides affective support. Norman's parents had planned for him to live in the hostel attached to the day centre he attended. In addition, Wendy described a strong implicit understanding that she would take responsibility for overseeing Norman's wellbeing. Although Norman is known to disability services, since he left the hostel he does not have any contact with disability services.

> Norman lives in a nursing home. He is 55 years old. He has Down syndrome and developed the first symptoms of Alzheimer's disease several years ago. He has an elder sister and two younger brothers who, between them, have nine children. His father is very frail and lives in another nursing home.
>
> Norman has a very close relationship with Wendy, who manages all his affairs and is regarded as next of kin by staff at the nursing home. Wendy visits Norman at least once a week. She brings him prune juice, takes him to visit his father and sometimes takes him home for tea. Wendy said, 'I do the banking. I buy the clothes and buy the little extras he needs. I tidy his wardrobe, clean his shaver, take him for a walk.' Wendy closely monitors the care Norman receives and has had several disputes with the nursing home about the quality of care. She said, 'I will complain again: I'm his advocate. He's got nobody else to speak for him. It's because I love him I care about him and because I've had the virtual looking after bit of him since my mother died. I care about him terribly. I have to speak up for him.'
>
> Wendy's husband works full-time but sees Norman regularly. Norman's brother Paul lives in the country and he and his wife see Norman about twice a year. His brother Chris lives in France and hasn't seen or contacted him for two years. Wendy said of her brothers, 'Even now they don't even ring me up to ask me how he is. The burden is just taken on my shoulders. When they are here, they

go and see him. They are very fond of him. It's not a lack of affection. It is just a lack of thought.'

All Norman's nephews and nieces are young adults and, although they have known him all their lives, only two of them, Wendy's children, visit him regularly.

Norman attended a day centre for adults with intellectual disability for many years where he had a number of friends. Talking about his life when he lived at home Wendy said, 'He was so much a "home body". He was just at home. Mother was very caring. There was the circle at the centre. He didn't need anyone else.' Norman moved to the hostel attached to the day centre after his mother died, thus retaining the same circle of friends.

He moved to a nursing home when he was 54 and has not seen any of his old friends since. Wendy said, 'I think it was a real shock going from the hostel to the nursing home. All his friends were in the hostel. I thought that they (staff from the hostel) would have gone to see him and take his friends. Perhaps that was my fault.'

Doreen Croxley

Doreen's network comprises two-thirds family members. Her network has 15 members, comprising ten family, four friends and a church minister. She sees 12 of these people at least monthly. Her sister Hilary is her key person and the only network member who provides instrumental as well as affective support. Her father had planned comprehensively for her future. He expected her to live in a hostel attached to the day centre she attended and her sisters to stay in contact with her. He had left money in trust for her.

> Doreen is 59. She lives in a hostel attached to the day centre that she has attended for 43 years. She has two older sisters, Hilary and Cath, six nieces and nephews, and nine grand nieces and nephews. Doreen's stepmother is in her 80s and, though she lives at home, is very frail.
>
> Doreen has always had a very close relationship with her sister, Hilary. She lived opposite Hilary for many years and then, after her father died, she lived with her for six years before moving to the hostel. Hilary described feeling sad rather than guilty when, because of her husband's illness, she was no longer able to care for Doreen at home.
>
> Hilary visits Doreen at the hostel at least once a week and has her home for the weekend monthly. She manages her affairs, takes her to church, to visit her stepmother, to the naturopath, and arranges for her children, Doreen's nieces, to visit Doreen when she is away on holiday. Hilary has been involved with the committee of the day centre and does some volunteer work in the hostel. She said, 'I have been and still am very close to her (Doreen). I have a commitment and it's not forced on me by anyone.'

Cath, her other sister, has never been as involved with Doreen but used to have her at weekends when she was living with Hilary. Cath visits Doreen at least once a month and sees her when she does voluntary work at the hostel. Doreen only sees her brothers-in-law and nephews and nieces incidentally, at family occasions and when she visits her sisters' homes.

Hilary considers that Doreen did not have the skills to make real friends but liked being around people. Doreen, with no hesitation, said that she had four friends who worked in the packaging department of the centre with her. She goes on outings from the hostel with other residents and, on occasions, has invited some of her friends from the centre to her sister's home for parties. The minister from the church visits Doreen irregularly but always does so when Hilary is away on holiday.

Nadia White

Family comprise half of Nadia's network of eight people. She has four siblings with whom she has contact at least monthly, and four friends who, with the exclusion of the church minister, she sees frequently. One sister is a key person, providing instrumental support, including primary care, and her other siblings provide affective support. She has four siblings-in-law and 13 nephews and nieces whom she rarely sees and who do not form part of her support network. As described in chapter 5, Nadia's sister had an implicit understanding with her mother that she would care for Nadia. She does not use any disability services and is not known to the disability service system.

> Since her mother died two years ago, Nadia has lived on her own. She is 56 and has lived in the same small block of walk-up flats for 32 years. She has two sisters, two brothers, 13 nieces and nephews, and 17 great nieces and nephews.
>
> Her sister Julie rings Nadia every morning to make sure she is all right. Julie helps her to budget, buy clothes and do the shopping. She comes over every Friday and they go out for lunch. Nadia said, 'Julie looks after me'. Julie commented that she acted as Nadia's 'rudder'.
>
> Nadia used to see more of the rest of her family when her mother was ill. Now she rarely sees her brothers or her other sister but she rings them regularly. She has photos of all her nieces and nephews but seldom sees them.
>
> Nadia knows most of the people in the block of flats and referred to two neighbours by name. She said, 'I know them all just about. I've got very good neighbours, Pam and Jude. If I want anything, they will do it.' One neighbour helps Nadia put tassels on the ends of the

scarfs that she knits. Since her mother's death, Nadia has developed a friendship with Stephen, a widower, who lives in the same block. She sees him most days. They go shopping and often have a meal together.

A community room is attached to the block of flats and Nadia participates in outings and activities arranged by the tenants' group. She has a good relationship with the tenant worker, whom she called her social worker. The minister, from the church she attended with her mother, visits now and again.

Alex Malin

Alex has no family, nor a key person who informally oversees his well-being. His network comprises one friend who lives in the room next door to him. No information is available about the plans his parents made for his future. Alex has never used disability services and is not known to this service system.

Alex is 75 years old and lives in an aged persons' hostel. After his parents' death, he continued to live at home with his sister. When his sister died he was left with no family. Alex showed me a picture of Mrs Stafford who had lived over the road from his house. He said that she and her husband looked after him when his sister died and eventually helped him sell the house and move to the hostel. Alex used to attend his local senior citizens club where he had lunch and played billiards. The secretary remembered him, but no one from the club has maintained contact with Alex.

Alex has been living at the hostel for ten years. The supervisor said that occasionally he used to be visited by some friends. According to the records, his closest friend or relative is Mr Stafford. However Mr Stafford had long since moved from the phone number that is in the hostel records, and could not be traced. The secretary at the senior citizens' club thought both Mr Stafford and his wife had died.

Alex said that he had a friend who lived in the room next door to him but was sad that nobody visited him any more. He said, 'I'm left on my own. Nobody comes to see me and no one rings.'

CONCLUSIONS AND SUMMARY

The structure and components of the informal support networks of older adults with intellectual disability have been described in this chapter. In the post-parental phase of their lives, older people with intellectual disability have significant others who primarily care about them rather than directly for them. Informal support is more significant in their lives than has previously been reported. Networks are larger and more robust than the existing literature in this area has indicated. For example, Ashman and his colleagues (1993) reported that only 47% of older people with intellectual disability had at least yearly contact with relatives, whereas this study found that 92% of older people had at least six-monthly contact with relatives, and most had much more. Both studies used similar definitions of intellectual disability and 'older', but Ashman's study included people from a variety of care backgrounds including those who had been institutionalised for many years. An explanation for the difference may be that this study focuses solely on older people who have remained at home with their parents until mid-life, suggesting that care background is a significant factor in later life informal support.

Parental expectations may also be associated with informal support in later life. The role of key person is usually negotiated and foreseen by parents, which suggests the efficacy of informally based parental plans and expectations. The presence of a proactive key person, in over three-quarters of their networks, suggests that key person succession plans are a useful mechanism for ensuring the ongoing involvement of a family member or friends in the life of an older person with intellectual disability.

The average network size of this group of older people with intellectual disability was six with a range of 0–20. This is smaller than the average size of seven and range of 3–21 reported in a study of people without intellectual disability, aged 60, living in Sydney, Australia (Mugford & Kendig, 1986). Networks are also smaller than the average of 7.5 among younger people with intellectual disability living at home with parents (Grant & Wenger, 1993). The family domination of networks is a particular characteristic of networks of older people with intellectual disability. For example, for three-quarters of the group, family comprised over half their network, compared to Mugford and Kendig's study where for only a third of the sample family comprised over half the network.

The network characteristics of older people with intellectual disability —density, lack of intergenerational members, the situation specificity of friendships, dominance of family members and the significance of key people and their importance in decision making for the older person— raise issues that require further discussion. These issues are taken up in chapter 10. However, first it is important to consider the nature of formal support in the lives of the study population, which is the subject of the next chapter.

CHAPTER 9

Formal support networks of older adults with intellectual disability

An overwhelming majority of the study population uses formal services, although the significance and degree of support they receive varies enormously. This chapter describes the role of formal services in the support networks of older adults with intellectual disability. A description of the types of services they use and their experience of service use is followed by four vignettes that illustrate the role of formal services in people's lives. The relationships and collaboration between disability and aged care services and between formal and informal sources of support are then considered. These various partnerships are examined from the perspective of informal network members and the older people themselves.

Formal service involvement in the processes of planning and transition from parental care and the provision of primary care are considered in previous chapters. In summary, attendance at disability day services is associated with a high level of parental planning and formal support during transition. Formal services do not play a major role in managing the transition from parental care but are more involved in subsequent residential moves. Provision by formal services of primary care increases steadily in the years following transition.

As they age, very few people use disability services for the first time, although several in this group had tried unsuccessfully to do so. In the years following transition, use of aged services steadily increases while contact with disability services diminishes, so that older people with intellectual disability are much more likely to use aged care services than disability services and few access both service systems. In later life, a third of the group use disability services compared to just over half at the time of transition from parental care. Older people no longer attend special schools or work-preparation centres, fewer attend disability day centres, and although quite a number of people had moved to a disability accommodation service after they left parental care, in the years that followed many had moved out again.

The most common types of service are residential and day activity services. Table 9.1 illustrates broad service types used from each system.

TABLE 9.1 **Broad types of generic aged and specialist disability services used**

Service type	Service system			
	Aged care	Disability	Total	
Residential primary care	40	6	46	74%
Respite care	1	2	3	5%
Domiciliary primary care	1	3	4	7%
Domiciliary support	7	0	7	11%
Supported employment, day or leisure activity	21	13	34	55%
Case management and caseworker	1	4	5	8%
Citizen advocacy	—	3	3	5%
Guardianship	13	N/A	13	21%

Note: Some people used several types of service.

TYPES OF FORMAL SERVICES USED

Supported employment, day activity and leisure services

Although ten people had left disability day centres (adult training and support services or ATSSs), either at the time of transition from parental care or since, they are still the most common disability day activity service used by older people. For the nine people who attend these services, they are more than just a 'day placement'. They are an integral part of people's lives. Most people have attended for many years, their friends are at the centre and their parents had worked with the voluntary associations that established and maintained these services.

ATSSs provide a range of age integrated and age specific programs and activities. They also provide a supportive base from which people can access aged care services such as senior citizens clubs. Staff at these centres often have a strong relationship with older people and their families and provide advice, support and encouragement for transition decisions. ATSSs, and the residential hostels attached to them, provide a comprehensive service that, in effect, forms a disability service subsystem. ATSS staff act as de facto case managers, and seldom refer families to regional disability services teams where such responsibility rests. Families who use these services often have very little knowledge of the wider disability service system and some are not aware of the role of disability service teams.

The retirement of older people from ATSSs is an unresolved issue for both voluntary associations and state governments in Australia. Older people themselves have not contemplated retirement and family members are generally opposed to it. Attitudes towards ATSSs by current users and their families are overwhelmingly positive. This, however, is not the case for former users, such as Morris (the subject of a vignette later in this chapter) who have unwillingly had to leave a day centre.

Three people attend social groups for people with intellectual disability, which are based in various community organisations such as neighbourhood houses. These groups occupy much shorter periods than ATSSs, only several hours once a week rather than five hours a day five days a week. They are less central to the lives of older people with intellectual disability and attendance is not usually on a long-term basis. Nevertheless, such groups provide valued opportunities for social interaction and participation in various recreational and educational activities. The element common to all the disability day and leisure activities is that programs are tailored to people with intellectual disability and aim to develop or maintain skills.

Just over a third of the group attend at least one aged care service that provides opportunities for leisure activities and social interaction external to their place of residence. These programs are usually organised by voluntary organisations such as churches, or local government aged services departments. Members of the study population resident in aged care facilities other than nursing homes often attend services in the local community en mass with other residents.

The older people interviewed spoke enthusiastically about the day programs they attend and comments about relationships with other participants were always positive. Daily attendance for lunch at a senior citizens' centre provides a vital central focus to the lives of people, such as Dot (the subject of a vignette in chapter 7) and Gina (whose case is vignetted later in this chapter), both of whom live at home alone.

Unlike disability services, the primary function of aged care day services is social and nutritional. Older people with intellectual disability do not participate in structured programs at these services, although no one criticised any aspects of people's attendance at these services.

Respite care

Two people living at home with relatives use a disability respite care service offered at a group home. Carers are satisfied with this service, which provides experience of being away from home for the person with intellectual disability and a break for carers. One person uses respite care offered by a nursing home and several more have used this type of care previously.

Domiciliary or outreach services

The primary care for three people is provided by a disability outreach service. Two of them, Godfrey and Gerry, share a flat, and the third, Bronwyn, lives alone in the family home. A support worker regularly supervises budgeting, meal planning, shopping, cooking and other domestic arrangements. A worker is on call to provide additional support if necessary. The services are managed by non-government organisations and funded by the Disability Services program of the Victorian state government.

These services are provided on an ongoing basis and are central to enabling Godfrey, Gerry and Bronwyn to live in the community. They provide regular reliable assistance, oversee household management and provide a valued safety net for the plethora of non-routine tasks that community living involves. The services have an important developmental aspect, aiming to develop skills as well as to provide support for the activities of daily living. Gerry, speaking of the service, said:

> 'Sometimes they come on Monday and sometimes they come on Thursday to do the budgeting. I can ring them. I've got a phone number. I can ring them any time I need them.'

The service these three older adults receive is similar to that Beatrice had received (which is described in chapter 4), although current service users had not experienced the problems of staff turnover and inadequate supervision that Beatrice experienced.

Primary care for one person, Dot, the subject of a vignette in chapter 7, is provided through a generic domiciliary service delivered by local government and funded through the Victorian state government HACC program. Dot lives alone in a block of older persons' flats and receives regular assistance with household management, shopping and cleaning. She received a similar service when she lived in her sister's flat in a different municipality. There is very little difference between the service Dot receives and that provided by disability outreach services described above.

The disability outreach service three people receive is supplemented by a weekly home help or domestic cleaning service provided by local government and funded under the HACC program. Four other people with informal primary carers, who live either at home alone or with relatives, receive similar domiciliary services, which include home help, meals on wheels and personal care.

Residential primary care

Six people live in disability accommodation, two of whom are still awaiting a permanent place. All six have a long history of contact with disability services and continue to attend the disability day centre they have attended for many years. These services are age integrated; either group homes with three or four other residents or larger hostels with at least 20 other residents. All residents have their own room.

As considered in chapter 7, 22 people have moved to disability accommodation and 16 have moved out in the period since transition from parental care. The chief reasons were pressure from the service and increased support needs.

Almost two-thirds of this group of older people, whose average age is 65, live in an aged care facility; 21 in aged persons' hostels, 11 in nursing homes and eight in special accommodation houses. The 40 members of the study population who live in this type of accommodation are clustered together in 23 of the 174 aged care facilities in the two regions in which the study was conducted. For example, eight people live in one aged persons' hostel, four in another and several clusters of two people exist. Most of these facilities also have other residents with intellectual disability who are younger or do not meet the criteria for inclusion in the study. Despite this concentration, older people with intellectual disability form a small proportion of the total residents. Most are large facilities with more than 50 residents and some are part of larger retirement complexes. Those who live in hostels (except the married couple who share a room) have their own room, while the majority in nursing homes or special accommodation houses do not.

Case management services and other services

Very few people have ongoing contact with a case manager or other type of worker from a regional disability services team. The case managers perform varied functions. For example, Ted's worker is helping him to consider alternative accommodation and has referred him to a citizen advocacy program, whereas Morris's worker rings the nursing home where he lives at irregular intervals. None of the workers have a long-term relationship with the older people or appear to play a central role in their lives.

Over three-quarters of older people who are known to regional disability services teams have not seen a worker from the team for more than 12 months. Vagueness surrounds the services available from disability service teams and informants, both family members and service providers, do not generally have a clear understanding of their mandate or the extent and duration to which these services can become involved in peoples lives.

Three people are matched with a community volunteer through a citizen advocacy program. The volunteers mainly provide opportunities for social interaction by taking people on outings or arranging for them to attend community-based social groups. For example, Frank's advocate has arranged for him to attend a senior citizens' club and Gerry attends an over-50s group at a leisure centre with his advocate.

In contrast to relationships with disability case managers, two older people have a very warm, long-term relationship with a social worker from an aged care service who provides a case management service for them. One of these is Nadia, described in chapter 8, and the other is Beth, who does not have an informal key person to oversee her wellbeing. Her social worker undertakes some roles fulfilled for other people by an informal key person. For example, she negotiated Beth's access to an aged persons' hostel, monitored the services she received previously from a regional disability service team and the State Trustee, advocates with service providers and liaises with other informal members of her network such as her cousin and the church community.

Most of the older people who live in supported accommodation have had short-term contact with aged care assessment services or hospital social workers. Informants frequently remarked upon the value of these services in helping informal key network members to find accommodation. Only one adverse experience was reported with an aged care assessment team and that was by Morris's family who were not involved in the assessment or allowed to see the report.

Guardianship

In Victoria, Australia, the Guardianship and Administration Board (GAB) has power to appoint either a guardian or an administrator for people with a disability who cannot make decisions for themselves and, at the time, requires a formally appointed person to make decisions in an area of their life or manage their financial affairs (Carney & Tait, 1997; Victorian Government, 1986b). The Board operates on the principle of the least restrictive alternative and will not appoint a guardian unless it is necessary and informal arrangements are not working satisfactorily.

Twenty per cent of the older people had been in touch with the GAB, several a few times. No one has a legal guardian but since the transition from parental care, time-limited guardians have been appointed for several people to make accommodation or medical decisions. It was predominantly formal services which initiated guardianship proceeding, when a major care or accommodation issue arose and the older person had no informal key person to whom they could refer or who was willing to make a decision. The application to the GAB by a regional disability service team, in respect of Frank and Bert (see the vignette later in this chapter), whose sister was unwilling to make decisions for them, is one illustration of such an application.

Officers with the Office of the Public Advocate acted as guardian when time-limited guardianship orders were made in respect of decisions about accommodation. The guardians, working with workers from regional disability teams, made the decision about accommodation and then withdrew from the person's life. An example of the poor quality of accommodation a guardian was forced to accept is described in the vignette of Bert and Frank in a later section of this chapter. The power of formal guardians (like informal guardians) in regard to the service system is very limited, they cannot guarantee appropriate services are available and can only make decisions within the parameters of existing services. They cannot require the provision of appropriate services, nor does the legislation require the state government to provide such services (Carney & Tait, 1997; Patterson & Hardy, 1991).

Family members successfully applied for guardianship only when formal consent to medical procedure was required by a hospital. In these cases, the key network member was appointed as a formal guardian with the power to sign medical consent forms. The role of key informal network members in the lives of older people with intellectual disability resembles very closely that of a guardian. This is reflected by formal service providers acknowledging their role and decision making functions on behalf of the older person which is in accordance with the least restrictive principle on which the GAB and Australian disability law operates (Creyke, 1995).

Only one example was found where a service provider suggested the person with the intellectual disability should make the decision rather than the key person. The circumstances which prompted this did not, however, appear to be overly concerned with safeguarding the wishes of the older person. Gerry's sister questioned a decision to move Gerry out of the disability hostel that his mother had hoped he would remain in for the rest of his life. His sister did not agree with this move and in her view, the decision was taken inappropriately by the residential service provider. She said:

> 'I didn't agree with it. I wasn't happy about the move. I didn't really have any say in it. They (hostel staff) said Gerry could have his say.'

However, from Gerry's perspective, the imperatives of the service rather than his wishes influenced the decision; he said:

> 'The people at the hostel wanted me to [leave]. They were trying to get people out into the community to live independently. They wanted

the space in [the day centre] and also up at the hostel. They reckoned I was getting too old for the place and they had a lot of other people who would be able to take my spot. They kept on at me, so I made up my mind that I would go out and try it (living in the community).'

Gerry's sister did not pursue this matter with the GAB.

In Morris' case, described in a vignette later in this chapter, his brother sought the assistance of the GAB to resolve a dispute with a service provider. However, this application for guardianship was rejected as being unnecessary because the dispute stemmed from a decision about the provision of services to Morris. It was not about who had the right to make decisions for Morris or the failure to acknowledge the informal decision-making role of Morris's brother. Rather, the issue for Morris was his lack of residency rights in the group home and rights to a disability service appropriate to his needs.

No examples were found where a decision, or the legitimacy of an informal network member to make a decision for an adult with intellectual disability, was questioned, resulting in an approach to the GAB to resolve a dispute. The fundamental issue of who has the right to make decisions about or for the person with intellectual disability or whether they have the capacity to make decisions for themselves seldom came to the fore to be debated openly.

Administration

Seven people have an administrator, six of whom are family members. A trustee company was appointed as administrator for one person, Beth, who does not have any family members willing to undertake this role. Her problems with the way the company fulfils this role illustrate the vulnerability of people who lack a key informal network member. Beth's social worker feels the company's response to Beth's needs is tardy and inappropriate and, in consultation with the minister from Beth's church, has appointed a solicitor to represent Beth's interests to the trustee company.

Beth's situation also raises a critical issue of the financial interdependence between adults with intellectual disability and their parents. Beth has no one able to resolve her situation informally and the trustee company is taking a strictly legal approach to the issue outlined below.

> While Beth and her widowed mother lived at home they had shared their resources, although the house was owned by her mother. Her mother developed Alzheimer's disease and moved to a nursing home and Beth remained in the house for several years alone before moving to an aged persons' hostel. During this time she incurred heavy debts

to Telecom and other utilities. The administrator appointed for Beth and her mother treats them as completely separate entities. Beth has no assets, her only income is her pension. The administrator refuses to use any of her mother's substantial assets to pay Beth's debts or supplement her pension. Beth's mother is in a nursing home and Beth is the beneficiary of her will. However, the administrator insists on using part of Beth's pension to pay the debts and consequently she cannot pay fees to the aged persons' hostel where she lives.

Family members are critical of the Board's operations and the manner in which administrators are treated. They feel mistrusted and resent the detailed annual report they must make to the GAB. Some resent the intrusion of a formal body into what they perceive as a family matter and a role they have performed informally for many years. For example, on the advice of a hospital social worker, Lewis's brother applied to be Lewis's administrator, since his father was not coping and had refused to hand over the management of Lewis's affairs. Lewis's sister-in-law said:

> 'I feel we have been treated like criminals by them (GAB). Having to be accountable when it's a brother and a sister. I don't think there's any need for all this court business and treating you like a criminal. All these questions you've got to answer.'

One key network member is very critical of the after hours service offered by the GAB and its slow response to his sister's medical emergencies that required the immediate appointment of a guardian. Overall, informal key network members are generally disillusioned and feel mistrusted and disempowered by their experiences with the GAB.

ROLES OF FORMAL SERVICE STAFF

Staff of formal services are integral members of the support networks of many older people with intellectual disability, particularly those who rely on formal services for primary care. Six older people named staff of a formal service provider as friends and many more, particularly those who live in supported accommodation, nominated a staff member as the person they would talk to if they had a problem. Only one older person had a friend who was an ex staff member of a service.

Staff of aged care facilities often organise and encourage access to external programs, helping the older person to find educational or day activity services. Staff have formed close relationships with several of the study population and their roles resemble that of a case manager. However, they recognise the relationship and their involvement is limited. For example,

Bertha lives in a special accommodation house and the proprietor has organised for her to attend a range of social groups in the community and fosters her friendships with other participants. When Bertha was persuaded to return home, despite previous allegations of sexual abuse by her step father, the proprietor considered this was not in Bertha's best interest but felt powerless to intervene. She said:

> 'I am very fond of her and really over three years I'm all Bertha has in relation to dependency, the only one who understands her routines and structures. When she left, I was quite devastated because I had put so much time into getting her organised. I could see she was being manipulated but there was nothing I could do because I was just a carer.'

However, the impression was sometimes conveyed that service providers have decision-making power and some degree of ownership of the person with intellectual disability. For example, Wilbur and his brother spent some time in hospital because they had not been coping at home. Their niece said:

> 'They (staff at the hospital) decided that Wilbur and his brother weren't allowed to go home and had to go to an accommodation place. So I did the running around. They (Wilbur and his brother) wanted to stay in their own home but they (staff at the hospital) said they weren't allowed to.'

Another example is the comment made by a special accommodation house proprietor who said:

> 'They (regional disability services) put me on trial for three months, so she (Bertha) actually belonged to them for three months'.

VIGNETTES

Two vignettes are drawn from each of the two main groups of the study population: those who were known to disability services and those who were not.

Morris Riley

Morris's family moved around the state when he was younger and he had intermittent contact with both community-based and institutional services for people with intellectual disability. His parents planned carefully for his future care and oversaw his move to a disability group home. As Morris aged, the group home was unable to adapt to his changing needs and, in an atmosphere of conflict and dissatisfaction, he moved to a nursing home. His family bitterly resents this move, considering it occurred prematurely, hastened the decline of his abilities and has severely reduced his quality of life.

> Morris began attending a disability day centre when he was 27. The association that managed the centre built a group home and Morris moved into this when he was 45. He maintained regular contact with his parents and siblings, participating in family events and going home for weekends. His sister-in-law suggested that, while living in the group home, he was more independent than ever before. During this time, his parents died and his siblings maintained a close relationship with him, particularly his brother who took over the management and supervision of his affairs.
>
> When Morris was 52, his behaviour began to change. He became forgetful and started getting up in the night. The group home found it increasingly difficult, with the existing staff resources, to meet Morris's additional needs for support. There was no active night staff, he disturbed other residents and doors had to be kept locked to prevent him wandering. A protracted period of conflict between the house staff and Morris's brother followed. Staff suggested that Morris move to a nursing home, while his brother considered that insufficient effort was being made to accommodate Morris's changing needs. His offer to pay for some additional support was refused.
>
> At a general service plan meeting convened by the regional disability services team and attended by his brother, it was resolved to seek a neuro-psychological assessment through the aged care assessment team to investigate Morris's condition. None of his family was involved in the assessment or was allowed to see the report that recommended he was eligible for a nursing home. When Morris broke his foot and went to a geriatric extended care centre for rehabilitation, the management of the service refused to take him back. The regional disability services team arranged for his admission to a respite care house for people with intellectual disabilities that had a three-month residency limit. This house had an active night staff and Morris, who was still able to do many things for himself, managed extremely well.
>
> All parties agreed that Morris needed a permanent place in a group home with a high level of staffing. However, the regional disability services team indicated that there was little hope of getting a place and assigned a caseworker to assist the family to find alternative accommodation. Morris was 53 and showing the first signs of Alzheimer's disease. His family was strongly opposed to the idea of a nursing home. They approached the Guardianship Board, hoping it could intervene and force the group home to take him back. They appointed his brother as administrator and considered Morris did not need a guardian but were willing to reconsider his case if suitable accommodation was not found.

Finding a nursing home that would accept Morris was difficult but eventually one accepted him. A volunteer from a specialist disability service was organised to take Morris out weekly but this arrangement only lasted several months.

At the time of the study Morris was 56. Perceptions of him contrasted sharply. The director of nursing at the home said that he could not comprehend or communicate. However, his sister-in-law said that he could express himself and was aware of people and his surroundings. Morris's family is frustrated with many aspects of his care. For example, staff never put his glasses on for him and they feel that he lacks any stimulation and activity. Since he moved to the nursing home, Morris has had a collapsed lung and renal problems and has lost many of his functional skills. The caseworker from the regional team has not visited him there, although a worker (not the original one, who left) rings up now and again to ask how he is. His general service plan has not been reviewed though his sister-in-law would like this to occur. His sister-in-law summed up the family's concerns, saying, 'It was very frustrating. They said he's got to go to a nursing home and he wasn't ready for a nursing home. I still say if he hadn't gone into a nursing home he wouldn't be as bad as he is now.'

Bert and Frank Roberts

Bert and Frank are brothers aged 57 and 64. No data is available about the planning that their parents had done for the future. When they were younger, they lived with their mother and two sisters, one of whom also had intellectual disability. When their mother went into a nursing home, they remained at home with their sisters, the elder of whom sought out specialist disability services for the first time four years later when she found it increasingly difficult to cope with them. The ensuing shift to supported accommodation resulted in considerable upheaval and dislocation for Frank and Bert and has restricted their opportunities to move independently around the community.

> Frank and Bert lived in the same inner city neighbourhood for many years. They knew the area well, moving around both on foot and by using public transport. They used local facilities such as shops and hotels. However, when their mother left home, their sister Doris found it increasingly difficult to provide care for Frank and Bert and to manage their behaviour. After four years she sought assistance from a regional disability services team. Bert and Frank were referred to the Guardianship Board and a guardian was appointed to make residential decisions for them. The guardian, with assistance from the regional team, found them a place in a special accommodation house in an outer suburb some 50 km away, which has a reputation among service providers as being of very poor quality but easy to get into. It is

isolated from shops and other facilities and access to public transport is limited. The house caters for a broad age range of people with psychiatric and intellectual disabilities.

Bert and Frank are taken annually to visit their mother, who suffers from dementia. Their sister Doris is no longer involved with either of them. They have another sister who has not seen them for many years. Bert said that his only friend was 'the boss', the proprietor of the special accommodation house. The proprietor said that Bert had an advocate from the local Citizen Advocacy Association who takes him out for drives every now and again but Bert did not mention him. Bert said that he didn't do anything all day apart from just sit around. He attends a senior citizens' centre one afternoon a week which was arranged by his advocate. The guardianship order has now lapsed and neither Frank nor Bert has had any contact with the regional team for over 12 months.

Harry Bedford

Harry is 55 years old. His mother died when he was 49. She had hoped he could stay in the family home although, other than developing a key person succession plan that nominated his sister and leaving her estate to Harry, she did not make any detailed plans as to how the wish would be implemented. Since his mother's death, Harry has remained in the family home, supported primarily by one of his sisters who lives about 20 minutes away by car. Harry continues to work in the job he has had since he was 15 years old but has now negotiated a shortened day. He attended a special school when he was a child but has not used any disability services since he left school. His case illustrates the frustrations experienced in trying to locate formal services appropriate for middle-aged and younger old people with intellectual disability, as well as the potential that exists for a combination of formal and informal sources of support to maintain a person in the community when they lose the support of their parents.

> Harry lives alone in the family home. He has frequent contact with his sister Marg who provides both primary care and organises and manages his affairs. She rings him every day when he gets home from work, shops for him, cooks all his meals at the weekends, manages his finances and coordinates additional support from her children and one of Harry's brothers. She has sought out and organised formal services for Harry, which has been a time consuming and frustrating experience for her. When her mother was in hospital, she said that the staff could not understand Harry's limitations in providing support for her at home. After her mother died, she tried to find assistance for Harry from government departments, such as Veterans Affairs and Disability Services, local community-based agencies such as the

Catholic Family Welfare Bureau and voluntary agencies such as Legacy. She said, 'Originally we rang everywhere. No one wanted to know. They just sort of said no there was nothing they could do. Everybody has a bit of a mental block when you say he is 55. When he was in his 40s, they were horrified I was trying [to get services] for a 48-year-old. He is not retiring age and doesn't come under the geriatric people.'

She has found the advice and support of her local doctor and the church minister useful. The domiciliary program of the local government community services department, which is funded through the HACC program, provides the only formal services Harry uses. These are meals on wheels five days a week, which are collected by a neighbour, and a home help who cleans the house and does the laundry once a fortnight.

Gina Watson

Gina is 57 years old and has lived alone since her mother died six years ago. Her mother tried to arrange for herself and Gina to move to an aged persons' hostel but Gina was considered too young. Instead, they moved to a small unit. Her mother made financial arrangements for Gina in her will and expected her brother to oversee her wellbeing in the future. Gina has never used any specialist disability services, having had a private tutor when she was young. She demonstrates that an older person with intellectual disability can successfully attend a range of day activities available to the general community and the difficulty of gaining access to specialist services in later life.

> Gina's brother lives interstate but maintains regular contact by phone and arranges for her to visit him twice a year. He oversees her financial affairs and liaises with Gina's church elder, Jane. Gina has a strong network of friends and church members who provide social and instrumental support for her day-to-day life. At the centre of the network is Jane, with whom Gina has almost daily contact. Jane monitors how Gina copes with the activities of daily living, such as household chores, washing and shopping. She checks her expenditure and makes sure she is not exploited. Jane has taught Gina to use public transport. She invites Gina to dinner, ensures she plays a valued role in one church group and informally coordinates others in the community who Gina relies on for help. Jane described Gina as a friend and her own role as anything from cutting toenails to discussing cremation. She attempts to make their relationship more reciprocal by asking Gina to help her out sometimes.
>
> Gina attended several social groups with her mother and continued to attend these groups after her mother's death. She regularly goes to

two ladies groups run by the Salvation Army and participates in social activities at her own church. Daily, she lays the tables and has lunch at a multi-purpose elderly persons' centre. She attends several classes held at the centre and is a member of the senior citizens' club based there. For a period Gina attended a group for elderly and disabled people organised by the local government social worker. However, this collapsed when the worker left. She has declined to attend a specialist group for people with intellectual disability at a neighbourhood house. The welfare officer at the elderly persons' centre thought that Gina had been integrated into the real world and, though aware of her limitations, did not identify with people with intellectual disability. Gina's church elder is very conscious of her heavy involvement in Gina's life. Soon after the death of Gina's mother the elder contacted the regional disability services team. She said, 'We contacted the regional team's office, to see if they would help us. At the time, we were given to understand that she (Gina) had so many support networks and they were so stretched that she really wouldn't fall into their category because she managed very well thank you. We were thinking it would be good to have a regional team worker come in and help her budgeting because it was too interfering for us to be doing it.' She has not followed up this contact.

ACCESSIBILITY OF FORMAL SERVICES

The study population depend on informal network members, or other formal services, to locate and arrange access to formal services. Help is primarily sought from aged care rather than disability services. The reasons for this are not clear. It may be from choice, their greater knowledge of aged care services, or reflect the relative accessibility of the two service systems to older people with intellectual disability.

Informal network members generally have a very poor knowledge of the disability service system and are better informed about aged care and domiciliary services. This is often a result of their parents' use of a wide range of these services. While they were still middle-aged, some of the study population had attended aged care day services with their elderly parents and continue to attend after the transition from parental care.

Negotiating access to domiciliary or aged care day services for an older person with intellectual disability did not appear to be problematic. Some informants raised the reluctance of aged care facilities to accept people with intellectual disability. This may account for the clustering of people with intellectual disability in a few facilities. A discriminatory attitude by these facilities was also evident during the case finding process when some stated quite categorically that they did not cater for people with intellectual disability.

For most of those who use disability services, their point of entry was an ATSS rather than a regional disability services team. However, this is potentially problematic since three-quarters of the study population have never used ATSSs. The disability service system has few recent new users; those who use it have generally done so for many years. Some evidence suggests the inaccessibility of disability services to older people wanting to use them for the first time is one reason for low use. In several instances, either informal network members or aged care service providers have approached a regional disability services team for assistance and been given the impression that no services could be offered to an older person and that pursuing the enquiry is not worthwhile. As a consequence, informal inquiries are not followed through to formal requests for services. The vignettes of Gina and Harry illustrate this occurrence.

Additionally, key people acting for two older people have been told informally that they are not eligible for disability services, although a formal, thorough assessment had not been undertaken. Both these older people met the criteria for inclusion in this study; they had intellectual disability in the view of service providers and close friends or family, and corroborating evidence exists that documents a history of intellectual disability. Dot's friend spoke about her experience of trying to obtain access to a regional disability services team for Dot. She rang disability services when Dot's sister died, as she didn't think Dot should be left on her own. However, after a short visit, the worker told her that Dot was not eligible for services. She was very frustrated with the regional disability services team but did not formally challenge the decision. She said:

> 'Why follow it up when he (regional team worker) said it [was] no longer their concern and that Dot was perfectly capable of looking after herself. [He had] no other contact except that 20 minutes [in which] he assessed her on the night her sister died. He hadn't met her before. I talked to him and said why can't community services look after her; keep an eye on her. No, no they didn't give me a formal letter. He said that it's out of their (regional disability team) hands because he felt that she was perfectly capable of looking after herself. The whole trouble is she just had nobody. They just make these bloody great decisions and just walk away. Somebody's got to pick up the tab.'

Very few of the study population have been referred to disability services, or provided with information about them by aged care service providers. Possible reasons are that aged care providers lack knowledge of the disability system or they consider they are inaccessible and have nothing to offer older people with intellectual disability. This latter view was expressed with considerable frustration by one aged care assessment team geriatrician, who remarked that he never referred anyone to regional disability services teams as they have a two-year waiting list just for assessment.

The disability service system does not usually maintain an ongoing relationship with older people after they leave a disability day centre, residential or outreach service. This trend, together with the shift towards residence in aged care facilities, helps explain why so few older people use services from both the aged care and disability service systems. For example, Beatrice's niece, speaking about Beatrice's move to the special accommodation house, said:

> 'They (regional disability services team) seem to have given her the flick. I don't see that they have any connection with her now. They don't see her, they don't come and they never check up on her.'

Another example is Vera who fell and broke her leg in a respite house run by an ATSS and spent almost a year in hospital. Her niece said, 'They (ATSS) discharged her and wanted nothing more to do with her'.

EXPERIENCES OF USING FORMAL SERVICES

The concerns expressed about disability services differ from those regarding aged care services. For example, informants are critical of the quality and appropriateness of aged care services but not of disability residential services. In contrast, they are critical of the processes, decisions and availability of disability residential services but not so of aged care facilities. All informants with experiences of regional disability service teams expressed concern about both quality and availability of those services.

Disability services

Informants' experiences of the services provided by regional disability teams spanned the last seven years and, for most, more than 12 months had elapsed since their last contact. Yet their views are remarkably similar; typically these services are considered to be over-stretched and superficial. For example, Madge's brother said:

> 'Their (regional disability services) general service plans and their individual program plans are just paperwork. Nothing has been actioned from any of her (Madge's) plans. When you question them (regional disability services) or ask for support, it's always in the too hard basket. When we started to have this wandering in the night I asked for an opinion because it had come up in individual program plans. We were referred to the psychologist. We followed it up on numerous occasions. I never even spoke to the psychologist. The caseload was too big. The waiting list was too long.'

Family members consider that team workers have a superficial understanding of the individuals on which they base their action plans. Family members feel that team workers do not listen to them or utilise their knowledge about the older person. The view is also expressed that team workers interfere too much and do not really understand the needs of people with intellectual disability. The following examples are typical of the views about team workers expressed by informants. Doreen's sister said:

> 'The general service plan was perfunctory. It was inappropriate for her (regional disability service team worker) to bring up retirement. The problem was they (team workers) had had no contact with Doreen. It would have been quite good if they had got to know her.'

George's sister-in-law discussed the way George was assessed by a team worker. She said:

> 'They had paperwork to fill out. I have a strong feeling that you can't just fill in forms, that people like George need someone to interpret and tease out things for them. When they try and reduce everything to numbers and boxes, it's very easy to get the wrong impression. She (team worker) heard George's response and was making an interpretation from it; I had to say that's not what George's really trying to say. He naturally has a limited capacity for choice of words, I teased it out by asking questions about that thing she assumed. I didn't tell her. I asked a lot more questions and then she got a completely different response and yet she was ready to take the first thing he said.'

Brendan's sister said:

> 'They (team workers) came here on several occasions to try and persuade us to have Brendan buy a unit and share it. We knew it would be an absolute disaster and they didn't know it until they got to know Brendan better. They (regional disability services) took us to court to find out how much money Brendan had. All they knew was there was some money that Brendan had. They wanted to know how much and get control of it. They can take over all management and control of an intellectually disabled person.'

Only a few older adults had been assigned a case manager to assist with the transition from parental care or a later transition. Some family members had felt unsupported and left to manage difficult transitions alone. Paradoxically, George had a case manager during his transition from parental care but, his sister-in-law, when asked what would have made the process easier, described the need for a competent case manager by saying:

> '[It would have helped if there was] one person who specialises in that process. Who knows how to traverse this minefield? There were lots of little people along the way to keep me company but there was no one

whose hand I could hold all through. That knowledge didn't appear. There was nobody really knowing what either side was about.'

Excepting the services provided by regional disability service teams, discussed above, current users and their key network members are very positive about disability services. General anxiety is expressed, however, about possible future redevelopment of services and budget cutbacks.

In contrast, a substantial number of informants connected with ex service users are not so positive. Hostels, outreach services and, to a lesser extent, ATSSs are criticised. The concerns raised by informants are illustrated in earlier chapters. For example, the vignette of Beatrice in chapter 4 illustrates problems experienced with a disability outreach service. The vignettes of Godfrey in chapter 7 and Morris in this chapter, exemplify the criticisms of disability residential services about encouraging adults with intellectual disability to move to independent living situations and the unwillingness of services to adapt and accommodate to people's increased need for support.

Lack of flexibility and withdrawal of specialist services to older people

Morris's case illustrates the most common issue of concern expressed about disability services, which was a decision by the service provider that the service was no longer appropriate for an older person. Such decisions are made in respect of residents in hostels and groups homes. Nursing homes are often suggested as the appropriate alternative residential service. Informants consider that, if disability services are more flexible and provide additional support, they can meet the changing needs of an older person, at least for a period. In their view, often when a decision is made that a service is no longer appropriate, the older person is functioning at too high a level for a nursing home. They also feel that the milieu of a nursing home hastens dependency and a deterioration of skills.

The core of these concerns is the merit of a decision by a service provider that a particular service is no longer appropriate for an older person. The issue then becomes whether the service should continue to be provided to the older person. Informants consider that these decisions are based on service system requirements, such as budget constraints or ideological commitments that preclude full consideration of the optimum outcome for the person with intellectual disability. Morris's sister-in-law has no doubts. She said:

> 'The hostel wanted him out. They had reduced their staff and increased their numbers.'

The supervisor of the group home where Morris had lived was very explicit about the reason the service was no longer considered appropriate for Morris and why he had to leave. She said:

> 'It was costing an absolute fortune [for Morris to continue to live here] with extra hours for staff to assist Morris. We were calling in some casual staff, we had two who had a nursing background and experience, to keep him here.'

In retrospect and with limited information, judging the merits of decisions made by service providers about the appropriateness of services is very difficult. The subjective views of those involved, who are the informants, provide only part of the picture, although their views should be considered in any service decision, together with objective assessment of needs. Nevertheless, the merits of decisions that a service is no longer appropriate for an older person were questioned in relation to 15% of the group and across several different services. Decisions such as this resulted in residential moves for all of the older people and for most, a move to a more restrictive living situation in an aged care facility rather than a disability service. It is, however, somewhat paradoxical that, because of the decision that a service was no longer appropriate and because pressure was applied by the service provider for the older person to move, two people moved to a less restrictive, more independent, living situation.

The questioning of decisions about the appropriateness of services by informal network members and the outcome of such decisions for most older people suggests that service flexibility, and willingness to adapt and attempt to meet changing needs as people age are important issues. These elements should be examined to avoid the movement of older people with intellectual disability to environments that are more restrictive than necessary. They also raise the broader issue of the right of older people with intellectual disability to age in place and to have continuing access to disability services as they age. Policy decisions, both implicit and explicit, regarding the respective places of the disability and aged care service systems in addressing the needs of older people with intellectual disability underscore these issues and are considered in the next chapter.

RELATIONSHIPS BETWEEN INFORMAL NETWORK MEMBERS AND FORMAL SERVICES

A common issue of process arose across all the substantive areas of concern expressed about disability services. As the case examples illustrate, most informants with experience of disability services felt that service providers do not pay regard to their concerns and implement service delivery decisions in the face of their opposition. Some service decisions are taken in a climate of conflict between formal providers and informal network members which leaves family members feeling powerless and frustrated in their quest to ensure the wellbeing of the person with intellectual disability. Conflicts of this nature amount to more than a few isolated incidents. They occurred to almost half of the older people using disability services, which suggests this is a systemic issue that cannot be put down to the failings of individual workers.

The amount of conflict between informal network members and aged care service providers is less than that between informal network members and disability service providers. Conflict is mainly about the quality of aged care facilities and not the merits of staff decisions.

Generic aged services

No consistent issues are raised about the quality of aged care domiciliary, day or case management services. The lack of consultation by the aged care assessment team staff with Morris's family is an exceptional occurrence. However, concerns are consistently expressed about the quality and appropriateness of nursing homes, special accommodation houses and aged persons' hostels for older people with intellectual disability. Quality concerns are reflected in the rates and reason for movement into and out of accommodation types, illustrated in chapter 7 and summarised in table 7.3. A central concern across all three types of accommodation is that the environment is considered to foster dependence rather than independence, provide insufficient stimulation, comprise people much older than the person with intellectual disability and have staff who are not attuned to the needs of people with intellectual disability.

The vignette of Morris illustrates family concerns about a nursing home environment. Norman's sister had similar concerns. She said:

> 'Since he's been there (nursing home) the deterioration has been so great. There's no stimulation. They are just left to sit, left to rot. One of the things was there are no activities for him. You know he went into the nursing home and they didn't watch his bowels and he got grossly constipated and he was crying all the time. They weren't really listening to him. It's his condition, Down syndrome. I know Norman very very well and I said there's something wrong with him. He's in pain in his tummy. I forced the issue and demanded he was treated.'

The remarks by Nora's brother illustrate concerns about the environment of a special accommodation house. He said:

> 'The next step will be a nursing home and the thing that annoys me so much is I believe there is no need for this. If they (staff) made Nora walk and made her do a bit more, I believe she would be one hell of a lot better, physically and mentally. They are showering her and dressing her. Having everything done for her she's just become very, very lazy. I can understand those people (staff). It's a lot easier for them.'

Beatrice's niece is also concerned about the few demands the environment of a special accommodation house makes on Beatrice. She said:

> 'You know, it's still not the best spot for Beatrice. They (other residents) just sit around in a great semi-circle watching TV all day. The only difference is that someone says, "Let's go for a walk around the corner". Beatrice has been used to doing the housework, doing some washing. The proprietor is good and understands but she is in an environment of mainly old people, not very active old ladies. There's not enough stimulation and she (Beatrice) has taken on the characteristics of those around her.'

Ted, who lives in a special accommodation house, commented about the age difference between him and the other residents, 'I would prefer to be amongst people of my own age or younger'.

Critical comments about the environment of aged care residential services far outweigh positive ones. Nevertheless, a few older people with intellectual disability and their families are happy with the quality of these services. However, their opinions are often coloured by their negative experiences of previous services. Wilbur had lived in a special accommodation house which was a converted motel and had to stay in his room all day. He moved to an aged persons' hostel, about which he said:

> 'I'm very happy. I like it very much mixing with the ladies. I think it's much better [than the special accommodation house].'

Jim lives in an aged persons' hostel in a retirement village. His friend said:

> 'They are lovely to him over there (hostel). The men like him. He's very popular. Their little boy, they call him.'

PERCEPTIONS OF UNMET SERVICE NEEDS

Although informants are critical of various aspects of formal services, most found it very difficult to pinpoint what type of formal support would have been useful in the past, present or the future. Knowledge and information about available services is one need that is highlighted. For instance,

Michael's sister, who had provided primary care for both Michael and his mother, said:

> '"People sitting" would have been a good service. They probably thought I knew about all the services. You know, people think that you know about these things. They take it for granted that you know.'

Options for the provision of primary care are seen as being too limited and, very often, nursing homes are presented as the only available alternative. Informants consider that older adults with intellectual disability fall into a service gap between disability and aged care services and are too old for the disability system but too young for aged care services. This is particularly the case for adults at the time of the transition from parental care but also later on as well. For example, Vera lived in a disability hostel for 17 years after she left parental care. Eventually she was asked to leave, as she was no longer considered to be independent enough. Her brother said:

> 'There's a system for the young, a system for the geriatrics. No alternatives for the younger old. It's frustrating when they are just past looking after themselves and need a bit more supervision and there's nowhere in between a nursing home.'

The domiciliary services coordinator said about Joyce:

> 'She doesn't fit into intellectual disability services. They said they didn't have much to offer and she's too young for aged services.'

Humphrey's sister summed up these issues, saying:

> 'Everybody has a bit of a mental block when you say he is 55. When he was in his 40s they were horrified I was trying [to get] a 48 year old [into an aged persons' hostel]. He is not retiring age and doesn't come under the geriatric people.'

Despite an inability to express what services would have been useful, informants who are key people consistently feel they had been let down by formal services, particularly disability ones. When they have sought help, little had been forthcoming or there has been conflict and dissatisfaction with services. Nevertheless, formal services play a significant role in the lives of most of the study population, mainly by providing primary care and opportunities for social contact.

SUMMARY

This chapter has highlighted the significance of formal services in the support networks of older people with intellectual disability but raises issues regarding the nature and quality of these services. In particular, the absence of any systemic responses by the disability services system to accommodate to the people's changing needs as they age, the impact of this on the quality of life of older adults and the consequent sense of frustration and powerlessness by their key informal network members. The failure of the disability and the aged care service systems to intersect successfully and pool their expertise in the interests of this group is particularly evident. The lack of partnership between formal and informal sources of support is also apparent by the failure of services to fully utilise the vast store of knowledge informal network members have about the life, skills and interests of these older people. Older people with intellectual disability are particularly vulnerable to decisions being made about them and, in view of the contentious nature of some of these decisions, the vulnerability of those with no one to question them on their behalf is very evident. The next chapter takes these issues further and considers the manner in which formal service systems at both a practice and policy level can begin to address the support needs of older people with intellectual disability.

CHAPTER *10*

Understanding the post-parental care phase and ensuring adequate sources of support for ageing adults with intellectual disability

Answers to the central questions of this book, 'What happens when parents die?' and 'Who or what services replace the roles of parents?' are neither simple nor static. A substantial period of their life follows the transition of adults with intellectual disability from parental care. This 'post-parental care phase' is characterised by change and spans both middle and old age for people with intellectual disabilities. It can be a period of broadened horizons and new opportunities but also a time of vulnerability to inappropriate restrictive lifestyles, poor quality services and loss of informal support. No single model of support exists. At different times, different individuals or services replace parental tasks. Some people live alone with support from family or the church, some live alone with support from disability or aged care services, some live with family, some move to disability accommodation and others to aged care accommodation. During the post-parental care phase, some people will live in several of these alternatives and experience greater upheaval and change than at the time of transition from parental care. Most receive affective support from a small number of friends or relatives and have a key informal network member who acts as their 'advocate or case manager'.

Five central themes characterise the post-parental care phase of the lives of people with intellectual disability:

- the splitting of parental roles between formal and informal sources of support
- the significance of informal support
- the existence of both opportunities and vulnerabilities
- the declining use of specialist disability services, and the problematic nature of formal supports
- the efficacy of key person succession plans in achieving a smooth transition and longer term security.

The length and nature of the post-parental care phase suggests that the focus of policy, service developments and intervention strategies must be broader than work with ageing parents regarding planning and the transition from parental care. The years following transition from parental care present new challenges for professionals who work with middle-aged and older people with intellectual disability. These include recognising and working with non-parental informal sources of support, countering ageist stereotypes, creating environments for optimal personal development, and confronting structural pressures for residential mobility which requires balancing the need for stability with the benefits of change. At a broad policy and service development level, the challenge is to ensure appropriate policies are developed and implemented to enable both aged care services and disability services to assist people with intellectual disability to age successfully. This chapter examines the five themes that characterise the post-parental care phase and develops a series of policy and practice proposals to ensure the optimisation of opportunities and minimisation of vulnerability for adults in this period of their lives.

SOURCES OF SUPPORT IN THE POST-PARENTAL CARE PHASE

Splitting parental functions

Despite the change experienced during this phase, clear trends in the provision of support are evident. No one person or service substitutes for all the tasks that parents have previously fulfilled. During the process of transition, the two central parental tasks, primary care and overseeing wellbeing, are separated and progressively fulfilled by different sources of support. The differentiation of tasks between groups increases in the years that follow transition from parental care, as groups gravitate towards the tasks most suited to their characteristics. Formal services become the dominant providers of primary care as people age. The percentage of those in receipt of informal primary care drops on entry to and throughout the post-parental care phase; in this study from 100% to 53% to 19%. Informal sources are the dominant substitute for the provision of the other major parental task: overseeing and managing the person's wellbeing. Formal services generally do not assume responsibility for this task on a continuing basis.

Primary care

Following the transition from parental care, a substantial proportion of adults continue to receive primary care informally, but from a family member or friend rather than parents. However, informal provision of primary care is unlikely to last for the entire post-parental phase. It is generally a short- rather than long-term arrangement. As informal primary carers find they are unwilling, or unable, to continue in this role they are seldom replaced by other informal carers. The need for 'placement' and the provision of primary care by formal services is therefore not as great at the time of transition from parental care as has been anticipated in the literature (Lakin et al., 1991; Walz et al., 1986) but increases during the post-parental phase.

Litwak's theory of task specificity helps to explain why parental roles are split and only a few kin or friends replace parents as primary caregivers in the long term (1985). It also explains why some informal network members provide primary care in the short term but are unable to sustain this role.

Provision of primary care tasks by kin or friends requires a high degree of commitment, proximity and face-to-face contact on a daily basis. Normally only a spouse, or for an adult with intellectual disability, their parent, has the characteristics required for this role. Other informal network members do not generally have these characteristics and the theory suggests they are unlikely to substitute for primary care formerly provided by parents. Kin with atypical characteristics, such as being single, being proximate and having daily face-to-face contact are more likely to substitute as primary carers as their characteristics more closely match the dimensions required for the task. Substitution may also be likely if a residential move results in a better match to the dimensions required; for example, the adult with intellectual disability moves to co-reside with a sibling, thus achieving close proximity. However, despite the existence of congruent dimensions, the prerequisites for substitution to occur are commitment and adequate physical resources by a primary group member.

In this study, an informal network member substituted for their parents and provided primary care for 53% of adults with intellectual disability directly after their transition from parental care. Most of these informal primary care providers had some of the atypical characteristics that Litwak suggests make substitution for domestic or household tasks more likely. A majority were siblings, who, Litwak suggests, are the kin most likely to have sufficient commitment to provide primary care. Many had also made some form of negotiated commitment to the adult with intellectual disability during the parental planning process. Alternatively, the commitment of church members to the individual was seen as part of a broader social responsibility. Another factor that explains the relatively high number of informal primary carers at the time of transition was the relative youth of adults with intellectual disability (average age 52 years) and their primary carers. Diminished physical resources were not an obstacle to the provision of primary care as would be the case with an older population.

The main reasons that informal primary care was relinquished were death, incapacity and an unwillingness of the carer to continue due to strain. They reflect the reasons found in Litwak's theory explaining either why primary groups do not substitute or the high cost involved in doing so.

SIGNIFICANCE AND STRENGTH OF INFORMAL SUPPORT

Informal support continues to play a central role in the lives of most of middle-aged and older people with intellectual disabilities during and after their transition from parental care. Relationships with friends and family provide opportunities for social interaction, shared activities, and a sense of self-esteem and belonging. Significantly, most people have a strong relationship with a 'key informal network member' who takes responsibility and is proactive in overseeing and managing their wellbeing.

The assumption of this role by particular individuals is not determined according to a hierarchical pattern of kin ties. The nature and history of the relationship with the person with intellectual disability and a commitment to the role is often more important than particular kin relationships. The kin and friends who become key network members have the pivotal characteristic that Litwak's theory suggests is required for the task: long-term commitment but not necessarily proximity or frequent face-to-face contact. Their commitment had often been negotiated with parents and encapsulated in a key person succession plan.

The roles played by key people were similar to those described in the mainstream gerontological literature by Sussman (1985) as indirect care and by Cantor (1989) as case management. They involve a myriad of unspecified, idiosyncratic tasks, such as monitoring the quality of services, negotiating with professionals, advocating on behalf of the adult with disability, taking major life decisions, managing finances, and providing affective support such as visits and ensuring the celebration of key life events occurred.

The key person, or their predecessor, plays a critical role in managing the transition from parental care and subsequently in dealing with the contingencies and transitions that confront the older person. Their role is crucial for dealing with the relationship between older people and formal organisations. It is particularly critical for those who rely on formal services for primary care.

Formal organisations find it difficult to fulfil non-uniform tasks with many contingencies such as management of financial affairs and advocacy. Litwak suggests that when people move into supported accommodation, tasks such as these, which were previously performed by primary groups and which cannot be routinised are neglected unless a primary group member takes them over (1985). He suggests the importance of service users having a strong independent source of advocacy to mediate the tensions that arise from the conflicting needs of formal organisations and primary groups. The importance of this for older people with intellectual disability is illustrated in chapter 9 which explores examples of the tension between organisations and the families of older people when their respective needs and priorities clash.

The suggestion that informal support, particularly that of a key person, is crucial to the quality of life of an older person with intellectual disability in residential care is reinforced by the evidence that formal services cannot easily or adequately substitute for key person roles. Formal services lack the characteristics to fulfil non-uniform tasks requiring long-term commitment and cannot replicate the commitment and flexibility possessed by key informal network members necessary to oversee another's wellbeing. Exceptionally, for one person a formal service fulfilled this role in the long term, but in his case many of the tasks were delegated to an informal volunteer.

Inability of formal services to substitute

The characteristics of formal services, particularly residential services, and economic imperatives, make it difficult to fulfil non-routinised tasks. The ability of service providers to advocate for their clients effectively or to adequately monitor service quality is hampered by the restraints imposed by their organisational positions and conflicts of interest. Several examples were found where a formal service, such as a guardian from the Office of the Public Advocate or a trustee company, assumed a fragment of the informal key person's role. But this was only for a time-limited period and the task was not performed particularly well. The case management service offered by regional disability services teams is not based on a long-term care management model and does not replicate the continuing comprehensive overseeing of wellbeing undertaken by key informal network members. For short periods, case management services can fulfil some key person functions. However, the inability of formal providers to substitute for continuing overseeing of wellbeing emphasises the vulnerability of those older people who lose their key person and do not get a replacement.

Network changes after transition from parental care

The informal network characteristics of older people with intellectual disability are similar, in some respects, to those reported for their younger peers living at home with ageing carers, in so far as they are dense, dominated by kin and show a concentration of instrumental support in the hands of one or two people (Grant, 1993; Krauss & Erickson, 1988; Seltzer et al., 1991). However, the nature of informal instrumental support received by older adults is different from that received by younger adults living with parents. Informal support for older adults generally includes the oversight wellbeing but not provision of primary care. The role of siblings in the support networks of the two groups is also very different. For example, almost three-quarters of older adults have a key person relationship with one of their siblings that meant they undertook at least three instrumental tasks. In contrast, only 20% of younger adults living with parents receive instrumental support from a sibling (Seltzer et al., 1991).

The contrast between the two age groups lends support to the conclusion that the role of some informal network members changes during, or after, transition from parental care. This is most clearly seen in relation to siblings who gradually take over responsibility for the wellbeing of the person from parents. The notion of change in sibling relationships is also supported by Zetlin's work that, similar to this study, indicates siblings are involved in the provision of instrumental support and occasionally assume what she terms a surrogate parent role when parents are not available or become frail (1986). The likelihood of some network members increasing their involvement in the lives of people with intellectual disability after the transition from parent care suggests that preparation for this role may be warranted.

OPPORTUNITIES IN THE POST-PARENTAL CARE PHASE

Myriad additional changes which are unplanned and unforeseen occur in the lives of adults with intellectual disability following the transition from parental care. These changes are often more contentious, less gradual and involve more conflict between families and formal services than those that occur in the initial transition. Many adversely affect the strength of informal support networks.

Nevertheless, not all changes experienced have a negative impact. Expanded horizons, new social relationships and increased independence are the positive changes experienced by many people. These later-life experiences resemble descriptions of the 'third age', as the time when people are chronologically old but still healthy and change the focus of their life activities, seeking out new roles and experiences (Laslett, 1989). Edgerton noted similar positive changes and increased competency occurring in old age among the cohort of ex-institutional inmates in his longitudinal study. These people experienced a striking improvement in their life satisfaction, social competence and quality of life as they grew older, as a result of increased competencies and the decreased expectations placed by society on older people. Edgerton suggests that, in old age, people with intellectual disability are more like their age peers than at any time previously in their lives: 'In fact when they are in their 60s these people are not only more competent in absolute terms than they have ever been before, they are also seen to be relatively more competent than in any prior period of their lives' (1994, p. 60).

CREATING POSITIVE EXPECTATIONS FOR OLDER ADULTS WITH INTELLECTUAL DISABILITY

Positive expectations, the creation of opportunities and sufficiently challenging environments are crucial to continued development and expansion of horizons in later life. However, staff in disability services often have little understanding of the ageing process and tend to impose negative stereotypical views of ageing on relatively young older people with intellectual disabilities. People with intellectual disability are often assumed to be 'older' at a much earlier age because of the premature ageing experienced by people with Down syndrome and as a cohort, people who are in their 50s are the oldest in many services. For example, Walker and Walker suggest that low expectations of staff alone are the primary barrier to social inclusion of older people with intellectual disability (1998b, p. 141). Also, as a group, older people with intellectual disability experience fewer choices, less programming, decreased access to day services and lower quality programs than their younger peers (Cooper, 1997b; Walker & Walker, 1998b).

The potential of middle-aged and older adults with intellectual disability to develop new skills and explore new interests contrasts to the way they are often portrayed in the literature and the view expressed in Australian policy documents. The common perception that older people with intellectual disability are in double or triple jeopardy and fall into two or more disadvantaged or devalued groups, conveys a negative conception of later life. Policy documents characterise this group as less independent, more frail and less motivated or capable of societal participation or individual achievement (CSV, 1992b; H&CS, 1993c, 1995b). The views in policy documents are similar to those expected in regard to the frail aged and people entering the 'fourth age' rather than the 'third age'. Too often those in the disability field assume that people can simply transfer to the aged care system when they are 60 years old. However, as suggested in chapter 4, the majority of older people with intellectual disability are the younger old rather than the frail aged at whom the aged care system is targeted.

These factors together suggest that, if the potential of middle-aged and older people with intellectual disability is to be realised, the disability service system needs to revise its preconceptions about older people. By adopting a more positive, optimistic stance towards later life a climate can be fostered that will ensure the full range of primary care, day activity and leisure options can be considered for adults in the post-parental phase. One way of fostering a more positive outlook is equipping direct care workers and other professionals in the disability field with a better understanding of ageing processes and the nature of the aged care system. By actively exposing discriminatory stereotypes and creating more positive images of older people negative preconceptions can be countered.

VULNERABILITY TO CONTROL BY OTHERS

A feature of both parental planning and the post-parental phase is the extent to which others take decisions and exert control over the lives of people with intellectual disability. Parents make key person succession plans in which others are nominated to exercise some control over the life of the adult with intellectual disability. Parents and nominated informal key people manage their transition and subsequently key people manage, advocate, decide, supervise and coordinate their affairs and relationships with services.

Some exceptional cases in this study highlight issues regarding the legitimacy of the role adopted by key informal network members and whether key people always act in the best interests of the older person. Their role, though not formally sanctioned, is accepted and recognised as legitimate by formal service providers. Fulfilment of a key person role is usually firmly embedded in a strong relationship and commitment to the older person's welfare, which provides some safeguards and from which legitimacy for such a high degree of involvement and decision making is derived.

Most key people adopt a collaborative approach that involves discussion and input from the person with intellectual disability. However, several older people found the fulfilment of a key person role unacceptable and had questioned the involvement of this person in their life. These exceptional cases raise the question of whether formal mechanisms are necessary to monitor informal arrangements and to safeguard the interests of the older person.

SAFEGUARDING INTERESTS AND ENSURING ADVOCACY

In Victoria, Australia, the Guardianship and Administration Board and Office of the Public Advocate provide the formal means to safeguard the interests of all people with disabilities. If problems surrounding informal decision-making arrangements arise, the Public Advocate can represent the interests of the individual and the GAB can arbitrate and replace informal, with formal, arrangements.

The success of the Public Advocate and GAB relies on two conditions. First that others, family, friends or service providers, are willing to question informal arrangements and initiate action. No evidence was found of the existence of this condition. The density of informal networks and their small size may reduce the likelihood of other informal sources being available to question the key person's role. Such action requires an advocacy perspective that may be problematic for formal service providers. Second, the success of formal safeguards relies on the replacement of unsatisfactory informal arrangements with more satisfactory, possibly formal, long-term ones. This condition was also problematic, as considered previously. Formal services do not have the characteristics required for long-term overseeing of wellbeing. Two interrelated issues that need to be addressed at a service planning and policy level are the availability of independent advocacy for older people with intellectual disability should they need it and the question of how to replace the crucial roles, such as indirect care and overseeing of wellbeing, that are best fulfilled by primary groups when an older person's informal support network lacks members with sufficient commitment to undertake these tasks.

Formal services exercise considerable control over the day-to-day lives of many older people with intellectual disability. They assess needs, formulate plans and make decisions about the appropriateness of services. These decisions are based on the discretion and judgment of service providers. The lack of explicit policy regarding disability service provision for older people with intellectual disability means that there is little basis on which to challenge service decisions. Additionally, in Australia, people with intellectual disability have no enforceable rights to receive services and no residential tenancy rights in disability services (Patterson & Hardy, 1991;

Villamanta Legal Service, 1995). Few avenues of redress exist for key people to challenge service decisions, which highlights the powerlessness of this group. Those without a key network member to monitor decisions are particularly vulnerable. The powerlessness experienced in relation to formal services could be addressed by the formulation of more explicit policy on services provision for this group, development of tenancy rights, and clearer service entitlements.

VULNERABILITY OF INFORMAL SUPPORT NETWORKS TO LOSS AND CHANGE

The informal support networks of older people with intellectual disability are vulnerable to shrinkage owing to characteristics such as lack of inter-generational support, shared network members and situation-specific contact and friendships. Vulnerability to loss of network members is accentuated by the effects of ageing and other characteristics such as the high propensity for residential mobility and the trend towards living in supported accommodation. The death or incapacity of parents is only one factor that contributes to the decline in size of older adults' informal networks.

The dominance in networks of people from the same, or an older, generation means that members are often lost owing to death or incapacity. Contact with network members who have been shared with a parent often ceases or is reduced when parents die. Either at the time of transition or later, most people move out of their locality and leave behind neighbourhood relationships established over many years. Incidental contact with other family members that commonly occurs when an adult with intellectual disability lives with relatives at home is also lost when they move to supported accommodation. Older people with intellectual disability often lack the skills necessary to maintain context-specific friendships and are seldom assisted by others to do so. This means that, as people cease attending a day service or leave a residential service, friends are left behind and are not sustained in a new context.

Some people can compensate for network losses and expand their networks in later life by broadening their horizons and developing new friendships after leaving parental care. The vignettes of Godfrey and Nadia illustrate this expansion. However, unfortunately, as happened to Morris, some people subsequently experience the onset of age-related health problems that result in further residential changes and the contraction of networks.

Key informal network members are stable elements in informal networks. Their relationships are multidimensional and not tied to a specific context, and are thus unaffected by residential mobility. Significantly, many key network members plan for their own succession and, when they die, are replaced. Most of the actual successors and many of those nominated for succession in the future are from a younger generation, and thus provide some guarantee of continuing support. However, despite these characteristics and safeguards, as people with intellectual disability age, they are vulnerable to the loss of key network members. Fewer people had a key informal network member at the time of the study compared with when they made the transition from parental care.

STRATEGIES TO RECOGNISE INFORMAL SUPPORT AND REDUCE NETWORK LOSS AND DISRUPTION

A recognition by professionals of the importance of informal support, its complementarity to formal support and the roles played by different network members must be a prerequisite to working with adults in mid and later life. This will ensure support and nurturance to informal network members and their optimal contribution to the wellbeing of the person with intellectual disability. Strategies such as the adoption of a network or family centred approach to the delivery of services for adults with intellectual disability are needed to replace the prevalent individual orientation that can too often ignore the contributions of significant others.

For example, professionals need to understand and respect the role that siblings or other more distant relatives may play in the lives of older people with intellectual disabilities, which in comparison to older people generally is non-normative (Wenger, 1987). Recognition and utilisation of their knowledge is essential, especially in view of the often limited information that residential staff have about residents (Green & Wunsch, 1994; H&CS, 1995a, p. 97). Where interventions such as health assessments are conducted, plans for future discussed, or activities decided, involvement of a key informal network member with a long-term, close relationship to the older person is crucial, not only to represent the interests of the older person but to facilitate communication and provide insight into their needs, interests, medical and personal history.

A sustained emphasis on maintenance and development of informal support networks as people age is crucial. Some changes experienced by older people with intellectual disability and consequent losses to their informal support networks result from factors in their environment rather than their personal characteristics. For example, characteristics of network members alter, residential moves are imposed because of the decisions or policies of service providers or friendships are simply not recognised and no support is provided to maintain them. Some losses, through death or incapacity are unavoidable but many are not and are open to manipulation. They can be avoided by adopting a social network approach to intervention. For example, if it is not recognised that an older person has friends, little effort will be made by either informal or formal sources to maintain friendships when a residential move or cessation of attendance at a day centre occurs. Attention to social networks and recognising the existence of friends, and that changes often disrupt networks is a first step to avoidance of disruption.

Once these factors are recognised, greater effort may be given to prevention of residential mobility and other changes by tackling their cause. This relies on policy changes occurring, some of which are suggested below. Specialist residential and day services could be encouraged to continue to care for ageing clients by being more flexible and willing to adapt to their changing needs. A greater acknowledgment, among service providers and informal network members, that a realistic option for some middle-aged and older adults with intellectual disability is to remain in the community with appropriate support is necessary. This could be developed and supported, along with efforts to improve access to both aged care and disability services that provide in-home support. More adequate monitoring and quality control of aged care facilities would ensure that poor quality services are not a reason for mobility. Formal supportive services to reduce the strain and cost to informal primary carers may make this role more attractive and able to be fulfilled on a long-term basis.

If residential or other changes are inevitable, greater account must be taken of their effect on informal networks. Plans should be formulated to minimise disruption of networks and facilitate the continuation of relationships.

Older people without a key informal network member had difficulties negotiating their relationship with formal service providers. This group was particularly vulnerable to poor quality, or inappropriate, services although they often had others in their informal, or formal, support networks who undertook some, but not all, of the tasks of a key person. This suggests the importance of attempting to ensure that key people are replaced. Similar to the emphasis placed on supporting elderly parents to plan for transition, support could also be provided to key network members who are elderly, to plan and negotiate a continuing commitment from potential successors. In the absence of key people, consideration should also be given to the manner in which these functions can be more adequately fulfilled by formal services; for example, by ensuring long-term case management, perhaps at a monitoring level, is available to this group.

Alternatively, consideration should be given as to how formal services can foster the development of informal relationships that can replicate some of the key person functions. Utilising the growing aged population as volunteers and peer supports for older people with intellectual disability may be a useful strategy. Community friendship schemes, leisure buddy schemes and citizen advocacy programs for older people may be mechanisms for providing additional sources of informal support for older people with intellectual disability and reducing their reliance on formal services, or assuring the quality of such services.

VULNERABILITY TO UNSTIMULATING AND INAPPROPRIATE LIVING ENVIRONMENTS

Provision of primary care is the dominant function of formal services in the lives of older people with intellectual disability. A greater number rely on aged care facilities for accommodation support since use of disability services and the number of informal primary carers declines with age. For many people, the environments of aged care facilities are considered unstimulating and dependency enhancing. In comparison, others regard them as developmental, stimulating and assisting people to develop increased skills and autonomy. However, in contrast, few criticisms are leveled at the environments of disability accommodation. Rather, it is often credited with increasing the independence and skills of adults who move into it and efforts to move older people out of these services are strongly resisted by key informal network members.

Issues about the environment of accommodation services can be interpreted using the ecological theory of ageing. This theory uses the concept of environmental press and the fit between an individual's competence and the environment (Nahemow, 1988, 1990). It suggests that people adapt to the demands of their environment, which should provide sufficient challenge to test their limits but not overwhelm them. Environmental press should slightly exceed an individual's adaptive level to maximise their ability to learn new tasks and perform familiar ones. If the environmental press is below an individual's adaptational level, boredom, learned helplessness and dependence on others is likely to result. (Environment refers to the larger society, the community, neighbourhood or home, and press refers to the demands for adaptation, response or change made by the environment.)

In theoretical terms, the environment of aged care facilities is considered to have too little environmental press relative to the competence level of some individuals, resulting in a decline in functioning instead of stability or growth. Challenges presented to others by the environment are optimal and result in increased abilities. Thus, the level of environmental press of aged care facilities falls at several points along the spectrum; for some people it is too protective and for others it is optimal. Therefore, drawing general conclusions about the appropriateness of such environments for older people with intellectual disability is not a straightforward task.

In contrast, the environmental press of disability accommodation is generally considered optimal by family members for older people with intellectual disability. Therefore, an important question is, whether particular features of aged care facilities make them more liable than disability accommodation to provide inappropriate levels of environmental press for older people with intellectual disability. Another is whether these problematic environments result from the variable nature and poor quality of some aged care facilities.

Wolfensberger's position is clear. He considers that the characteristics of aged care services make them inappropriate for older people with intellectual disability. He argues that they are 'segregatory, demeaning, image and competency diminishing and quite possibly even socially and physically destructive' (Wolfensberger, 1985, p. 73). His view reflects the societal devaluation of aged people and the poor quality of aged services that may have been prevalent in the US 15 years ago. It cannot be argued that in Australia at the beginning of the 21st century aged services are as poor in quality as Wolfensberger asserted in 1985. Since then efforts have been made to counteract the devaluation of aged people and promote more positive attitudes (Bytheway, 1995; Friedan, 1993; Shenk & Achenbaum, 1994). A major reform of aged care policy has occurred, much of which has focused on service quality. The national Aged Care Reform Strategy that commenced in 1986 resulted in massive changes to policy and reorientation of the aged care system (Gibson, 1998; DHHLGCS, 1993; Howe et al., 1990; Kendig & McCallum, 1990; Sax, 1993). The prevailing ethos of supported accommodation for the aged in the mid 1980s was one of custodial care that aimed to keep patients safe, comfortable, fed, clean and supervised. Clearly, these residential services would have been low on environmental press. However, an approach has now been adopted that aims to provide a level of care that will support quality of life activities and keep the physical, social and mental capacity of each individual at a maximum (Sax, 1993, p. 94). Standards for residential services reflecting these aims have been established and are monitored (DHSH, 1994; Gibson et al., 1993; Ronalds, 1989).

Thus, residential services are likely to pay attention to ensuring optimum levels of environmental press. At the level of objectives and philosophy, little difference exists between the two systems and few indicators suggest that aged care facilities are more liable to result in inappropriate environments for older people with intellectual disability compared with disability services. However, at service delivery level, some characteristics of aged care facilities make their environments liable to result in an environmental press that is too low for older people with intellectual disability.

The focus of aged care policy is the 'old old' and frail aged who have a quite different profile of needs from the bulk of older people with intellectual disability who comprise the 'young old' who sometimes do not even match the aged care system's definition of an older person. The Age Care Reform Strategy shifted the balance of care towards community care and restricted the growth of nursing homes and hostels. These facilities are now carefully targeted towards the frail aged with high support needs. Most residents are in their eighties and have experienced a decline in health, adaptive functioning or cognitive skills. The characteristics of a few older people with intellectual disability are similar to that of typical residents in aged supported accommodation; in particular, the small group of people with Down syndrome who had the early onset of Alzheimer's and had experienced a considerable decline in their functional skills when still in their fifties or early sixties.

However, many older people with intellectual disability who are resident in aged care facilities have quite different characteristics from most other residents. They are younger than other residents, some do not have major health problems and, before admission, had not experienced a substantial decline of adaptive and cognitive skills. Primarily, the reasons they are in aged care facilities are external factors, such as a breakdown of informal care, and not because of their personal characteristics or increased needs for support. Their need for assistance with activities of daily living stems from their intellectual disability rather than a decline in skills due to age. As this study has demonstrated, many still had untapped potential for the development of adaptive skills.

A residential environment, however, reflects the competence level of the bulk of residents. Given the profile of residents in aged care facilities, this may be much lower than the actual or potential competence level of many residents with intellectual disability. Development depends on opportunities and experiences to which the person has access. Expectations have a powerful influence on the provision of opportunities (Cocks, 1998; Nahemow, 1988). The environmental expectations and milieu of aged care facilities, which reflect the needs of most residents, are likely to be insufficiently challenging for those older people with intellectual disability whose characteristics are different from other residents. This tendency is unlikely to occur in age integrated disability services where the developmental principle dominates and the milieu reflects the needs of the bulk of residents, who are likely to be younger and have higher expected competence levels.

This argument has demonstrated why, because of the characteristics of the bulk of other residents, aged care facilities may be more prone to providing insufficient environmental press to 'younger older' people with intellectual disability than disability services. However, this is a liability and not an inevitability and can by mediated by the quality or structure of services.

ENSURING OPTIMAL LIVING ENVIRONMENTS

If a liability to a less than optimal environment is recognised, strategies can be implemented to counteract it. These will inevitably involve collaboration between aged care and disability services. Consultation with specialist staff and training can equip aged care staff to recognise the particular needs of older people with intellectual disability and provide a service that involves challenge and stimulation as well as care and maintenance. Individualised programs could compensate for a mismatch of challenge and potential. Supplementing aged care services with specialist programs could also compensate for unstimulating environments. Clustering a small group of people with similar specialist needs within generic aged services is a strategy adopted in relation to people from non-English-speaking background (DCSH, 1995). This approach could be replicated for people with intellectual disability and would ensure special attention was paid to their needs within a generic service. These strategies all revolve around a recognition of the specific needs of people with intellectual disabilities and ensuring they are visible, and their needs actively addressed within aged care facilities. The strategies also rely on input from the disability services system, and a proactive policy towards the provision of specialist and generic services for older people with intellectual disability.

BROADENING POSSIBILITIES FOR HOUSING AND SUPPORT

Aged care facilities are only one option for providing housing and support to middle-aged and older adults in the post-parental care phase. Many adults with intellectual disability, particularly at the time of transition but in some cases during the period after transition, do not have major health needs and are too young for aged services.

An identified service gap is the lack of housing and support options for middle-aged and younger older people when they make the transition from parental care or later from a replacement informal carer. Innovative models must be developed for this group which should focus on maintaining people within their local community and preserving pre-existing, often lifelong, community support networks. They must also be geared to achieving the flexibility to adapt to increased support needs as people age. Models such as group homes with adaptable designs for people of similar ages, sharing a previous family home with visiting support, the UK 'key ring' model of several one- or two-person apartments within walking distance of each other supported by outreach staff, or the predominantly US model of adult home board may all be worth further investigation for this group. A key characteristic of models must be the separation of place of residence from type of support—the ability to increase or alter the nature of support with activities of daily living without the necessity to change residence. This will provide one safeguard to later life mobility.

Options, other than residential facilities to provide primary care, are seldom considered by key network members seeking to arrange care. Increasingly, the fields of aged care and disability are developing service models that separate accommodation from support and aim to maintain people in their existing home or other community based accommodation (Challis & Davies, 1986; Graham, 1993; Graham et al., 1992; Parmenter, 1994; Taylor et al., 1992). This study demonstrates that some older people with intellectual disability use such models, and disability outreach or generic domiciliary services can provide sufficient support for them to remain at home. Experience of these models is varied, with problems that occur relating to either quality, or the extent and consistency of support that is provided. Litwak's theoretical position and empirical research reflect such problems. He suggests that, because of the many contingencies involved in provision of these services and the instrumental motive of service providers, such services require considerable monitoring to ensure high quality (1985). However, programs such as these should be considered as viable alternatives to supported accommodation, particularly for those people who have access to a private home and frequent contact with a key network member who can oversee provision and monitor quality. However, their consideration depends on the availability of a person in the support network with knowledge about them and an attitude that sees their utilisation as a possibility.

DISABILITY SERVICES POLICY AND PRACTICE

Older people with intellectual disabilities receive services from both the aged care and the disability service system; however, a much larger proportion use aged care than disability services. Very few use services from both systems. Contrary to anecdotal evidence, the process of transition from parental care is largely handled informally and does not result in a deluge of service requests by adults with intellectual disability previously unknown to the disability service system. Only a few additional people contact, register with or use the disability service system during or following transition. Indeed, in later life, fewer people use disability services than do so directly after transition. Inaccessibility, inflexibility, lack of knowledge by relatives or an unwillingness to refer to disability services by professionals are suggested as possible reasons for the decline of specialist service use. Choice is rarely a reason. In contrast, the issue of accessibility to aged services is rarely mentioned. Concerns with these services focuses more on quality and appropriateness than access.

Five trends characterise the disability service system in respect to services provided to middle-aged and older adults in the post-parental care phase of their lives:

- The numbers served by specialist services reduces considerably in the period following transition from parental care.
- As people age, specialist disability services are replaced by aged services.
- The disability system does not retain a monitoring role for previous clients when they cease to use its services.
- Little or no collaboration is evident between the disability and aged care services, either at the systemic level or in relation to particular individuals.
- Informal network members experience considerable disillusionment and conflict with the disability service system.

IMPLICIT POLICIES OF REDIRECTION TO AGED CARE SERVICES WITHOUT SPECIALIST COLLABORATION

Few explicit policies or specific programs relating to older people with intellectual disability exist at either the Federal or state level in Australia. However, the trends noted above demonstrate an implicit policy, at the service delivery level, which redirects older people with intellectual disability towards the aged care system, and away from disability services. This involves the deflection of new requests for services and shifting services for existing older clients to aged care services. Support for the suggestion of an implicit policy is found in the annual reports of the Office of the Public Advocate that document several examples of older people being moved, in their view precipitously and inappropriately, from a disability to an aged care service (Office of the Public Advocate, 1993). In addition, some H&CS documents (H&CS, 1993c) base arguments for use of aged care services on questions of eligibility rather than on choice, or the quality and appropriateness of these services.

This implicit policy represents a thrust towards integration and the use of generic services that is consistent with the principles in both State and Federal legislation and those adopted by international bodies (Victorian Government, 1986a; Commonwealth Government, 1986a; Larnaca Resolution, 1999; United Nations, 1994). However, the manner in which such a policy is put into practice is problematic. In particular, there is an absence of collaboration between the two systems which is essential to ensure that generic services provide effective, appropriate services and achieve quality outcomes for people with intellectual disability. The lack of a continuing role for disability service provision and a collaborative approach results in aged care services not being monitored to ensure their environments match the needs of older people with intellectual disability. Neither is consultation and training for working with people with intellectual disabilities provided to staff of aged care services. The need for such staff support and the nature it should take has been extensively researched overseas and noted as being fundamental to the provision of appropriate services for older adults with intellectual disability (Kultgen & Rominger, 1993).

Another consequence of this implicit policy is the frustration and dissatisfaction suffered by members of informal support networks who often consider that transfers of an older person to an aged care service results in a less appropriate, more restrictive residential environment. In their view, decisions to move a person from disability to aged care services are sometimes based on organisational imperatives and cost instead of evidence that aged care services are better able to meet an individual's needs.

The outcomes of the implicit policy of diverting older people with intellectual disability towards aged care services without complementary disability services or collaboration can be contradictory to established policies and detrimental to the quality of services available to this group. The notions of ageing in place, and community care policies that aim to assist elderly and disabled people to remain in their own homes as long as possible, are not followed. Disability services become a home for some middle-aged people with intellectual disability after their transition from parental care. Yet, few attempts are made to adapt disability services to the changing needs of ageing people with intellectual disability. Specialist residential services rarely draw on the broad array of flexible in-home supports developed by the Home and Community Care program to assist people to remain there.

STRUCTURAL FACTORS OBSTRUCTING COLLABORATION

One explanation of this implicit policy may be the simplistic, or dogmatic, application of ideology and service principles, such as normalisation and integration, that advocate the use of generic services available in the community. This approach neglects other important principles, such as freedom of choice and seeking the least restrictive alternative. Aged care assessments and decisions about place of residence should not just be concerned with eligibility requirements for generic services but offer a choice whether or not to use them, and ensure that all options are considered. The economic and funding environment in which the disability system operates also provides an explanation of the implicit policy. Victoria, Australia, has an enormous unmet demand for specialist disability services, and services operate on very tight budgets. In an environment such as this, and where there is no entitlement to disability services, little incentive exists to adapt to changing needs of older residents if this will result in increased costs. This is accentuated by Federal policies that restrict the availability of HACC services, except at full cost, to people living in state-funded specialist services, despite this being their home. The costs of aged care facilities are borne by the Federal government, and the costs of the bulk of disability services in Victoria are borne by the state government. This funding arrangement reduces further the incentive to adapt services to meet changing needs and provides a strong incentive to direct new requests for service towards the aged care service system rather than disability services. The operation of this implicit policy could be construed as cost shifting and one way of dealing with budget restrictions and waiting lists for specialist services.

DIRECTIONS FOR POLICY AND SERVICE DEVELOPMENT

Responsibility for the provision of services in the post-parental phase does not fall clearly under the responsibility of either the aged care or disability systems. The aged care system can provide appropriate services for some people while for others the disability system will do so, but essentially each system must contribute its services and expertise to ensure the optimal provision of services and reduce the vulnerabilities of adults with intellectual disability in the post-parental phase of their lives. To achieve this, several core policy strands are needed to counter the policy vacuum that currently exists in Australia in respect of this group.

Strategically, one sector must take a leading role to develop and implement policy for older people with intellectual disability. This has been absent to date in most states in Australia. This does not infer that one sector must 'own' older people with intellectual disability, merely that one must take the initiative in tackling cross sectorial boundary issues and ensuring the needs of this group are adequately represented in both service systems.

Several cogent arguments that the disability sector should take the lead role are put forward. First, a major part of needed policy and service development revolves around ensuring that aged care services are accessible, appropriate and sensitive to the needs of older people with intellectual disabilities. Tasks of this nature, for people of all age groups with intellectual disability, clearly fall within the existing parameters of intellectual disability policy (DHS, 1996). Second, even in later life, when differences between those with and without an intellectual disability are narrower than at any other stage of the life course (Edgerton, 1994), intellectual disability will still be a defining factor in many people's lives. The life history of being 'intellectually disabled' will have affected educational and work histories, friendships and family networks, financial resources and security, as well as a person's ability to advocate for themselves. Lifelong intellectual, functional and communicative limitations will underlie any health or disability related impairment acquired in later life. Finally, many minority groups exist within the ageing population, and responsiveness of the aged care system is not only reliant on identification of a group's special needs but also effective external advocacy to ensure they are met. The aged care system on its own cannot ensure responsiveness to all minority groups.

Other strands of policy and service development to effectively meet the needs of older people with intellectual disability can be broadly categorised as:

- systematically bridging gaps with specialist services where neither sector has appropriate services to meet needs
- supporting inclusion and ensuring that older people with lifelong disability are visible within the aged care system

- adapting and resourcing disability services to facilitate ageing in place
- developing partnerships and joint planning aimed at the removal of cross- and intra-sector obstacles.

Policy and service developments rely on cooperation between the two sectors. Mechanisms to achieve this, which have been successful in the US, are mandatory joint planning between sectors and the establishment of research and teaching consortiums on ageing and lifelong disabilities at key universities. These have resulted in strategies such as regional joint planning forums between the sectors, regular conferences to share service development ideas, provision of educational and resource materials, and joint initiatives between sectors to trial and demonstrate innovative programs. Creation of a continuing focus through development of similar mechanisms can be achieved in Australia at both a state and regional level and will serve to maintain a momentum to address the complex issues that confront service systems in responding to older people with lifelong disabilities.

ENSURING EFFECTIVE KEY PERSON SUCCESSION PLANNING

Key person succession plans centre on the nomination of an informal network member to replace one element of the parental role, overseeing of wellbeing. These plans, made by the majority of parents, although often vague and open-ended, are usually successfully implemented. A clear connection exists between functions envisaged for those nominated in plans and those they or those who follow them eventually perform. By planning standards, these plans are not very thorough. Arrangements to ensure wellbeing are largely left up to the nominated key person. However, they provide a mechanism, in the form of a key person, to organise and plan the detailed provision of primary care for the adult with intellectual disability and this person's relationships with formal services. Thus, a critical feature of plans is flexibility and the potential for responsiveness. Other less common types of plans are financial and residential. Most of these plans are also successfully implemented at the time of transition from parental care, though residential plans often go awry in the longer term.

Transitions from parental care are gradual and managed informally without emergency recourse to formal services, and the indications are that parental planning contributes to the smooth nature of the transition process. Those nominated in key person succession plans step in to manage transitions and fill out the details of care that are often missing from parental plans.

Parental planning has two aspects. The first aspect is the facilitation of the transition from parental care and the immediate care needs following this transition. In this regard, key person succession plans have several demonstrated advantages. Someone else, less emotionally involved, can step in when necessary and relieve parents of transition arrangements that they are either unable or unwilling to make or are too difficult for them to face. The conservatism of parents towards their adult child with an intellectual disability is countered by key people with different, and perhaps less protective, attitudes. Adults with intellectual disability are not tied into the particular visions of their parents and earlier times. These plans allow for opportunities to be created and expectations held about their potential that parents have not foreseen.

The second aspect of parental planning is the procurement of security and stability for the adult with intellectual disability in the post-parental phase. Making a blueprint to determine the future of a middle-aged adult with intellectual disability with any certainty, even if a legitimate goal, is indeed a difficult task. Most adults make the transition from parental care in their fifties, with a life expectancy of 20 or 30 years ahead of them. This transition is just one of the many transitions and changes that occurs in their lives after their parents relinquish primary care. Personal characteristics such as health, skills, independence and autonomy develop or decline and factors in their external environment (such as organisational policies, resources and informal network composition and support capability) change. Some of these factors can be foreseen, although their impact cannot be accurately predicted, while others are unexpected. All are difficult to plan for.

Therefore, it is not surprising that many residential plans made by parents are only successful in the short term. No association between residential stability and parental residential plans is found in the years following transition from parental care. The length of time since a person has left parental care is associated with residential mobility, irrespective of parental planning. Attempting to make residential plans for the rest of their adult child's life may not be realistic for parents. It may be argued that nor is it appropriate that they try, particularly in view of the later life development experienced in the post-parental care phase. Such planning poses the risk of locking people into environments that may become inappropriate or are more restrictive than they need to be.

Key person succession plans have demonstrated advantages in respect of the longer-term element of security. They do not have the drawbacks of residential plans and rarely go awry. Those with such a plan, in the long term are effectively provided with security. Through the mechanism of an informal key person, they have a network member with a long-term commitment to their wellbeing. Nominated key people, with their open brief, are flexible and responsive to unexpected occurrences and the myriad changes that occur after transition. Thus, key person succession plans do not achieve stability but do provide the security of an advocate to ensure that the person's interests are foremost in any decisions that have to be made about residential or other aspects of their life.

Planning is not a task only to be undertaken once by parents as normally envisaged in the literature. It is an ongoing task faced by key people as they deal with changes that occur to individuals and their environments. Key person succession plans fail when key people die and are not replaced or, in exceptional cases, where they do not act in the best interest of the older person. However, they have the potential to deal with one of these contingencies. Just as parents had done, many key people plan for their own mortality, nominating a successor to ensure their role continues to be performed.

Most parents neglect to make comprehensive plans for the future but most, in this study, had done an excellent job of planning for the future. Key person succession plans are not inappropriately prescriptive. They ensure older people with intellectual disability have an advocate and a committed other to manage and monitor their care arrangements, which are tasks that formal services cannot replicate effectively.

EFFECTIVE PLANNING AND PREPARATION FOR THE FUTURE

The nature and efficacy of key person succession plans and the continuing role of family and friends in the lives of people with intellectual disability suggests that assisting families to build supportive informal networks with a pivotal informal key person may be more important to longer-term security than more detailed plans and securing of residential placements. This suggests that professionals working with elderly parents should encourage the negotiation of commitments from informal social network members. Parents may need assistance to locate an appropriate key person if one is not immediately obvious within their close family. Here a social network approach will facilitate consideration of all possible candidates for this role. The search for a future key person should not be confined to kin alone, since acceptance of the role of future key person is more likely to be connected to a person's long relationship to the adult with intellectual disability than the nature of their kin relationship.

The discussion of future care preferences with the adult with intellectual disability should be encouraged, and this is often less emotionally difficult between a nominated key person and the adult with intellectual disability than with a parent. Facilitation of such discussion will help to ensure future care arrangements reflect the preferences of the person concerned.

The likelihood of some network members increasing their involvement in the lives of people with intellectual disability after the transition from parental care suggests that education to equip them for their future role may be warranted. Preparation should focus on knowledge of available resources and the nature of the aged care and disability service systems. This could occur in the pre-transition planning stage on an individual or group basis. One mechanism for this could be to target community information sessions, focused on future planning for adult siblings as well as aged carers.

Families with no contact with disability day services do not generally receive any planning assistance, often lack peer support to tackle these issues and have the least knowledge of the disability service system. This is the group who are most likely to benefit from the interventions suggested but may require a more dedicated outreach approach than other groups. As with other strategies suggested in this chapter, a proactive approach from the disability system is required to achieve this.

SUMMARY

This chapter has discussed the central elements of parental planning and the post-parental phase of the lives of people with intellectual disability. The efficacy of parental key person succession plans and the continuing significance of informal support for ageing people with intellectual disability is highlighted. It suggests that the post-parental care phase can include broadened horizons and expanded opportunities, the achievement of which relies on creating a climate of expectation and appropriate responsive policy and services. Without these, older people with intellectual disability are vulnerable to disruption and shrinkage of their informal support networks, control by other, inappropriate environments and disconnection from specialist services, all of which negatively affect their quality of life. Table 10.1 summaries the challenges for human service systems and professionals that arise out of the transition from parental care and during the post-parental care phase in the lives of people with intellectual disability. The chart includes some of the suggested strategies to effectively meet these challenges, optimise the quality of life, and minimise the identified vulnerabilities of older people with intellectual disability.

TABLE 10.1 **Challenges in the post-parental care phase: service and policy strategies**

Challenges	Strategies	
	Practice and service delivery and design	Policy

Broaden horizons and optimise opportunities for adults

Create a climate of positive expectations for ageing people with intellectual disability.	Develop staff knowledge of ageing processes, positive ageing strategies and awareness of ageist stereotypes.	Fill policy vacuum with clearly articulated policy directions and visions for older people with intellectual disabilities.
Recognition of varied options for housing and support in post-parental care phase. Recognition of possibilities for remaining within local community rather than moving to supported accommodation.	Develop innovative housing and support models, for example: • local clusters of supported independent living with central system of support • extend availability of domiciliary support to those who remain in the community • mechanisms to facilitate sharing of accommodation and support for those who remain in private homes in the community • extend support to informal carers who replace parents • development of flexible, adaptable group homes • explore possibilities for adult home board schemes.	

Reduce later life vulnerabilities of adults

Reduce vulnerability to control by others: safeguard interests and ensure independent advocacy.	• Use formal mechanisms to challenge inappropriate decisions by service providers or informal network members. • Ensure avenues of redress exist to challenge service system decisions. • Ensure older people with intellectual disability are visible within aged care system and services are responsive to their needs.	Increase rights to tenancy and services Development of explicit policy for people ageing with intellectual disability. Service decisions policy not resource driven.
Reduce vulnerability to inappropriate living environments, particularly in aged care facilities.	• Maximise environmental press of aged care facilities. • Staff sensitisation and training in needs of people with disabilities.	

TABLE 10.1 (cont'd)

Challenges	Strategies	
	Practice and service delivery and design	Policy
Reduce vulnerability to mobility: foster ageing in place.	• Develop cluster arrangements for people with intellectual disability within aged care facilities. • Provide specialist disability consultation and support to aged care facilities. • Remove structural barriers to ageing in place. • Adaptable physical designs and flexibility of staff support to residents of group homes. • Ability to increase support, reconfigure profile of staff skills and modify the home environment. • Extend use of aged care expertise to residents of disability group homes via use of domiciliary services. • Develop processes to ensure adequate assessments occurs utilising both aged care disability expertise when considering a change of residence, in particular relocation to a nursing home or more restrictive environment. • Improve quality of aged care facilities to reduce movement due to quality issues.	Collaboration between aged care and disability services. Joint responsibility between two sectors. Policies that support strategies and provide resources to enable ageing in place within disability supported accommodation. Remove barriers that obstruct ageing in place. Negotiation of joint responsibility by aged care and disability sectors. Remove incentive to shift people and move costs from one sector to another.
Reduce vulnerability to shrinkage and disruption of informal support networks: preserve and strengthen informal support networks.	• Recognition of friendships, the importance of informal support, the expertise and knowledge of informal support network members. • Recognition of the difficulty formal services have in replicating non-routine and idiosyncratic roles fulfilled by informal support that require ongoing commitment. • Nurturance of and respect for informal network members by services and professionals.	

- Adoption of a network or family centred approach to work with older people with intellectual disabilities.
- Recognition of non-normative role played by distant relatives or unrelated friends.
- Recognition and respect for knowledge of person, possessed by informal network members.
- Proactive attention to identification and maintenance of friendship and community links if residential mobility or change of regular day activity occurs.
- Develop mechanisms to compensate for loss of network members or extend networks (e.g., citizen advocacy, peer companions).
- Assist key network members to plan for their own succession.

Deliver an optimal mix of aged care and disability services that are available and accessible for older people with intellectual disability

- Replace functions of informal support for those who lack key informal network member. For example, by the availability of long-term care management to negotiate with formal services and monitor quality of care for those without a continuing key informal network member.
- Disability service system to adopt a lead role in service and policy development for ageing people with intellectual disability.
- Bridge gaps and develop new services where neither sector has appropriate services. For example, housing and support for those in middle age or the young old, and mechanisms to support integration into activities undertaken by older people in the general community.
- Raise the visibility of older people with disabilities in the aged care system (see above).
- Develop responsive policy and service system for ageing people with intellectual disability
- Remove barriers to ageing in place such as cross- and inter-sector funding and program barriers.
- Develop joint funding, collaborative programs, and cross-sector planning between aged care and disability service systems.

TABLE 10.1 (cont'd)

Challenges	Strategies	
	Practice and service delivery and design	Policy
	• Develop a mechanism to facilitate eligibility assessment for those seeking entry to the disability service system in later life. • Adapt and resource the disability sector to be more flexible and responsive to older people and those who seek first-time access in later life.	

Ensure effective planning for transition from parental care, and longer-term security

- Extend planning focus beyond parents and involve broader family and informal network in planning for the future.
- Provide education and support for siblings and others involved in future plans to understand service systems, and the potential of people ageing with intellectual disability.
- Awareness of the dangers of locking people into long-term housing and support options that reflect limited visions and possibilities for changing needs.
- Recognise the efficacy of key person succession plans that are flexible and responsive over the longer term.
- Recognise the importance of building supportive informal networks as well as more concrete aspects of future planning.
- Proactive support to parents and informal network members to undertake planning.
- Establish peer support groups for siblings, parents, and adults with intellectual disability to enable tackling of issues of the future and the transition from parental care.
- Conduct public education forums and outreach strategies.

Appendixes

APPENDIX 1: STUDY DESIGN

Overview

The study sample of 62 older people with intellectual disability was derived by an intensive area-based case finding strategy. This ensured that the sample included some of the older people with intellectual disability who are 'hidden' in the community, unknown to specialist disability services. Data were collected using in-depth semi-structured interviews with multiple informants. For each older person, the primary informant was a person with whom they had a close, long-term relationship. This was supplemented by data from formal service providers and, in most cases, an interview with the older person themselves. The primary informants were mainly siblings but also included more distant relatives, friends and service providers. Interviews sought information regarding parental planning, the transition from parental care and the present and past informal support networks of the person with intellectual disability.

Data were analysed using quantitative and qualitative methods. Data that were easily quantifiable, such as personal characteristics or types of residence, were entered on a database designed by the author using a program called Dataflex and analysed using descriptive statistics. The qualitative data were analysed using an interpretive approach (Tesch, 1990) and constant comparative method (Huberman & Miles, 1994). A qualitative data analysis program, The Ethnograph, was used to facilitate this latter analysis.

Design issues

The design took into account the complex issues that arise in research about older people with intellectual disability. These include defining what is meant by an 'older' person and 'intellectual disability', operationalising these definitions, determining the size of the population in question, selecting and locating an appropriate sample, and choosing data collection methods that provide an opportunity for the perspective of people with intellectual disability to be heard as well as other informants, and establishing the reliability and validity of data. Ethical concerns such as confidentiality and informed consent were also important in the design. A further issue was the constraints imposed by the resources available to a lone researcher.

Rationale for the case finding strategy

Although the size of the population of older people with intellectual disability is not clear, researchers generally agree that they are more likely to be unknown to the specialist intellectual disability service system than their younger counterparts (Hogg et al., 1988; Jacobson et al., 1985; Seltzer & Krauss, 1987). Reference has been made to the 'hidden' population (Horne, 1989a, 1989b) and estimates of the proportion who are unknown to specialist services range from 60% to 75% (Jacobson et al., 1985).

The Victorian *Intellectually Disabled Persons' Services Act 1986* requires that all people who receive intellectual disability services, either directly from the Department of Human Services (H&CS) or from non-government agencies funded under the Act, be registered with H&CS. As a result, a comprehensive database of people with intellectual disability is maintained by H&CS that includes not only all current service users but also people who are no longer in receipt of services. Because the database existed in a rudimentary form before the 1986 legislation, it includes some people who have been out of touch with the system for as long as 20 years (Ashman et al., 1993; CSV, 1992c). However, the accuracy and comprehensiveness of the database have been criticised by researchers (Bigby, 1990; Neilson, 1987, 1988). For example, the Neilson report (1987) estimated that only 30% of people with intellectual disability in Victoria were registered with H&CS.

The literature indicates that it is the subjects of this study, people who remain at home with families, who are least likely to be known to specialist services. Elderly parents caring for an adult with intellectual disability at home have been found to use few services (Heller & Factor, 1991; Janicki et al., 1999). Additionally, anecdotal evidence suggests that for many middle-aged people with intellectual disability, their first contact with disability services is at the time of the death or illness of their parents.

Methodological imperatives

Most studies of older people with intellectual disability have been based on samples of those who are in touch with disability services or who are volunteers, and such designs have been criticised (Duffy et al., 1991; Hogg, 1990; Seltzer et al., 1991). Duffy et al. (1991), in a lengthy discussion of methodology, suggest that commonly no systematic sampling procedure is used and samples of convenience, those in touch with disability services, are used. In their view, such samples are biased against people with a milder intellectual disability, as they are less likely to be in touch with services. Hogg (1990, p. 462) writes:

> A critical concern in such studies in the community is the fact that we know many people with mental handicap are unknown to service providers. Purely administratively based surveys, therefore, inevitably involve an underestimate of numbers and are likely in unspecified ways to result in somewhat distorted data.

Compelling evidence suggests that only a proportion of older people with intellectual disability is known to disability services and strong methodological reasons exist for using a broader sample than one based on people known to such services. This study used a case finding strategy to address these methodological issues and ensure that the sample of older people with intellectual disability was drawn from a broader frame than those known to disability services.

Criteria used to define the sample frame

The sample frame comprised older people with intellectual disability who had lived at home until mid-life. An older person is defined as 'a person aged 55 years or over'. There is no consistent definition of an older person with intellectual disability but, as noted in chapter 4, generally a lower age than for the broader community is used. The definition used is consistent with that used by the Australian National Survey of Older People with Intellectual Disability (1993) and should facilitate comparisons with it and help to establish and maintain a consistent definition for Australian studies.

Intellectual disability is defined as having 'a significant sub-average general intellectual functioning existing concurrently with deficits in adaptive behaviour and manifested during the developmental period' (Victorian Government, 1986a, 1 (3)). This is the definition used in legislation and generally accepted in Victoria, Australia at the time the study was conducted.

Living with parents till mid-life was defined as meaning 'remaining in the family home with at least one parent until at least the age of 40 years'. The timing, particularly the life course stage, that the person with intellectual disability, their parents and siblings are at when the transition is made from parental to non-parental care affects the nature of the transition, the processes involved, informal support available and the impact for the person with intellectual disability. Remaining at home until the age of 40 years was used, since this is commonly perceived as middle age. Also, a person having a life span of 80 years or more will have lived with their parents for half their lives or more.

Case finding strategy

The design of this strategy drew on the studies conducted by Hand and Reid (1989) in New Zealand and Horne (1989a) in the UK, which successfully located older people with intellectual disability unknown to specialist services. Horne's study, conducted in a metropolitan area, showed that front line personnel in generic aged services were the most promising group for identifying older people with intellectual disability.

The current study used non-government disability organisations to identify older people already in touch with services and, similar to Horne's methodology, used front line personnel in a range of aged services to identify older people with intellectual disability unknown to disability services. It was conducted in 12 municipalities of metropolitan Melbourne that, at the time of the study, formed two H&CS administrative regions. These two regions had a total population of 791 134 people and an aged distribution that reflected the state population (ABS, 1995). It was confined to the metropolitan area since evidence suggests that geographic location, particularly the rural–metropolitan distinction, is an important factor affecting the nature of older people's informal support networks (Wenger, 1991; Ashman et al., 1990). The scale of this study was too small to allow for two subsamples of rural and metropolitan residents to be drawn and compared. Also, by restricting the study to a specific geographic area, local knowledge and networks could be utilised.

Case finding procedure

The process had three stages. First, building up a statistical picture and identifying as many as possible of the older people with intellectual disability living in the two regions. Second, establishing from this the sample frame of people who had remained at home until mid-life. Third, compiling the sample, which involved seeking permission to contact the older people, inviting their participation in the study and verifying the opinion of the identifier that sample members had intellectual disability.

Cooperation was sought from personnel of aged services and disability services to identify older people with intellectual disability living in the community. Community services directories, listings of supported accommodation from aged care assessment teams and discussions with local government aged services coordinators were used to identify generic aged services. In addition, non-government residential services for people with intellectual disability and disability day services, including vocational services and adult training and support services, were approached. These services were identified by using a directory of disability organisations, community service manuals and discussions with personnel from peak disability organisations. A total of 337 organisations fitted these categories and were contacted by a letter which was followed by a phone call asking if anyone in their service was aged 55 years or over with intellectual disability.

Raw data on the number of older clients registered with H&CS in the municipalities, which included their type of residence, were obtained and analysed. These data did not identify individuals but provided a background against which the results of the case findings could be compared.

When agency personnel identified older people with intellectual disability, non-identifying information was sought regarding basic socio-demographics, registration status with H&CS and the age at which they had left parental care. For people who had lived with parents until mid-life, the service provider who had identified them was asked to seek permission for the author to make contact to explain the study and invite their participation.

In practice, this last stage often involved a close family member or friend who was regarded as the older person's guardian (though most had no legal status) being contacted by the service provider. Service providers felt that it was from these people that the researcher should obtain permission for the involvement of the older person in the study rather than directly from the older people. This raised some ethical issues considered in a later section of this appendix.

The case finding process involved the identification of older people with intellectual disability by service providers who often had little experience of intellectual disability. Therefore, it was important to ensure that information was provided to assist them in this task and to include a mechanism for validating their opinion that a person had intellectual disability. This study used an amended version of an explanatory definition developed by Horne to explain intellectual disability to service providers. In addition, phone contact following a formal letter provided an opportunity to explain intellectual disability further and ensure that the definition was understood. Several methods were used to confirm the opinion of informants that the person had intellectual disability. This validation process was comprehensive for people who formed the study sample but not as thorough for people identified through the case finding process who did not meet the sample criteria.

As has been discussed, those people who use state-funded specialist services have, as a prerequisite, been assessed as having intellectual disability and must be registered with H&CS. For these people, the use of specialist services is an indicator that they have been previously assessed as having intellectual disability and this was accepted as validation of their status. For people who did not use disability services, informants were asked about registration status with H&CS and if the older person agreed to participate in the study, their status was checked with H&CS. Similarly, registration was taken as validation of their intellectual disability. The assumption was made that all people identified who were living, or had previously lived, in state intellectual disability training centres were registered with H&CS.

In addition, a family member or person well known to the person was asked to confirm that in their view the person had intellectual disability in the case of people not currently using or previously registered with the disability service system. Attempts were made to substantiate this opinion by asking for indicators from the person's developmental years. Additionally, after the older person had agreed to participate in the study, access was sometimes provided to files held by generic services, and these frequently included medical records or referrals that noted the person's intellectual disability.

Thus, for those who participated in the study, at least two sources identified a person as having intellectual disability—the original identifier and a family member or H&CS. In some cases, agency records provided further verification.

Results of the case finding and the sample composition

Two hundred and fifteen older people with intellectual disability were identified by staff from a range of generic and specialist agencies. Although this result endorsed reliance on service providers as the main method of case finding, it meant that the sample was essentially a service population, although not just a disability service population.

Of the 215 older people with intellectual disability identified, 164 (76%) were known to disability services and 51 (24%) were not. Eighty-four (39%) people had lived at home until mid-life and 131 people (61%) had left home earlier. Many of these had spent much of their lives in institutions. Significantly, people who had remained at home with parents until the age of 40 were more likely to be out of touch with H&CS than those who left home earlier.

As a result of the case finding strategy, data was gained about the population of older people with intellectual disability in these two regions that was not directly relevant to the aims of this study. These findings are available in Bigby (1995). The case finding strategy was successful in its main purpose of identifying a sample frame for the study. Eighty-four people met the sample criteria and 65 of these agreed to participate in the study. Three, however, were still living at home with parents and, as they had not yet made the transition from parental care and were too small a group to use for comparative purposes, they were not included. Thus, the study sample comprised 62 older people with intellectual disability who had lived with their parents until mid-life but had since left parental care. Chapter 4 presents a detailed description of their characteristics.

Data collection

To address the questions this study sought to explore, two types of data were collected. First, biographical details and 'social facts' such as how often people had moved since they had left parental care, where they had lived, the types of services they had used, how many family members they had and their frequency of contact. Such details and social facts are easily quantifiable but may not always be known, neatly ordered or easily recalled by informants. Second, detailed descriptions of social processes, relationships, experiences, and the interpretations and meanings of these for people involved was collected. For example, social processes included the transition from parental care, the nature of relationships between older people and others in their social world and the kinds of support they received from them.

In-depth semi-structured interviews conducted by the author, a skilled interviewer, were used to collect both types of data. This method allowed respondents to raise issues not included in the interview schedule. It provided the opportunity for informants to use and describe their own unique ways of defining their social worlds and recognised that the phenomena under study, are largely uncharted and thus not easily reduced to pre-structured dimensions or variables.

The data collection process

An important issue, once the sample had been identified, was who should be the major informants. A number of studies of older adults with intellectual disability, particularly where people do not live with family members, have relied on formal service providers as informants (Hand & Reid, 1989; Krauss & Seltzer, 1986; Maaskant & Haveman, 1990; Moss et al., 1989). Sometimes service providers are used in conjunction with the person with intellectual disability (Ashman et al., 1993; Krauss & Erickson, 1988).

A drawback to this approach, particularly for the current study, is that service providers often have a poor knowledge about the background of the older person with intellectual disability (Ashman et al., 1993; Green &

Wunsch, 1994; H&CS, 1995a; Horne, 1989a). Many studies, mainly of middle-aged and older adults with intellectual disability living with relatives, rely on the primary caregiver, usually a parent or sibling, to act as informant (Grant, 1988; Prosser, 1989; Seltzer & Krauss, 1989; Seltzer & Krauss, 1994). Although this approach means the informant is likely to have a good knowledge of the person's background, it has been criticised for relying on the perspective of one informant (Seltzer et al., 1991).

Some research has directly involved older people with intellectual disability as informants (Edgerton & Gaston, 1991; Erickson et al., 1989; Grant et al., 1995; Urlings, 1992). This approach recognises that people with intellectual disability are a valid source of information and can speak for themselves (Atkinson 1988; Erickson et al., 1989).

It is suggested that the most effective designs for research about people with intellectual disability use a combination of data collection strategies to allow for checking and cross-referencing of data (Atkinson, 1988; Seltzer, 1983; Sigelman et al., 1982; Wyngaarden, 1981). This approach is particularly important where biographical information is sought, since people with intellectual disability often have difficulty providing details about their past, often confusing sequences of events (Flynn, 1986). The nature of the data reinforced the importance of having informants who knew the background of the older person.

Accordingly, the study was designed to have three informants for each member of the sample: a person with whom they had a close long-term relationship, the older person her or himself, and a service provider. In practice, however, it was not always possible to achieve this aim.

For each older person, an informant was sought with whom they had a close long-term relationship. The nature of the relationship was standardised as 'a close long-term one', but the formal, or kin, relationship was not standardised. The age of the sample members and possible variation in the constellation of their social world meant that if the formal relationship with informants had been predetermined, and/or relational consistency obtained, inevitably some sample members would not have had the specified relationship or some informants may not have been well acquainted with the older person. Adopting a more flexible approach allowed the uniqueness of each person's family constellation and social relationships to be recognised and an emphasis was placed on collecting as much data as possible from the most appropriate person.

It had been intended to ask the person with intellectual disability to nominate the person who should act as this informant but mostly the person 'emerged' from the research process. Usually they were the people who, as described previously, had been contacted by the service provider during the case finding process to seek permission for the involvement of the older person in the study.

Several older people had a number of people with whom they had close long-term relationships. These were often siblings and siblings-in-law and, in such cases, they decided who would act as informant. In three instances, people chose to be interviewed jointly. Where this occurred, the person with the closest kin relationship was recorded as the informant. For 13 people, in the absence of close family or friends or in accordance with their wishes, a service provider acted as the informant in this category. These service providers, who were not always the original identifiers of the person, usually had a long-term relationship with the older person and many had known their parents.

The formal relationships of informants to the sample members were 30 siblings, eight friends, five nieces, three cousins, one aunt, two parents and thirteen service providers. Interviews were conducted in either service agencies or the informant's private home and lasted from between one and four hours. A detailed interview schedule was designed and used as a prompt for the interviewer. Formal documents such as wills, trusts, letters, service plans and case files were often shown to the interviewer during interviews.

Although the importance of involving people with intellectual disability in the research processes is recognised, as Atkinson suggests, the challenge remains for researchers to involve individuals effectively (1988). A small literature has addressed the most appropriate methods to involve people with an intellectual disability in the research process. A review of this literature indicates that people with intellectual disabilities who have mild to moderate disability are responsive in interview situations and, if attention is paid to the appropriate format of questions and structure of interviews, they can provide reliable, valid information. However, there can be little doubt that a single interview with an unknown interviewer only provides a very limited opportunity for the person with intellectual disability to give an account of their feelings, experiences, or insight into their personal world. As the work of Edgerton and his colleagues demonstrates, such opportunities and insights often only occur in the context of a long-term relationship between the researcher and the subject, and many hours of discussion and observation (Edgerton, 1994).

With an awareness of the limitations, it was decided, if at all feasible, to interview each person with intellectual disability to ensure they had some voice in the research and that their perspective on relationships and processes was included. Fifty-one of the 62 older people with intellectual disability were interviewed. One person chose not to be interviewed and the researcher was advised by other informants that an interview with the other ten would not be possible. This was usually because, in their view, the person's communication or cognitive skills were too impaired. Usually, where a person was not interviewed, the researcher visited and sat a while with them. An interview schedule was designed but, again, this was used as a guide only. The order and wording of questions were altered to fit people's differing communication skills. Many people had family photos, albums and other keepsakes that they talked about and that sometimes acted as the focus for the interview. The interviews lasted between ten minutes and an hour and were very variable. For ten people they were very limited, with few topics being covered and little information obtained. Most people, with varying degrees of clarity and detail, covered all the topics, recalled past events and discussed relationships and their feelings. A few people described their experiences and current life situation with ease and at considerable length. As the literature suggests, a common feature was people's difficulty in recalling sequences of events, dates, elapsed periods of time and details of services attended.

Service providers who originally identified the older person with intellectual disability during the case finding process were the third type of informant. Their inclusion was expedient because, as part of the case finding process, they had already provided information about people they had identified. Their inclusion provided another source of data, particularly about the current situation and service use of sample members.

All interviews with informants were conducted by the researcher, an experienced social worker in the field of intellectual disability. They were conducted in a setting nominated by the informant, usually a residential or day service or their private home. Notes were taken during the interviews, and except for interviews with some service providers, interviews were audiotaped.

Data management and analysis

A mixture of quantitative and qualitative methods of data management and analysis was undertaken which relied on careful description and inductive analysis (Silverman, 1993; Taylor & Bogdan, 1984). Extensive notes were written up directly after each interview using a format with broad headings. Audiotapes were listened to and further notes compiled using the same headings. A series of notebooks was kept which recorded comments and reflections about the data.

Examination of notes and comparison of data supplied by different informants about a person enabled a set of biographical details and social facts to be pieced together for each sample member. These details were entered on a relational database designed using a computer program called Dataflex. Using this database, descriptive and some basic statistical techniques were used to analyse and describe these data.

The method of data collection eased the development of ideas and analytical categories from the data rather than from preconceived and pre-structured operational definitions. The qualitative data were analysed using a method broadly termed the constant comparative method (Huberman & Miles, 1994). The aim of qualitative analysis is to identify patterns and themes from the data and generate categories of things, persons or events, and look for explanations and linkages between them. This involves a process of questioning and reflection on the data. It is difficult, complex, creative and ambiguous (Marshall & Rossman, 1989), and is 'a creative process that requires making carefully considered judgments about what is really significant and meaningful in the data' (Patton, 1980, p. 313).

The data analysis involved three sub-processes comprising data reduction, data display and conclusion drawing or verification (Huberman & Miles, 1994). These were not carried out, however, in a purely linear fashion. A qualitative data analysis computer program, The Ethnograph, characterised as a store and retrieve program (Richards & Richards, 1994), facilitated the data reduction. The data were read and re-read, during which themes and categories were identified and coded using the computer program. This process often involved several layers of coding, moving to different conceptual levels. Hypotheses and ideas about patterns in the data developed from this process that were then further developed and verified by comparison across data records. The computer program facilitated this process by the extraction of coded segments from each data record and the compilation of similarly coded segments from every record.

The data display involved the assembly of condensed sets of data such as diagrams, matrices and summaries that provided the basis for thinking about meaning and drawing conclusions. This process mainly involved writing analytical summaries that led to further development of explanation and interpretation of the data. As suggested by Silverman (1993), it also involved counting and presenting the occurrence of different but related categories in tables. Data display merged with the process of drawing conclusions and verification that continued with the process of writing up and presenting the findings.

Ethical considerations

The issue of consent is complex for people with intellectual disability who may have difficulties understanding the purpose of research and, therefore, in giving their informed consent. Current legislation and service ideologies, however, clearly recognise the rights of people with intellectual disability to exercise maximum choice and control over their lives. A least restrictive approach is emphasised which recognises the importance of well developed informal arrangements that support their decision-making (Creyke, 1995). Following this principle, the research design aimed to seek consent directly from each older person with intellectual disability and, if this was not feasible, from others with whom they had a close relationship. This was difficult to achieve in practice because the process of obtaining consent relied on the cooperation of others. First, when a person was identified by the case finding strategy as meeting the sample criteria, their consent had to be sought for the researcher to contact them to explain the study. Second, their consent to participate in the study then had to be obtained.

Reliance for the first stage rested with personnel who originally identified the person. Some of these people, particularly those from generic aged services, imposed their own perspectives on this process. Rather than directly seeking consent from the older person, they sought it from a family member or close friend whom they regarded as the older person's guardian. Consequently, it was sometimes this person who consented to participate in the study on behalf of the older person.

Despite this de facto consent by others, every effort was made to ensure that people with intellectual disability fully understood what was being asked, and consented themselves. An outline of the study and its purpose was given, or read, to all participants when their agreement to participate was sought. It was made clear that participants were under no obligation to participate, free to withdraw at any time and that the research was not connected in any way with the provision or receipt of services.

Potential risks for participants

The subject matter of interviews often related to an informant's personal relationships and life history. For people with intellectual disability, it included the recall and discussion of emotional events such as the death of parents and leaving a lifelong home. Consequently, the interviews may have evoked unresolved feelings and memories of catastrophic lifestyle disruptions that were distressing. Interviews were structured to minimise any distress and sensitive issues were raised towards the end when the people were more likely to be at ease with the interviewer.

Confidentiality

All information collected about individuals during the study was treated as confidential and kept securely. Neither the individuals nor the regions and municipalities in which the study was conducted were identified in this or other reports. To ensure anonymity, pseudonyms have been used for the names of all participants, their family members and services.

Strengths and limitations

Unlike quantitative methods, few standard tests of a structural nature can be applied to qualitative research. The applicability of concepts such as validity and reliability to this kind of research has been questioned by some authors (for discussions see Silverman, 1993) and replaced by notions of plausibility and credibility.

However conceptualised, the rigour of the research must be demonstrated. One way in which this has been done is to explicate clearly and show the integrity of the processes of the research, the design, data collection and analysis procedures. This study design also addressed some of the specific issues raised by researchers in this field as discussed above. Particularly, the inclusion of a case finding strategy ensured a broader and more representative sample of older people with intellectual disability than has been the case for many studies.

Collection of data, from two or more sources for each member of the sample provided the opportunity to cross check and validate data relating to biographical details and social facts. Selection of informants was designed to ensure they had sufficient knowledge of the older person's life history and to avoid relational biases. Although, the views and recollections of one primary informant were usually complemented by other sources, the design attempted to avoid total reliance on only one 'reporter' (Seltzer et al., 1991). It also provided the opportunity to compare different perceptions of a particular relationship. Within the confines of resources available and with an awareness of the limitations, the perspectives of people with intellectual disability were included. This avoided total reliance on secondary informants.

Although the study was primarily exploratory, it was theoretically driven. It drew on a range of theoretical concepts from the fields of gerontology, sociology, intellectual disability, social policy and social work.

In the analysis of the data, counting and presentation of simple tabulations was used. This provides a valuable means of validating impressions obtained from the data, providing a flavour of the data as a whole and avoiding reliance only on the selected case examples or fragments of dialogue (Silverman, 1993). Also, deviant cases have been analysed and, in some instances, documented.

The research was undertaken by a lone researcher, not a team. Thus, opportunities for reliability to be demonstrated by comparing analysis of data by several researchers was not possible. The limitations of the design of the study relate particularly to its scale and restraints imposed by available resources.

The data collected related to past events and relationships, as well as current ones. This design relied on the ability of informants to recall past events in their lives accurately. Because of this, the data may be incomplete and subject to distortion by the processes of time and memory. It also means that some social processes described are situated and influenced by different historic times. For example, sample members made the transition from parental care from one to 46 years ago. The age span of the sample was wide. The oldest and youngest members were separated by 32 years, resulting in the inclusion of not one, but several cohorts of older people.

A more effective study design to address the first two research questions would have been a longitudinal approach. Events could then have been observed and data collected from a narrower time span, closer in time to their occurrence. However, such an approach would require a high level of resources over an extensive and unpredictable period.

As with any research concerning older people, this study is limited by the cohort effect. Each generation or cohort is exposed to different and unique environmental and social influences that differentiate them from other cohorts and restricts the generalisation of findings to other cohorts and the predictive value of findings. Another limiting factor is the confounding effects of age and generational effects, which makes it difficult to determine whether findings are a result of the particular generational experiences or age per se.

The sample size was small and its representativeness hard to predict, since the number of older people with intellectual disability who have remained at home until at least the age of 40 years is unknown. Previous studies have not focused on this group, meaning comparative results are not available. The study was drawn exclusively from the metropolitan area which restricts the generalisation of findings thereto.

Some bias may have resulted because people with more severe disability, due to health factors, were not able to speak for themselves. The sample was not stratified by age or level of disability. Thus, people with a more severe disability and the very old, who are a small minority, may be under-represented. Neither is the sample stratified by diagnostic category. Accordingly, the question of differences between diagnostic groups is only dealt with broadly.

The strength of the study's design was that instead of collecting superficial information about a large number of people, a detailed data set was compiled about a relatively small number of individuals who were fairly representative of a group of people whose biographies and relationships with formal and informal sources of support had not been investigated previously.

APPENDIX 2: GLOSSARY

ACAT	Aged care assessment team. Multi-disciplinary team responsible for assessment of older people and determination of eligibility for nursing homes and aged persons' hostels.
ATSS	Adult training and support service. Specialist day centres for adults with intellectual disability, funded by H&CS and auspiced by community-based committees of management. Many were established by parent groups in the 1950s and later, with little government support or funding until the 1980s. Committees which manage these services often run other specialist services such as residential hostels.
CRU	Community residential unit. Group home for four to six people with intellectual disability, situated in the community. Funded by H&CS and consumer fees, and managed directly by H&CS or by non-government organisations.
CSV	Community Services Victoria. Predecessor to H&CS as the state government department responsible for administration of the *Intellectually Disabled Persons' Services Act 1986*.
GAB	Guardianship and Administration Board. Responsible for the appointment of guardian and administrators under the *Guardianship and Administration Board Act 1986*. What about all the Departments e.g. DCS&H, DHM&CS, etc
GSP	General service plan. All people who receive specialist services under the *Intellectually Disabled Persons' Services Act* are required to have a GSP which must be reviewed at least every five years. Defined in the Act as 'a comprehensive plan prepared for an eligible person which specifies the areas of major life activity in which support is required and the strategies to be implemented to provide that support' (*IDPS Act 1986*, pt. 1, s. 3)
HACC	Home and Community Care Program. A central plank of aged care policy which aims to assist

	people to remain in their own home. Targeted at the frail aged and younger people with disabilities.
H&CS	Health and Community Services. Victorian government department responsible for the a range of human services, including health, aged care and disability services. Responsible for the direct provision, administration and funding of disability services under the *Intellectually Disabled Persons' Services Act*. Each of the 9 state regions has a disability client services team.
Disability hostel	Congregate care setting for between five and 30 adults with intellectual disability.
IPP	Individual program plan. Defined in the *Intellectually Disabled Persons' Services Act* as 'a plan prepared for an eligible person which specifies activities and methods to achieve goals in areas identified in the general services plan'. Such a plan must be prepared for all people using services funded under the Act.
SAH/SRS	special accommodation houses, also known as supported residential services. Provide supported accommodation in the community for older people and younger people with disabilities. Facilities vary in size and quality. They do not receive government subsidy but are regulated by government and are run as for-profit businesses. Fees may exceed aged or invalid pension levels.

APPENDIX 3: ADDITIONAL TABLES

TABLE A.1 **Detailed summary of residential moves**

Living situation moved from	Home with relative	Home alone	Home, friend	Aged hostel	Nursing home	Special accommodation	Disability hostel	Disability respite	Group home	Hospital respite	Psychiatric hospital	Total
Parental home	9	1		9	1	3	6	1	4			34
Home with relative	10	1		4	1	8	4			1		29
Home alone	1			4		3						8
Home, friend			2									2
Aged persons' hostel					2							2
Special accommodation	1			5	2	3		1				12
Nursing home					3							3
Disability hostel					2	2			2			6
Disability respite					1				1			2
Group home	1		1	1				1	2	1	1	8
Hospital respite					2							2
Psychiatric hospital						1						1
Total	21	3	3	23	14	20	10	3	9	2	1	109

TABLE A.2 **Detailed summary of first residential moves**

Living situation moved from	Living situation moved to											
	Home with relative	Home alone	Home, friend	Aged hostel	Nursing home	Special accommodation	Disability hostel	Disability respite	Community residential unit	Hospital respite	Psychiatric hospital	Total
Parental home	10	1		8	1	3	6	1	4			34
Home with relative	3			1	1	7				1		13
Home alone		1		2		3						6
Home, friend												
Aged persons' hostel												
Special accommodation												
Nursing home												
Disability hostel												
Disability respite												
Community residential unit												
Hospital respite												
Psychiatric hospital												
Total	13	2		11	2	13	6	1	4	1	1	53

TABLE A.3 **Detailed summary of second residential moves**

Living situation moved from	Living situation moved to										
	Home with relative	Home alone	Home, friend	Aged hostel	Nursing home	Special accommodation	Disability hostel	Disability respite	Community residential unit	Hospital respite	Psychiatric hospital	Total
Parental home	5											34
Home with relative		1		1		2	1					10
Home alone			1									1
Home, friend												
Aged persons' hostel				1								1
Special accommodation	1		2	1	3							7
Nursing home				1								1
Disability hostel			2	2	2			1				5
Disability respite								1				1
Community residential unit	1							1	1	1		4
Hospital respite			1									1
Psychiatric hospital												
Total	6	1	3	7	5	2	1	3	1	1		31

TABLE A.4 **Detailed summary of third residential moves**

Living situation moved from	Living situation moved to										
	Home with relative	Home alone	Home, friend	Aged hostel	Nursing home	Special accommodation	Disability hostel	Disability respite	Community residential unit	Hospital respite	Psychiatric hospital	Total
Parental home												
Home with relative	1			2					1			4
Home alone				1								1
Home, friend												
Aged persons' hostel												
Special accommodation				3		1						4
Nursing home					1							1
Disability hostel									1			1
Disability respite												
Community residential unit		1										1
Hospital respite										1		1
Psychiatric hospital						1						1
Total	1	1		6	1	2		1	2	1		14

TABLE A.5 **Detailed summary of fourth residential moves**

Living situation moved from	Living situation moved to										
	Home with relative	Home alone	Home, friend	Aged hostel	Nursing home	Special accommodation	Disability hostel	Disability respite	Community residential unit	Hospital respite	Psychiatric hospital	Total
Parental home												
Home with relative	1											1
Home alone												
Home, friend		1										1
Aged persons' hostel												
Special accommodation			1									1
Nursing home												
Disability hostel			1									1
Disability respite												
Community residential unit		1							1			2
Hospital respite												
Psychiatric hospital												
Total	1	2	2						1			6

TABLE A.6 **Detailed summary of fifth residential moves**

Living situation moved from	Home with relative	Home alone	Home, friend	Aged hostel	Nursing home	Special accommodation	Disability hostel	Disability respite	Community residential unit	Hospital respite	Psychiatric hospital	Total
Parental home												
Home with relative				1								1
Home alone												
Home, friend			1									1
Aged persons' hostel												
Special accommodation												
Nursing home					1							1
Disability hostel												
Disability respite												
Community residential unit				1								1
Hospital respite												
Psychiatric hospital												
Total		1	2	2	1							4

TABLE A.7 **Detailed summary of sixth residential moves**

Living situation moved from	Home with relative	Home alone	Home, friend	Aged hostel	Nursing home	Special accommodation	Disability hostel	Disability respite	Community residential unit	Hospital respite	Psychiatric hospital	Total
Parental home												
Home with relative												
Home alone												
Home, friend												
Aged persons' hostel					1							1
Special accommodation												
Nursing home												
Disability hostel												
Disability respite												
Community residential unit												
Hospital respite												
Psychiatric hospital												
Total					1							1

TABLE A.8 **Characteristics of informal support networks**

Type of members	Frequency of contact by network members					
	Monthly or more		Twice a year, less than monthly		Minimum of twice a year	
	average	range	average	range	average	range
Family	3	0–7	2	0–9	4	0–16
Friends	1	0–5	1	0–4	2	0–5
Total	4	0–12	2	0–9	6	0–20

Note: Friends included neighbours and church connections.

TABLE A.9 **Network characteristics and living situation**

Living situation	Network characteristic			
	Average size	Average no. friends	Average no. family	Average % family
Aged persons' hostel	5	2	3	59%
Supported residential service	5	2	2	65%
Nursing home	6	0	6	99%
Specialist disability accommodation	9	2	7	55%
Home with relatives	8	1	8	95%
Home alone or with friend	7	4	3	33%

Note: Figures have been rounded. Neighbours are included with friends.

Bibliography

Adlin, M. (1993). Health care issues. In E. Sutton, A. Factor, B. Hawkins, T. Heller & G. Seltzer (eds), *Older adults with developmental disabilities: Optimising choice and change* (pp. 49–60). Baltimore: Brookes.

American Association on Mental Retardation (1998). *News and notes. Special issue on older carers.* Washington: Author.

Anderson, D. (1989). Healthy and institutionalised: Health and related conditions among older persons with developmental disabilities. *Journal of Applied Gerontology*, 8, 228–241.

Anderson, D., Lakin, K., Hill, B. & Chen, T. (1992). Social integration of older persons with mental retardation in residential facilities. *American Journal on Mental Retardation*, 96, 488–501.

Antonucci, T. & Akiyama, H. (1987). Social networks in adult life and a preliminary examination of the convoy model. *Journal of Gerontology*, 42, 519–527.

Ashman, A., Hulme, P. & Suttie, J. (1990). The life circumstances of aged people with an intellectual disability. *Australia and New Zealand Journal of Developmental Disabilities*, 16, 335–347.

Ashman, A., Suttie, J. & Bramley, J. (1993). *Older Australians with an intellectual disability.* (A Report to the Department of Health, Housing and Community Services, Research and Development Grants Committee). Queensland. Fred and Eleanor Schonnell Special Education Research Centre, The University of Queensland.

Ashman, A., Suttie, J., & Bramley, J. (1996). The health and medical status of older people with an intellectual disability in Australia. *Journal of Applied Gerontology*, 15, 57–72.

Atkinson, D. (1988). Research interviews with people with mental handicaps. *Mental Handicap Research*, 1, 75–90.

Australian Bureau of Statistics. (1995). *Focus on families. Caring in families: Support for persons who are older or have disabilities* (cat. no. 4423.0). Canberra: Australian Government Publishing Service.

Australian Institute of Health and Welfare, (1997). *Australia's welfare, 1997: Services and assistance.* Canberra: Author.

Baker, B., Seltzer, G. & Seltzer, M. (1977). *As close as possible: Community residences for retarded adults.* Boston: Little, Brown & Co.

Balandin, S. & Morgan, J. (1997). Adults with cerebral palsy: What's happening? *Journal of Intellectual and Developmental Disability*, 22(2), 109–124.

Baldock, J. & Evers, A. (1991). Innovations and care of the elderly: The frontline of change for social welfare services. *Ageing International*, June, 8–21.

Beange, H., McElduff, A. & Baker, W. (1995). Medical disorders in adults with intellectual disability: A population study. *American Journal on Mental Retardation*, 99, 595–604.

Beange, H. & Taplin, J. (1996). Prevalence of intellectual disability in northern Sydney adults. *Journal of Intellectual Disability Research*, 40(3), 191–197.

Bear, M. (1990). Social network characteristics and the duration of primary relationships after entering institutional long term care. *Journal of Gerontology*, 45, S156–162.

Biegel, D. (1985). The application of network theory and research to the field of aging. In W. Sauer & T. Coward (eds), *Social support networks and care of the elderly* (pp. 251–273). New York: Springer

Bigby, C. (1990). *The needs of older people with intellectual disability for day activity and leisure services*. Unpublished Master of Social Work thesis, University of Melbourne, Melbourne.

Bigby, C. (1992). Access and linkage: Two critical issues for older people with intellectual disability in utilising day activity and leisure services. *Australia and New Zealand Journal of Developmental Disabilities*, 18, 95–108.

Bigby, C. (1994). A demographic analysis of older people with intellectual disability registered with Community Services Victoria. *Australia and New Zealand Journal of Developmental Disabilities*, 19, 1–10.

Bigby, C. (1995). Is there a hidden group of older people with intellectual disability and from whom are they hidden? Lessons from a recent case-finding study. *Australia and New Zealand Journal of Developmental Disabilities*, 20, 15–24.

Bigby, C. (1997). Later life for adults with intellectual disability: A time of opportunity and vulnerability. *Journal of Intellectual and Developmental Disability*, 22(2), 97–108.

Biklen, J. & Moseley, C. (1988). 'Are you retarded? No I'm a Catholic'. Qualitative methods in the study of people with severe handicaps. *Journal of the Association for Persons with Severe Handicaps*, 13, 155–162.

Blacher, J. (1993). Siblings and out-of-home placement. In Z. Stoneman, & P. Waldman Berman (eds), *The effects of mental retardation, disability and illness on sibling relationships. Research issues and challenges* (pp. 117–141). Baltimore: Brookes.

Bornat, J., Johnson, J., Pereira, C., Pilgrim, D. & Williams, F. (1997). *Community care: A reader* (2nd edn). London: Macmillan Press.

Bowes, J. & Hayes, A. (1999). *Children, families, and communities: Contexts and consequences*. Melbourne: Oxford University Press.

Brubaker, E. & Brubaker, T. (1993). Caring for adult children with mental retardation. Concerns of elderly parents. In K. Roberto (ed.), *The elderly caregiver. Caring for adults with developmental disabilities.* (pp. 51–61). Newbury Park, CA: Sage.

Bulmer, M. (1987). *The social basis of community care*. London: Allen & Unwin.

Bytheway, B. (1995). *Ageism*. Buckingham, UK: Open University Press.

Campbell, J. & Essex, E. (1994). Factors affecting parents in their future planning for a son or daughter with developmental disabilities. *Education and Training in Mental Retardation and Developmental Disabilities*, Sept, 222–238.

Cantor, M. (1989). Social care: Family and community support systems. *Annals of the American Academy of Political and Social Science*, 503, 99–112.

Cantor, M. & Little, V. (1985). Aging and social care. In R. Binstock & E. Shanas (eds), *Handbook of aging and the social sciences* (2nd edn, pp. 745–781). New York: Van Nostrand Reinhold.

Card, H. (1983). What will happen when we've gone? *Community Care*, 28, 20–21.

Carers Association of Australia. (1995). *Listen to the carers: The many voices of care* (Report of the national carers consultation). Canberra: Author.

Carney, T. & Tait, D. (1997). *The adult guardianship experiment: Tribunals and popular justice*. Sydney: Federation Press.

Carter, C. & Jancar, J. (1983). Mortality in the mentally handicapped: A fifty year survey at the Stoke Park group of hospitals. *Journal of Mental Deficiency Research*, 27, 143–156.

Caserta, M., Connelly, R., Lund, D. & Poulton, J. (1987). Older adult caregivers of developmentally disabled household members: Service needs and fulfilment. *Journal of Gerontological Social Work*, 10, 35–50.

Challis, D. & Davies, B. (1986). *Case management in community care*. Aldershot, UK: Gower.

Chappell, N. (1990). Aging and social care. In R. Binstock & L. George (eds), *Handbook of aging and the social sciences* (3rd edn, pp. 438–454). San Diego: Academic Press.

Cicirelli, V. (1992). Siblings as caregivers in middle and old age. In J. Dwyer & R. Coward (eds), *Gender, families and elder care* (pp. 84–101). Newbury Park, CA: Sage.

Cocks, E. (1998). *An introduction to Intellectual Disability in Australia*. (3rd edn). Canberra: Australian Institute on Intellectual Disability.

Cocks, E. & Ng, C. (1983). Characteristics of those persons with mental retardation registered with the mental retardation division. *Australia and New Zealand Journal of Developmental Disabilities*, 9, 117–127.

Collins, A. & Pancoast, D. (1976). *Natural helping networks. A strategy for prevention*. Washington DC: National Association of Social Workers.

Collinson, W. (1997). *Succession planning. Providing a future for people with intellectual disabilities, families and parents. Project report*. Townsville, Qld: Endeavour Foundation, Townsville.

Commonwealth Government. (1986). *Disability Services Act*. Canberra: Australian Government Publishing Service.

Community Services Victoria. (1988). *Interim report: Accommodation for intellectually disabled people who are currently living at home with older parents* (Unpublished report). Melbourne: Author.

Community Services Victoria. (1992a). *The planned care approach: Future partnerships in residential care for people with intellectual disabilities* (Unpublished report). Melbourne: Author.

Community Services Victoria. (1992b). *Annual report 1991/2*. Melbourne: Author.

Community Services Victoria. (1992c). *Services for older people with an intellectual disability (research papers included)*. Melbourne: Author.

Cooper, S. (1997a). A population-based heath survey of maladaptive behaviours associated with dementia in elderly people with learning disabilities. *Journal of Intellectual Disability Research*, 41(6), 481–487.

Cooper, S. (1997b). Deficient health and social services for elderly people with learning disabilities. *Journal of Intellectual Disability Research*, 41(4), 331–338.

Cooper, S. (1998). Clinical study of the effects of age on physical health of adults with mental retardation. *American Journal on Mental Retardation*, 102(6), 582–589.

Creyke, R. (1995). *Who can decide? Legal decision making for others*. Canberra: Department of Human Services and Health, Aged and Community Care Division.

d'Abbs, P. (1982). *Social support networks: A critical review of models and findings* (Monograph no. 1). Melbourne: Australian Institute of Family Studies.

d'Abbs. P. (1991). *Who helps? Support networks and social policy in Australia* (Monograph no. 12). Melbourne: Australian Institute of Family Studies.

Dalley, G. (1988). *Ideologies of caring: Rethinking community and collectivism*. Basingstoke, UK: Macmillan.

Dalley, G. (1997). The principles of collective care. In J. Bornat, J. Johnson, C. Pereira, D. Pilgrim & F. Williams (eds), *Community care: A reader* (2nd edn, pp. 153–159). London: Macmillan.

Dalton, A., Seltzer, M., Adlin, M. & Wisniewski, H. (1994). Association between Alzheimer disease and Down syndrome: Clinical observations. In J. Berg, A. Holland & J. Karlinsky (eds), *Alzheimer disease and Down syndrome* (pp. 1–24). London: Oxford University Press.

Department of Community Services & Health. (1995). *The efficiency and effectiveness review of the HACC program* (Final report, June). Canberra: Australian Government Publishing Service.

Department of Health, Housing & Community Services. (1991). *Aged care reform strategy: Mid term review, 1990–1991* (discussion papers). Canberra: Australian Government Publishing Service.

Department of Health, Housing, Local Government & Community Services. (1993). *Aged care reform strategy. Mid term review* (Stage 2. Report). Canberra: Australian Government Publishing Service.

Department of Human Services & Health. (1994). *Your guide to residents' rights in nursing homes* (2nd edn). Canberra: Australian Government Publishing Service.

Department of Human Services. (1996). *State plan for Intellectual Disability Services 1996–1999*. Melbourne: Author.

Department of Human Services. (1997). Raw data. February 1997.

Dobrof, R. & Litwak, E. (1977). *Maintenance of family ties of long term care patients: Theory and guide to practice* (Report by US Department of Health, Education and Welfare, Public Health Service, Alcohol, Drug Abuse and Mental Health Administration). Maryland: National Institute on Mental Health.

Duffy, S., Widaman, K. & Eyman, R. (1991). Life-span development and age related trends in adaptive behaviour and mortality. In M. Janicki & M. Seltzer (eds). *Aging and developmental disabilities: Challenges for the 1990s* (The proceedings of the Boston Roundtable on Research Issues and Applications in Aging and Developmental Disabilities) (pp. 76–100). Washington DC: Special Interest Group on Aging, American Association on Mental Retardation.

Edgerton, R. (1988). Aging in the community: A matter of choice. *American Journal of Mental Retardation*, 92, 331–335.

Edgerton, R. (1994). Quality of life issues: Some people know how to be old. In M. Seltzer, M. Krauss & M. Janicki (eds). *Life course perspectives on adulthood*

and old age (pp. 53–66). Washington DC: American Association on Mental Retardation.
Edgerton, R. & Gaston, M. (1991). *'I've seen it all.' Lives of older persons with mental retardation in the community*. Baltimore: Brookes.
Eloura Homes. (1995). *Report on family support program*. (Unpublished report). Melbourne: Author.
Encel, S. (1997). Work in later life. In A. Borowski, S. Encel & E. Ozanne (eds), *Ageing and social policy in Australia* (pp. 137–156). Melbourne: Cambridge University Press.
Erickson, M., Krauss, M. & Seltzer, M. (1989). Perceptions of old age among a sample of mentally retarded persons. *Journal of Applied Gerontology*, 8, 251–260.
Essex, E., Seltzer, M. & Krauss, M. (1994, November). *The end of caregiving. Transitions of older mothers of adults with mental retardation*. Paper presented at the 47th Annual Scientific Meeting of the Gerontological Society of America.
Essex, E., Seltzer, M. & Krauss, M. (1997). Residential transitions of adults with mental retardation: Predictors of waiting list use and placement. *American Journal on Mental Retardation*, 101(6), 613–629.
Eyman, R. & Borthwick-Duffy, S. (1994). Trends in mortality rates and predictors of mortality. In M. Seltzer, M. Krauss & M. Janicki (eds), *Lifecourse perspectives on adulthood and old age* (pp. 93–108). Washington DC: American Association on Mental Retardation.

Finch, J. & Groves, D. (1980). Community care and the family. A case for equal opportunities. *Journal of Social Policy*, 9, 487–511.
Finch, J. & Mason, J. (1990). Filial obligations and kin support for elderly people. *Ageing and Society*, 10, 151–175.
Finch, J. & Mason, J. (1993). *Negotiating family responsibility*. London: Routledge.
Fine, M. (1994). Supporting, exploiting or displacing the family. In J. Inglis & L. Rogan (eds), *Flexible families. New directions in Australian communities* (pp. 73–92). Sydney: Pluto Press/ACOSS.
Fine, M. & Thompson, C. (1995). *Three years at home. The final report of the longitudinal study of community support services and their use*. Sydney: Social Policy Research Centre.
Flynn, M. (1986). Adults who are mentally handicapped as consumers: Issues and guidelines for interviewing. *Journal of Mental Deficiency Research*, 30, 369–377.
Freedman, R., Krauss, M. & Seltzer, M. (1997). Aging parents' residential plans for adult children with mental retardation. *Mental Retardation*, 35(2), 114–123.
Freeling, B. & Bruggeman, R. (1994, October). *Guaranteed care: Progress in South Australia*. Paper presented at the joint National Conference of the Association for the Study of Intellectual Disability and the National Council on Intellectual Disability, Perth.
Friedan. B. (1993). *The fountain of age*. New York: Simon Schuster.
Fujiura, G. & Braddock, D. (1992). Fiscal and demographic trends in mental retardation services: The emergence of the family. In L. Rowitz (ed.), *Mental retardation in the year 2000* (pp. 316–338). New York: Springer.
Fullmer, E., Smith, G. & Tobin, S. (1997). Older mothers who do not use day programs for their daughters and sons with mental retardation. *Journal of Developmental and Physical Disabilities*, 9(2 June), 153–173.

Germain, C. & Gitterman, A. (1980). *The life model of social work practice*. New York: Colombia University Press.

Gibson, D. (1998). *Aged care: Old policies, new problems*. Melbourne: Cambridge University Press.

Gibson, J., Rabkin, J. & Munson, R. (1992). Critical issues in serving the developmentally disabled elderly. *Journal of Gerontological Social Work*, 19, 35–49.

Gibson, D., Turrell, G. & Jenkins, A. (1993). Regulation and reform, promoting residents' rights in Australian nursing homes. *Australian and New Zealand Journal of Sociology*, 29, 73–91.

Gold, M. (1987). *Parents of the adult developmentally disabled*. New York: Brookdale Center on Aging.

Goodman, D. (1978). Parenting an adult mentally retarded offspring. *Smith College Studies in Social Work*, 48, 209–234.

Gordon, R., Seltzer, M. & Krauss, M. (1997). The aftermath of parental death: Changes in the context and quality of life. *Quality of life. vol 2* (pp. 25–42). Washington DC: American Association on Mental Retardation.

Graham, S. (1993). Alternative approaches to the provision of community services for people with disabilities. In P. Saunders & S. Graham (eds), *Beyond economic rationalism. Alternative futures for social policy* (pp. 107–132). Sydney: Social Policy Research Centre.

Graham, S., Ross, R. & Payne, T. (1992). *The evaluation of community options in New South Wales*. Sydney: Social Policy Research Centre.

Grant, G. (1986). Older carers, interdependence and the care of mentally handicapped adults. *Ageing and Society*, 6, 333–351.

Grant, G. (1988). *Stability and change in the care networks of mentally handicapped adults living at home* (First report, Centre for Social Policy and Development, University of Wales). Bangor, UK: University of Wales.

Grant, G. (1989). Letting go: Decision making among family carers of people with mental handicap. *Australia and New Zealand Journal of Developmental Disabilities*, 15, 189–200.

Grant, G. (1993). Support networks and transitions over two years among adults with mental handicap. *Mental Handicap Research*, 6, 36–55.

Grant, C., McGrath, M. & Ramcharan, P. (1995). Community inclusion of older adults with learning disabilities. Care in place. *International Journal of Network and Community*, 2(1), 29–44.

Grant, G. & Wenger, C. (1993). Dynamics of support networks: Differences and similarities between vulnerable groups. *Irish Journal of Psychology*, 14, 79–98.

Green, J. & Wunsch, A. (1994). The lives of six women. *Interaction*, 7(4), 11–15.

Greenberg, J., Seltzer, M. & Greenley, J. (1993). Aging parents of adults with disabilities: The gratification and frustrations of later life caregiving. *The Gerontologist*, 33, 542–550.

Griffin, T. & Bennett, K. (1994, October). *Peering into the future: Focus group interviews with parents who have a child with an intellectual disability*. Paper presented at the joint National Conference of the Association for the Study of Intellectual Disability and the National Council on Intellectual Disability, Perth.

Griffith, D. & Unger, D. (1994). Views about planning for the future among parents and siblings of adults with mental retardation. *Family Relations*, 43, 221–227.

Griffiths, R. (1988). *Community care: Agenda for action* (The Griffith report). London: HMSO.

Hand, J. (1994). Report of a national survey of older people with lifelong intellectual handicap in New Zealand. *Journal of Intellectual Disability Research*, 38, 275–287.

Hand, J. & Reid, P. (1989). Views and recollections of older people with intellectual handicaps in New Zealand. *Australia and New Zealand Journal of Developmental Disabilities*, 15, 231–240.

Hareven, T. (1978). *Transitions. The family life course in historical perspective*. New York: Academic Press.

Harper, D. & Wadsworth, J. (1993). Grief in adults with mental retardation: Preliminary findings. *Research in Developmental Disabilities*, 14, 313–330.

Harris, J. (1998). *Working with older carers: Guidance for service providers in learning disability*. Kidderminster: Bild Publications.

Hawkins, B., Eklund, S. & Matz, B. (1993). Aging adults with Down syndrome. Biological and psychological considerations for caregivers. In K. Roberto (ed.), *The elderly caregiver. Caring for adults with developmental disabilities* (pp. 61–81). Newbury Park, CA: Sage.

Hayden, M. & Heller, T. (1997). Support, problem-solving/coping ability, and personal burden of younger and older caregivers of adults with mental retardation. *Mental Retardation*, 35(5), 364–372.

Health & Community Services. (1993a). *Review of placement of eligible aged clients into aged care facilities* (Draft, unpublished paper). Melbourne: Author.

Health & Community Services. (1993b). *Annual report 1992/3*. Melbourne: Author.

Health & Community Services. (1993c). *New directions. The changing face of disability services*. Melbourne: Author.

Health & Community Services. (1995a). *Options for older families*. Unpublished service proposal. Melbourne: Author.

Health & Community Services. (1995b). *Report to the Hon Michael John MP, Minister for Community Services of the Intellectual Disability Services Taskforce*. Melbourne: Author.

Heller, T. (1993). Mastery and control strategies throughout the life course among families of persons with mental retardation. In A. Turnbull, J. Patterson, S. Behr, D. Murphy, J. Marquis & M. Blue-Banning (eds), *Cognitive coping in families who have a member with developmental disability* (pp. 195–206). Baltimore: Brookes.

Heller, T. (1997). Current trends in providing support for families of adults with mental retardation. *Alert*, 9(1), 6–13.

Heller, T. & Factor, A. (1988a). Permanency planning among black and white family caregivers of older adults with mental retardation. *Mental Retardation*, 26, 203–208.

Heller, T. & Factor, A. (1988b). *Development of a transition plan for older adults with developmental disabilities residing in the natural home* (Public Policy Monograph Series, No. 37). Chicago: Illinois University at Chicago.

Heller, T. & Factor, A. (1991). Permanency planning for adults with mental retardation living with family caregivers. *American Journal on Mental Retardation*, 96, 163–176.

Heller, T. & Factor, A. (1993). Aging family caregivers: Support resources and changes in burden and placement desire. *American Journal on Mental Retardation*, 98, 417–426.

Heller, T., Miller, A. & Factor, A. (1997). Adults with mental retardation as supports to their parents: Effects on parental caregiving appraisal. *Mental Retardation*, 35(5), 338–346.

Hogg, J. (1990). Mental handicap, ageing and the community. In W. Fraser (ed.), *Key issues in mental retardation research. Proceedings of the eighth congress of the International Association for the Study of Mental Deficiency* (pp. 460–465). London: Routledge.

Hogg, J. & Moss, S. (1993). The characteristics of older people with intellectual disabilities in England. In N. Bray (ed.), *International review of research in mental retardation, vol. 19*, 71–92. New York: Academic Press.

Hogg, J., Moss, S. & Cooke, D. (1988). *Ageing and mental handicap*. London: Croom Helm.

Hooyman, N. (1983). Social support networks in services to the elderly. In J. Whittaker & J. Garbarino (eds), *Social support networks: Informal helping in human services* (pp. 133–164). New York: Aldine.

Hooyman, N. & Kiyak, H. (1991). *Social gerontology: A multidisciplinary perspective* (2nd edn). Boston: Allyn and Bacon.

Horne, M. (1989a). *Identifying a 'hidden' population of older adults with mental handicap. The outreach study in Oldham. A demographic study of older people with mental handicap in Oldham Metropolitan Borough* (part 4). Manchester, UK: Hester Adrian Research Centre.

Horne, M. (1989b). Identifying 'hidden' populations of older adults with mental handicap: Outreach in the UK. *Australia and New Zealand Journal of Developmental Disabilities*, 15, 207–218.

Horowitz, A. (1985). Family caregiving to the frail elderly. In D. Maddox (ed.), *Annual review of gerontology and geriatrics* (pp. 174–246). New York: Springer.

Howe, A., Ozanne, E. & Selby Smith, C. (1990). *Community care policy and practice: New directions in Australia*. Melbourne: Public Sector Management Institute, Faculty of Economics and Politics, Monash University.

Huberman, A. & Miles, M. (1994). Data management and analysis methods. In N. Denzin & Y. Lincoln (Eds.), *Handbook of qualitative methods* (pp. 428–444). Newbury Park: Sage.

Jacobson, J., Sutton, M. & Janicki, M. (1985). Demography and characteristics of aging and aged mentally retarded persons. In M. Janicki & H. Wisniewski (eds), *Aging and developmental disabilities: Issues and approaches* (pp. 115–143). Baltimore: Brookes.

Janicki, M. (1992). Lifelong disability and aging. In L. Rowitz (ed), *Mental retardation in the year 2000* (pp. 115–127). New York: Springer.

Janicki, M. (1996). *Help for caring—for older people caring for adults with a developmental disability*. Albany, NY: New York State Developmental Disabilities Planning Council.

Janicki, M., Dalton, A., Henderson, C. & Davidson, P. (1999). Mortality and morbidity among older adults with intellectual disability: Health services considerations. *Disability and Rehabilitation*, 21(5–6), 284–294.

Janicki, M., McCallion, P., Force, L., Bishop, K. & LePore, P. (1998). Area agency on aging and assistance for households with older carers of adults with a developmental disability. *Journal of Aging and Social Policy*, 10(1), 13–36.

Janicki, M., Otis, J., Puccio, P., Rettig, J. & Jacobson, J. (1985). Service needs among older developmentally disabled persons. In M. Janicki & H. Wisniewski (eds), *Aging and developmental disabilities: Issues and approaches* (pp. 289–304). Baltimore: Brookes.

Janicki, M. & Seltzer, M. (eds). (1991). *Aging and developmental disabilities: Challenges for the 1990s* (The proceedings of the Boston Roundtable on Research Issues and Applications in Aging and Developmental Disabilities). Washington DC: Special Interest Group on Aging, American Association on Mental Retardation.

Jarvis, C. (1993). *Family and friends in old age, and the implications for informal support: Evidence from the British attitudes survey 1986*. London: Age Concern Institute of Gerontology.

Johnson, C. & Catalano, D. (1981). Childless elderly and their family supports. *The Gerontologist*, 21, 610–618.

Johnson, J. (1998). The emergence of care as policy. In A. Brechin, J. Walmsley, J. Katz & S. Peace (eds), *Care matters: Concepts, practice and research in health and social care* (pp. 139–152). London: Sage.

Kahana, E., Biegal, D. & Wykle, M. (1995). *Family caregiving across the lifespan*. Thousand Oaks: Sage.

Kahana, E., Kahana, B., Johnson, J., Hammond, R. & Kercher, K. (1995). Developmental challenges and family caregiving: Bridging concepts and research. In E. Kahana, D. Biegal & M. Wykie (eds), *Family caregiving across the lifespan* (pp. 3–41). Thousand Oaks: Sage.

Kahn, R. & Antonucci, T. (1980). Convoys over the life course: Attachment, roles, and social support. In P. Baltes & O. Brim (eds), *Lifespan development and behaviour* (pp. 253–286). New York: Academic Press.

Kaufman, A., Adams, J. & Campbell, V. (1991). Permanency planning by older parents who care for adult children with mental retardation. *Mental Retardation*, 29, 293–300.

Kaufman, A., Glicken, M. & de Weaver, K. (1989). The mentally retarded aged: Implications for social work practice. *Journal of Gerontological Social Work*, 14, 93–110.

Kearney, G., Krishman, V. & Londhe, R. (1993). Characteristics of elderly people with a mental handicap living in a mental handicap hospital. A descriptive study. *British Journal of Developmental Disabilities*, 39, 31–50.

Kelly, T. & Kropf, N. (1995). Stigmatised and perpetual parents: Older parents caring for adult children with lifelong disabilities. *Journal of Gerontological Social Work*, 20, 3–16.

Kendig, H. & McCallum, J. (1990). *Grey policy: Australian policies for an ageing society*. Sydney: Allen & Unwin.

Kloeppel, D. & Hollins, S. (1989). Double handicap—mental retardation and death in the family. *Death Studies*, 13, 31–38.

Krauss, M. (1990, May). *Later life placements: Precipitating factors and family profiles*. Paper presented at the 114th annual meeting of the American Association on Mental Retardation, Atlanta.

Krauss, M. & Erickson, M. (1988). Informal support networks among aging persons with mental retardation. A pilot study. *Mental Retardation*, 26, 197–201.

Krauss, M. & Seltzer, M. (1986). Comparison of elderly and adult mentally retarded persons in community and institutional settings. *American Journal of Mental Deficiency*, 91, 237–243.

Krauss, M., Seltzer, M. & Goodman, S. (1992). Social support networks of adults with mental retardation who live at home. *American Journal on Mental Retardation*, 96, 432–441.

Krauss, M., Seltzer, M., Gordon, R. & Friedman, D. (1996). Binding ties: The roles of adult siblings of persons with mental retardation. *Mental Retardation*, 34, 83–93.

Kropf, N. (1994). *Older parents of adults with developmental disabilities: Issues for practice and service delivery*. Paper presented at the Young Adult Institute 15th Annual International Conference on Developmental Disabilities, New York.

Kropf, N. & Greene, R. (1993). Life review with families who care for developmentally disabled members: A model. *Journal of Gerontological Social Work*, 21(1/2), 25–40.

Kultgen, P. & Rominger, R. (1993). Cross training within the aging and developmental disabilities services systems. In E. Sutton, A. Factor, B. Hawkins, T. Heller & G. Seltzer (eds) *Older adults with developmental disabilities: Optimising choice and change* (pp. 239–256). Baltimore: Brookes.

Lakin, K., Anderson, S., Hill, B., Bruininks, R. & Wright, E. (1991). Programs and services received by older persons with mental retardation. *Mental Retardation*, 29, 65–74.

Land, H. (1995). Rewarding care: A challenge for welfare states. In P. Saunders & S. Shaver (eds), *Social policy and challenges of social change. Proceedings of the National Social Policy Conference* (pp. 1–24). Sydney: Social Policy Research Centre.

Larnaca Resolution. (1999). *Journal of Intellectual Disability Research*, 42(3), 262.

Laslett, P. (1989). *A fresh map of life*. London: Weidenfield and Nicholson.

Laughlin, C. & Cotton, P. (1994). Efficacy of a pre-retirement planning intervention for ageing individuals with mental retardation. *Journal of Intellectual Disability Research*, 38, 317–328.

Lehman, J. & Roberto, K. (1993). Current and future service needs of aging individuals with developmental disabilities living with relatives. In K. Roberto (ed.), *The elderly caregiver: Caring for adults with developmental disabilities* (pp. 108–124). Newbury Park, CA: Sage.

Lifskitz, H. (1998). Instrumental enrichment: A tool for enhancement of cognitive ability in adult and elderly people with mental retardation. *Education and Training in Mental Retardation and Developmental Disabilities*, 33(1), 34–41.

Litwak, E. (1985). *Helping the elderly*. New York: The Guildford Press.

Litwak, E., Jessop, D. & Moulton, H. (1995). Optimal use of formal and informal systems over the lifecourse. In E. Kahana, D. Biegal & M. Wykle (eds), *Family caregiving across the lifespan* (pp. 96–130). Thousand Oaks: Sage.

Lowy, L. (1985). *Social work with the aging. The challenge and promise of the later years* (2nd edn). New York: Longman.

Maaskant, M. & Haveman, M. (1990). Elderly residents in Dutch mental deficiency institutions. *Journal of Mental Deficiency Research* 34, 475–482.

McCallion, P., Janicki, M. & Grant-Griffin, L. (1997). Exploring the impact of culture and acculturation on older families caregiving for persons with development disabilities. (Family Caregiving For Persons With Disabilities.) *Family Relations*, 46(4), 347–358.

McCallion, P. & Tobin S. (1995). Social workers' perceptions of older adults caring at home for sons and daughters with developmental disabilities. *Mental Retardation*, 33, 153–162.

MacDonald, M. & Tyson, P. (1988). Decajeopardy—The aging and aged developmentally disabled. In A. Marchetti (ed.), *Developmental disabilities: A lifespan perspective* (pp. 256–291). San Diego: Grune Stratton.

McDonald, P. (1997). Older people and their families: Issues for policy. In A. Borowski, S. Encel & E. Ozanne (eds), *Ageing and social policy in Australia* (pp. 194–210). Melbourne: Cambridge University Press.

McGrath, M. & Grant, G. (1993). The lifecycle and support networks of families with a mentally handicapped member. *Disability Handicap and Society*, 8, 25–41.

Magrill, D., Handley, P., Gleeson, S., Charles, D. & Group, S. S. (1997). *The sharing caring project. Developing services for older carers of people with learning disabilities*. Sheffield, UK.

Marshall, C. & Rossman, G. (1989). *Designing qualitative research*. Newbury Park, CA: Sage.

Mengel, M., Marcus, D. & Dunkle, R. (1996). 'What will happen to my child when I'm gone?' A support and education group for aging parents as caregivers. *The Gerontologist*, 36(6), 816–820.

Meyers, C., Borthwick, S. & Eyman, R. (1985). Place of residence by age, ethnicity, and level of retardation of the mentally retarded/developmentally disabled population of California. *American Journal of Mental Deficiency*, 90, 266–270.

Minichiello, V., Alexander, L. & Jones, D. (1992). *Gerontology: A multidisciplinary approach*. Sydney: Prentice-Hall.

Morris, J. (1993). *Independent lives: Community care and disabled people*. London: Macmillan.

Moss, S. (1991). Age and functional abilities of people with mental handicap: Evidence from the Wessex Mental Handicap Register. *Journal of Mental Deficiency Research*, 35, 430–445.

Moss, S. (1994). Quality of life and aging. In D. Goode (ed.), *Quality of life for persons with disabilities* (pp. 218–234). Cambridge, MA: Brookline Books.

Moss, S. (1995). Ageing and learning disabilities. Guest Editorial. *BILD Bulletin*, 97.

Moss, S. & Hogg, J. (1989). A cluster analysis of support networks of older people with severe intellectual impairment. *Australia and New Zealand Journal of Developmental Disabilities*, 15, 169–188.

Moss, S., Hogg, J. & Horne, M. (1989). *Residential provision and service patterns in a population of people over the age of 50 years and with severe intellectual impairment. A demographic study of older people with mental handicap in Oldham Metropolitan Borough* (Part 2). Manchester, UK: Hester Adrian Research Centre.

Moss, S., Hogg, J. & Horne, M. (1992). Demographic characteristics of a population of people with moderate, severe and profound intellectual disability (mental handicap) age structure, IQ and adaptive skills. *Journal of Intellectual Disability Research*, 36, 387–401.

Moss, S. & Patel, P. (1997). Dementia in older people with intellectual disability: Systems of physical and mental illness, and levels of adaptive behaviour. *Journal of Intellectual Disability Research*, 41(1), 60–69.

Mugford, S. & Kendig, H. (1986). Social relations: Networks and ties. In H. Kendig (ed.) *Ageing and families: A social networks perspective* (pp. 38–60). Sydney: Allen & Unwin.

Nahemow, L. (1988, August). *The ecological theory of aging as it relates to elderly persons with mental retardation.* Paper presented to the Ninth Congress of International Association for the Scientific Study of Mental Deficiency, 1988, Dublin.

Nahemow, L. (1990). *The ecological theory of aging. How it has been used.* Paper presented to the American Psychological Association (Symposium on Environment and Aging), 1990, Boston.

Neilson & Associates Pty Ltd. (1987). *Ten year plan for the redevelopment of intellectual disability services* (interim report June). Melbourne: Community Services Victoria.

Neilson & Associates Pty Ltd. (1988). *Ten year plan for the redevelopment of intellectual disability services* (final report). Melbourne: Community Services Victoria.

Nolan, M., Grant, G. & Keady, J. (1996). *Understanding family care. A multidimensional model of caring and coping.* Buckingham, UK: Open University Press.

Office of the Public Advocate. (1993). *Annual report 1993.* Melbourne: L. V. North Government Printer.

Oliver, M. (1990). *The politics of disablement.* London: Macmillan.

O'Malley, P. (1996). Group work with older people who are developmentally disabled and their caregivers. *Journal of Gerontological Social Work*, 25(1–2), 105–120.

Parker, R. (1981). Tending and social policy. In E. Goldberg & S. Hatch (eds), *A new look at the personal social services* (pp. 17–34). London: Policy Studies Institute.

Parkinson, C. & Howard, C. (1996). Older persons with mental retardation/developmental disabilities. *Journal of Gerontological Social Work*, 25, 91–103.

Parmenter, T. (1994). Emerging trends in the provision of community living for people with an intellectual disability. *Interaction*, 7(3), 11–15.

Patterson, J. & Hardy, B. (1991). *Review of disability services. Head office functions* (Unpublished report). Melbourne: Community Services Victoria.

Patton, M. (1980). *Qualitative evaluation methods.* Los Angeles: Sage.

Pierce, G. (1991). *Regional review of ageing carers*. Unpublished paper. Melbourne: Community Services Victoria.

Pierce, G. (1993). *Who cares for ageing carers. Lifelong caring and coping has few just rewards.* Unpublished paper, Department of Social Work, University of Melbourne.

Pierce, G. & Nankervis, J. (1998). *Putting carers in the picture. Improving the focus on carer needs in aged care assessment.* Melbourne: Carers Association.

Prosser, H. (1989). *Relationships within families and the informal networks of older people with severe intellectual impairment (mental handicap), A demographic study of older people with mental handicap in Oldham Metropolitan Borough* (Part 3). Manchester, UK: Hester Adrian Research Centre.

Prosser, H. (1997). The future care plans of older adults with intellectual disabilities living at home with family carers. *Journal of Applied Research in Intellectual Disabilities.* 10(1), 15–32.

Prosser, H. & Moss, S. (1996). Informal care networks of older adults with intellectual disability. *Journal of Applied Research in Intellectual Disabilities*, 9(1), 17–30.

Richards, T. & Richards, L. (1994). Using computers in qualitative research. In N. Denzin & Y. Lincoln (eds), *Handbook of qualitative methods* (pp. 445–462). Newbury Park, CA: Sage.

Richardson, A. & Ritchie, J. (1986). *Making the break: Parents' perspectives on adults with mental handicap leaving home.* London: King Edward's Hospital Fund.

Richardson, A. & Ritchie, J. (1989). *Letting go: Dilemmas for parents whose son or daughter has a mental handicap.* Milton Keynes, UK: Open University Press.

Roberto, K. (1993a). *The elderly caregiver: Caring for adults with developmental disabilities.* Newbury Park, CA: Sage.

Roberto, K. (1993b). Family caregivers of aging adults with disabilities. A review of the caregiving literature. In K. Roberto (ed.), *The elderly caregiver: Caring for adults with developmental disabilities* (pp. 3–21). Newbury Park, CA: Sage.

Ronalds, C. (1989). *I'm still an individual. A blueprint for the rights of residents in nursing homes and hostels.* Canberra: Department of Community Services and Health.

Rosenman, L. (1991). Community care: Social or economic policy. In P. Saunders & D. Encel (eds), *Social policy in Australia. Options for the 1990s* (pp. 43–60). Sydney: Social Policy Research Centre.

Sach & Associates. (1991). *The housing needs of people with disabilities* (National Housing Strategy discussion paper). Canberra: Australian Government Publishing Service.

Sax, S. (1993). *Ageing and public policy in Australia.* Sydney: Allen & Unwin.

Schofield, H., Bloch, S., Herrman, H., Murphy, B., Nankervis, J. & Singh, B. (1998). *Family caregivers: Disability, illness and ageing.* Sydney: Allen & Unwin.

Seltzer, G., Begun, A., Magan, R. & Luchterhand, C. (1993). Social supports and expectations of family involvement after out of home placement. In E. Sutton, T. Heller, A. Factor, B. Hawkins & G. Seltzer (eds), *Older adults with developmental disabilities: Optimising choice and change* (pp. 123–140). Baltimore: Brookes.

Seltzer, G., Begun, A., Seltzer, M. & Krauss, M. (1991). Adults with mental retardation and their aging mothers: Impacts of siblings. *Family Relations*, 40, 310–317.

Seltzer, G., Finlay, E. & Howell, M. (1988). Functional characteristics of elderly persons with mental retardation in community and nursing homes. *Mental Retardation*, 24, 213–217.

Seltzer, M. (1983). Non-experimental field research methods. In J. Matson & J. Mulick (eds), *Handbook of mental retardation* (pp. 557–570). New York: Pergamon Press.

Seltzer, M. (1985). Informal supports for aging mentally retarded persons. *American Journal of Mental Deficiency*, 90, 259–265.

Seltzer, M. (1992a). Aging in persons with developmental disabilities. In J. Birren, R. Sloane & G. Cohen (eds), *Handbook of mental health and aging* (2nd edn, pp. 583–599). New York: Academic Press.

Seltzer, M. (1992b). Training families to be case managers for elders with developmental disabilities. Feasibility, effectiveness and implication, *Generations*, winter 1992, 65–70.

Seltzer, M. & Krauss, M. (1987). *Aging and mental retardation. Extending the continuum.* Washington DC: American Association on Mental Retardation.

Seltzer, M. & Krauss, M. (1989). Aging parents with mentally retarded children. Family risk factors and sources of support. *American Journal on Mental Retardation*, 94, 303–312.

Seltzer, M. & Krauss, M. (1993). Adult sibling relationships of persons with mental retardation. In Z. Stoneman & P. Waldman Berman (eds), *The effects of mental retardation, disability, and illness on sibling relationships. Research issues and challenges* (pp. 99–115). Baltimore: Brookes.

Seltzer, M. & Krauss, M. (1994). Aging parents with co-resident adult children: The impact of lifelong caregiving. In M. Seltzer, M. Krauss & M. Janicki (eds), *Life course perspectives on adulthood and old age* (pp. 3–18). Washington DC: American Association on Mental Retardation.

Seltzer, M., Krauss, M., Choi, S. & Hong, J. (1996). Midlife and later-life parenting of adult children with mental retardation. In C. Ryff & M. Seltzer (eds), *The parental experience in midlife* (pp. 459–492). Chicago: University of Chicago Press.

Seltzer, M., Krauss, M. & Janicki, M. (1994). *Life course perspectives on adulthood and old age.* Washington DC: American Association on Mental Retardation.

Seltzer, M. & Ryff, C. (1994). Parenting across the lifespan. The normative and non-normative cases. In D. Featherman, R. Learner & M. Perlmutter (eds), *Life span development and behaviour, vol. 12* (pp. 1–40). Hillsdale, NJ: Erlbaum Assoc.

Seltzer, M. & Seltzer, G. (1985). The elderly mentally retarded. A group in need of service. In G. Getzel & M. Mellor (eds), *Gerontological social work practice in the community* (pp. 99–120). New York: Haworth Press.

Seltzer, M. & Seltzer, G. (1992). Aging in people with developmental disabilities. A social work perspective. In F. Turner (ed.), *Mental health and the elderly: A social work perspective* (pp. 136–160). New York: Free Press.

Seltzer, M., Seltzer, G. & Sherwood, C. (1982). Comparison of community adjustment of older vs younger mentally retarded adults. *American Journal of Mental Deficiency*, 87, 9–13.

Sharkey, P. (1989). Social networks and social service workers. *British Journal of Social Work*, 19, 387–405.

Shearn, J. & Todd, S. (1996). Identities at risk: The relationships parents and their coresident adult offspring with learning disabilities have with each other and their social worlds. *European Journal on Mental Disability*, 3(9), 47–60.

Shenk, D. & Achenbaum, A. (1994). *Changing perceptions of aging and the aged*. New York: Springer.

Sigelman, C., Budd, E., Winer, J., Schoenrock, C. & Martin, P. (1982). Evaluating alternative techniques of questioning mentally retarded persons. *American Journal of Mental Deficiency*, 86, 511–518.

Silverman, D. (1993). *Interpreting qualitative data. Methods for analysing talk, text and interaction*. Thousand Oaks: Sage.

Sinason, V. (1992). *Mental handicap and the human condition: New approaches from the Tavistock*. London: Free Association Books.

Skeie, G. (1989). Contact between elderly people with mental retardation living in institutions and their families. *Australia and New Zealand Journal of Developmental Disabilities*, 15, 201–206.

Smith, G. (1996). Caregiving outcomes for older mothers of adults with mental retardation. A test of the two factor model psychological wellbeing. *Psychology and Aging* (11), 1–9.

Smith, G. (1997). Aging families of adults with mental retardation: Patterns and correlates of service use, need and knowledge. *American Journal on Mental Retardation*, 102(1), 13–26.

Smith, G., Fullmer, E. & Tobin, S. (1994). Living outside the system: An exploration of older families who do not use day programs. In M. Seltzer, M. Krauss & M. Janicki (eds), *Lifecourse perspectives on adulthood and old age* (pp. 19–38). Washington DC: American Association on Mental Retardation.

Smith, G., Majeski, R. & McClenny, B. (1996). Psychoeducational support groups for aging parents: Development and preliminary outcomes. *Mental Retardation*, 34(3), 172–181.

Smith, G. & Tobin, S. (1989). Permanency planning among older parents of adults with lifelong disabilities. *Journal of Gerontological Social Work*, 114, 35–59.

Smith, G. & Tobin, S. (1993a). Casemanager's perceptions of practice with older parents of adults with developmental disabilities. In K. Roberto (ed.), *The elderly caregiver: Caring for adults with developmental disabilities* (pp. 146–173). Newbury Park, CA: Sage.

Smith, G. & Tobin, S. (1993b). Practice with older parents of developmentally disabled adults. In T. Brink (ed.), *The forgotten aged: Ethnic, psychiatric and societal minorities* (pp. 59–77). Binghampton, NY: Haworth Press.

Smith, G., Tobin, S. & Fullmer, E. (1995). Elderly mothers caring at home for offspring with mental retardation: A model of permanency planning. *American Journal on Mental Retardation*, 99, 487–499.

Specht, H. (1986). Social support, social network, social exchange and social work practice. *Social Services Review*, 60, 218–240.

Stehlik, D. (1997). Learning to be 'consumers' of community care: Older parents and policy discourse. In M. Caltabiano, R. Hill & R. Frangos (eds), *Achieving inclusion: Exploring issues in disability* (pp. 129–146). Queensland: Centre for Social and Welfare Research, James Cook University, North Queensland.

Sussman, M. (1985). The family life of old people. In R. Binstock & E. Shanas (eds), *Handbook of aging and the social sciences* (2nd edn, pp. 415–449). New York: Van Nostrand Reinhold.

Swain, J. & French, S. (1998). Normality and disabling care. In A. Brechin, J. Walmsley, J. Katz & S. Peace (eds), *Care matters: Concepts, practice and research in health and social care* (pp. 81–94). London: Sage.

Taylor, S. & Bogdan, R. (1984). Introduction to qualitative research: The search for meanings (2nd edn). New York: John Wiley.

Taylor, S., Bogdan, R. & Racino, J. (1992). *Life in the community, Part 11, Housing, homes and support*. Baltimore: Brookes.

Tesch, R. (1990). *Qualitative research. Analysis types and software*. New York: Falmer.

Tippet, G. (1994, February, 13). What happens to Kenny when I die? *The Age*. Melbourne. pp. 1–2.

Todd, S., Shearn, J., Beyer, S. & Felce, D. (1993). Careers in caring: The changing situations of parents caring for an offspring with learning difficulties. *The Irish Journal of Psychology*, 14, 130–153.

Trevillion, S. (1992). *Caring in the community: A networking approach to community partnership*. Harlow, UK: Longman.

Twigg, J. & Atkin, K. (1994). *Carers perceived. Policy and practice in informal care*. Buckingham, UK: Open University Press.

United Nations. (1994). *The standard rules on the equalisation of opportunities for persons with disabilities*. New York: United Nations.

Urlings, H. (1992, April). *The important voice of the mentally retarded person in qualitative research on ageing*. Paper presented at the Manchester Roundtable on Ageing and Developmental Disabilities. Manchester, UK.

Victorian Government. (1986a). *Intellectually Disabled Persons' Services Act*. Melbourne: Victorian Government Printing Office.

Victorian Government. (1986b). *Guardianship and Administration Board Act*. Melbourne: Victorian Government Printing Office.

Villamanta Legal Service. (1995). *Submission to review of residential tenancies legislation* (Unpublished report). Geelong, Vic: Author.

Wadsworth, J. & Harper, D. (1991). Grief and bereavement in mental retardation. A need for a new understanding. *Death Studies*, 15, 281–292.

Walker, C. & Walker, A. (1998a). *Uncertain future: People with learning difficulties and their ageing family carers*. Brighton, UK: Pavilion Publishing and Joseph Rowntree Foundation.

Walker, A. & Walker, C. (1998b). Normalisation and 'normal' ageing: The social construction of dependency among older people with learning difficulties. *Disability and Society*, 13(1), 125–142.

Walker, C., Walker, A. & Ryan, T. (1995). What kind of future: Opportunities for older people with a learning difficulty. In T. Philpott & L. Ward (eds), *Values and visions. Changing ideas in services for people with learning difficulties* (pp. 232–243). Oxford, UK: Butterworth Heinemann.

Walker, A., Walker, C. & Ryan, T. (1996). Older people with learning difficulties leaving institutional care—A case of double jeopardy. *Ageing and Society*, 16, 125–150.

Walmsley, J. (1996). Doing what mum wants me to do: Looking at family relationships from the point of view of adults with learning disabilities. *Journal of Applied Research in Intellectual Disabilities*, 9(4), 324–341.

Walsh, P., Concliffe, C. & Birbeck, G. (1993). Permanency planning and material wellbeing. A study of caregivers of people with intellectual disability in Ireland and Northern Ireland. *Irish Journal of Psychology*, 14, 176–188.

Walz, T., Harper, D. & Wilson, J. (1986). The aging developmentally disabled person: A review. *The Gerontologist*, 26, 622–629.

Wenger, C. (1987). *Relationships in old age: Inside support networks* (A third report of a follow up study of old elderly people in N. Wales). Bangor, UK: Centre for Social Policy Research and Development, University of Wales.

Wenger, C. (1991). A network typology: From theory to practice. *Journal of Aging Studies*, 15, 147–162.

Wenger, C. (1992). *Help in old age: Facing up to a change. A longitudinal network study* (Occasional paper no. 5. Institute of Human Aging). Liverpool: Liverpool University Press.

Wenger, C. (1994). *Understanding support networks and community care. Network assessment for elderly people*. Aldershot, UK: Avebury.

Wenger, C. (1995). *Support networks of older people. A video based training and resource pack*. Brighton, UK: Pavilion Publishing.

Whittaker, J. (1986). Integrating formal and informal social care: A conceptual framework. *British Journal of Social Work*, 16, supp, 39–62.

Wolfensberger, W. (1985). An overview of social role valorisation and some reflections on elderly mentally retarded persons. In. M. Janicki & H. Wisniewski (eds), *Aging and developmental disabilities: Issues and approaches* (pp. 61–76). Baltimore: Brookes.

Wood, B. (1993). Planning for the transfer of care: Social and psychological issues. In K. Roberto (ed.), *The elderly caregiver: Caring for adults with developmental disabilities* (pp. 95–108). Newbury Park, CA: Sage.

Wood, J. & Skiles, L. (1992). Planning for the transfer of care. Who cares for the developmentally disabled adult when the family can no longer care? *Generations*, Winter, 61–62.

Wyngaarden, M. (1981). Interviewing mentally retarded persons: Issues and strategies. In R. Bruininks, C. Meyers, B. Sigford & K. Lakin (eds), *Deinstitutionalisation and community adjustment of mentally retarded people* (Monograph no. 4) (pp. 107–113). Washington DC: American Association on Mental Deficiency.

Zetlin, A. (1986). Mentally retarded adults and their siblings. *American Journal of Mental Deficiency*, 91, 217–225.

Zigman, W. (1997). The epidemiology of Alzheimer disease in intellectual disability: Results and recommendations from an international conference. *Journal of Intellectual Disability Research*, 41(1), 76–80.

Index

(Page numbers in italics indicate tables and diagrams.)

A

accommodation
   changes in during post-parental phase 99–107, *222–8, 229*
   ensuring optimal 191–2
   inappropriateness of services for some people 188–91
   reasons for changes in 100–5
administrators 159–60
adult training and support services 153–4, 167–8
adults with intellectual disabilities *see* older people with intellectual disabilities
advocacy 184–5
affective support 126
aged care
   inappropriateness of services for some people 188–91, 193–5
   policy 3, 57, 183, 184, 193–5
   see also disability care; formal care and support
   services 20–1, 172–3
aged population 47–8, *48*
   'hidden population' of adults with intellectual disabilities 53–5
   number of adults with intellectual disabilities 48–50
ageing of adults with intellectual disabilities 46–66
   health and physiological ageing of 50–1, 56
   'hidden population' 53–5
   increased life expectancy of 3
   number of 48–50
   premature 47, 56
   psychological aspects of 51
   social attitudes to 52

Alzheimer's disease
   early onset of 19, 56
   and people with Down syndrome 56

C

carers 32, 44, 102, *see also* primary carers
case management services 156–7
case vignettes 60–6, 110–13, 147–50, 161–6
community care 33

D

data collection, management and analysis 211–14
day activity services 153–4
death of parents 90–2, 129, 185
deinstitutionalisation 33
dementia 55
disability care
   and collaboration with aged care services 193–7
   policy 3, 57, 183, 184–5, 193, *201–4*
   see also aged care; formal care and support
   services 20–1, 43, 152–60, *153*, 168–71, 191–3
   withdrawal of services 170–1
domiciliary services 155
Down syndrome 19
   Alzheimer's and 56
   premature ageing and 47, 56, 182

E

ecological systems theory 7

249

F

family care and support 16, 20, 31, 33, 36, 39, 40–1, 138–43
  distant relatives 141–3
  see also friends and acquaintances as support; informal care and support; siblings; siblings-in-law
financial plans 15, 75
formal care and support 17, 18, 20–1, 22, 25–6, 34, 42–4, 152–75, 177–9, 180
  accessibility of 166–8
  administrators 159–60
  adult training and support services 153–4, 167–8
  case management services 156–7
  challenges for services 27, 180, 186–8, *201–4*
  day activity services 153–4
  domiciliary services 155
  experiences of service users 168–71
  formal service staff 160–1
  guardianship 157–9
  and informal network members 171–3
  intersection with informal support 42–4, 171–3
  leisure services 153–4
  residential primary care 155–6
  respite care 154
  see also aged care; disability care; informal care and support
  in transition management 89–90, 97
  unmet needs 173–4, 180
friends and acquaintances as support 41–2, 143–6
  church connections 146
  neighbours 145–6

G

guardianship 157–9, 160, 184
  legislation 14–15, 79, 157–8
  planning 14

I

independence of adults with intellectual disability 17, 183–5
  in post-parental care phase 113–17, 181–3
informal care and support 3–5, 17, 30–44, 88, 125–51, *130–1*, 177–9
  changes to networks 185–6
  composition of networks 128–38, *229*
  dimensions of networks 125–6
  family networks 138–43
  and formal services 171–3
  intersection with formal support 42–4, 171–3
  in the post-parental phase 38–42
  reducing disruptions to 186–8
  see also family care and support; formal care and support
  significance of 33–4, 179–81
  structure of networks 127–8
  theories of 36–8
instrumental support 126–7
Intellectually Disabled Persons Services Act 1986 (Vic) 54
interdependence 20, 35, 76

K

key people
  changes of 134, 185–6
  friends 144
  parents 138
  relationships with 134–7
  role of 128–9, 176, 179–80
  see also primary carers
  siblings 132–3
  who they are 129, 132–4
key person succession plans 69–81, 94–5, 96
  definition of 71–4
  difficulties associated with 69–70
  ensuring effectiveness of 197–9
  explicit 73
  implicit 72–3
  see also parental planning

L

leisure services 153–4
life expectancy, increased 3
Litwak 4, 7, 17, 178

M

mutual support groups 26

O

older parents 19–27
  death of 90–2, 129, 185
  formal intervention and 23–4
  and interdependence with adult children with intellectual disabilities 20, 35, 76

see also parental planning; key person succession plans
support needs of 25
older people with intellectual disabilities 46–66
  ageing and 46–66
  characteristics of 50–2
  definition of 46–7
  diversity of group 55–7
  informal support networks of 125–51
  psychological disturbance and 51
  rights of 29, 34–5, 81, 90, 91, 183–5
  size of population of 47–50
  social attitudes to 52
outreach 25–6, 27, 155
overprotectiveness of parents 34–5, 183

P

parental care, transition from *see* transition from parental care
parental planning 5–6, 14–29
  avoidance of 15
  continuing process of 117–18, 199–200
  and expectations 16–17
  explicit plans 70–1, 73–4, 79
  extent and nature of 15–16
  factors associated with 76–7
  family characteristics and type of *77*
  financial plans 15, 75
  implicit plans 16, 71, 72–3, 79
  involvement of day centres and organisations in 77–8
  key person succession plans 69–81, 197–8
  low level 28
  obstacles to 18
  plans not implemented 93–4
  residential plans 74–5
  and rights of their children with intellectual disability 29, 34–5, 183–5
  see also transition from parental care
  timelines for implementing 75–6
  types of plans *71*
parents
  death of 90–2, 129, 185
  and interdependence with adult children with intellectual disabilities 20, 35, 76
  older 19–27, 90–2, 129, 185
  overprotectiveness of 34–5, 183
  relationships with children 24, 35

see also parental planning; key person succession plans
personal development in late life 113–17, 181–3
  explanations for 115–17
plan of book 10–13
planning *see* key person succession plans; parental planning
post-parental care phase 99–121, 176–204
  challenges in *201–4*
  living situations in *100, 229*
  opportunities in 181–2
  personal development in 113–17
  and residential changes 99–107, *222–8*
  see also transition from parental care
  sources of support in 177–9, 181
premature ageing 47, 56
primary carers
  changes of 107–9, 177–9
  and inability to continue caring 102, *109*, 179
  informal 137–8
  see also carers; key people
professionals
  roles of *24*
  see also formal care and support
  staff of formal services 160–1

R

reciprocity in caregiving 20, 35, 76
residential plans 74–5, 99–107
residential primary care services 155–6, *see also* accommodation
respite care 154
rights of adults with intellectual disability 29, 34–5, 81, 90, 91, 183–5

S

siblings
  as key people 132–3
  as primary care givers 5, 16, 20, 36–7, 39, 40, 72
  relationships with 138–40, *139*
  role of in planning 78
  role of in transition from parental care 89
siblings-in-law
  relationships with 140–1
social networks 37, 38–42
  dynamic nature of 38
  importance of 36
  see also informal care and support

spouses 138
study design and methodology 7–10, *8*, 205–19
　data collection, management and analysis 211–14
　ethical considerations 215–17
　strengths and limitations 217–19
study population
　case vignettes 60–6, 110–13, 147–50, 161–6
　description of 57–9, 207
　type of accommodation of *59*
succession plans *see* key person succession plans
support
　characteristics of support networks 39–40
　intersection of formal and informal support 42–4, 171–3
　in the post-parental phase 38–42
　predictors of support networks 35–8
　see also aged care; disability care; formal care and support; informal care and support
　sources of 30–44

T

task specificity, theory of 4, 7, 94, 178
transition from parental care 82–98
　changes at time of 82–8
　formal services and 89–90, 180
　gradual 92
　involvement of person with intellectual disability 90, 183–4
　living situation after *84*
　losses involved in 92
　management of 88–90
　parental planning and 93–5
　partial transitions 88
　processes of 90–2
　reasons for 82
　see also parental planning; post-parental care phase
　sources of support in process 95–7
　sudden transitions 87–8, 90
　transferral of responsibility 85–7, 181
　types of residential changes made after *83*

V

vignettes 60–6, 110–13, 147–50, 161–6